SEABROOK (NH) LIBRARY
W9-AJL-004

HUMAN
HARVEST

Human Harvest

The Sacramento Murder Story

DANIEL J. BLACKBURN

KNIGHTSBRIDGE PUBLISHING COMPANY
NEW YORK

Published in the United States by
Knightsbridge Publishing Company
255 East 49th Street
New York, New York 10017

Library of Congress Cataloging-in-Publication Data

Blackburn, Daniel J., 1943–
Human harvest : the Sacramento murder story / by Daniel J. Blackburn.
p. cm.
ISBN 1-877961-10-8 : $19.95
1. Murder—California—Sacramento—Case studies. 2. Puente, Dorothea. 3. Socially handicapped—California—Sacramento—Crimes against. 4. Welfare recipients—California—Sacramento—Crimes against. I. Title.
HV6534.S16B57 1990
364.1'523'0979454—dc20 89-71630
CIP

Designed by Stanley S. Drate/Folio Graphics Co. Inc.

10 9 8 7 6 5 4 3 2 1
FIRST EDITION

To Mom and Dad,
lucky in life's lottery;
and to Bert, who was not.

Contents

ACKNOWLEDGMENTS

This was a journalistic endeavor that sprinted while others of similar intent waited at the starting gate, a fast-moving project made possible only by a symphony of people whose fingerprints are evident in the final results:

Maria Centrella, wife, helpmate, fellow writer, understanding the vacant expression, tolerating my often-missing self, always supportive; project shepherd Shelly Usen, whose original perceptiveness, subsequent persuasiveness, and fine-line editing got it into print; Tim Grieve, Wayne Wilson, and Dick Schmidt, whose on-the-spot journalism stands the test of time; Mike and Pru Coonan, Jim Meyers, Kerry Kaiser, Arnie Frank, Claudia Engel, and Curt Childs, for their help along the way; all of my interview subjects, willing and unwilling; and Gerry Sindell and Tony Edens, for their initial courage and ongoing sense of adventure.

Prologue

She was perfectly at ease, tastefully dressed, expensively bejeweled—the prototypical grandma with watery, cornflower blue eyes and carefully coiffed, fine white hair. As she bustled into Henry's Lounge, a workingman's bar in downtown Sacramento, she ordered up a tall vodka and grapefruit juice for herself and a round of cocktails for the house. That consisted of only about six male customers and Marjorie (Mitch) Harper, the early-shift bartender.

After settling herself on a barstool, she casually surveyed the clientele, one of whom was me, elbow-deep in a research project. The fact that I wore a tie set me apart from the others, and she noted this with a cordial smile before walking over to me.

It was August 1986. There was no way to know it at the time, but I was witnessing firsthand the method of operation of an individual whose alleged crimes would soon earn her a prominent spot among the world's most infamous women.

Today, Dorothea Gray Johanson Montalvo Puente stands accused in Sacramento, California, of mass murder in the deaths of nine people—seven of whom were found buried in the carefully tended yard of her rented, blue and white, two-story Victorian flat. (Because of her many surname aliases and their intermingled usage throughout her life, she usually will be referred to as "Dorothea" in this text for purposes of clarity, not casualness.)

During our first conversation at Henry's and in subsequent chats, Dorothea painted a very revealing self-portrait whose finer details would not be discernible to me until several years later. In retrospect, I suppose she was just rehearsing her role on me, but her delivery was polished, earnest, convincing.

After her arrest on November 16, 1988, Dorothea telephoned and corresponded with me whenever her lawyer permitted, and often when he didn't. On nearly every occasion, she steadfastly proclaimed her innocence of the nine murders with which she is charged.

The charges of homicide notwithstanding, Dorothea's personal history is replete with unsuccessful confrontations with the law, and she has spent a decade of her sixty-one years in jail or prison doing hard time. Forgery of old folks' monthly assistance checks and tinkering with dosages of prescribed medications while caretaking have been her professional mainstays.

Over the years, Dorothea managed to develop her criminal craft to a near art form, dancing around the law like an aging ballerina. This provided her with a tax-free income that would delight most top-level executives in America today, grossing as much as $11,000 monthly during various phases of her professional life.

The felonies to which Dorothea informally admits among her current bag of troubles—forgery and other forms of larceny and grand theft—are crimes she was able to continue year after year, with only intermittent official interference.

Prosecutors allege that Dorothea is a female serial killer, an extremely rare phenomenon in the annals of American crime. They will attempt to prove that she took advantage of a flaw in the Social Security laws to carve a lifelong career out of exploiting elderly, ill, often helpless people. They will further charge that she established herself in positions of trust in order to steal these people's only source of income, then drugged them to expedite her chicanery and, finally, murdered them.

However, Dorothea did not exist in a vacuum. She simply took full advantage of a system that fails to protect America's most helpless citizens. A stubborn and unreasonable refusal to correct a faulty administrative code has perpetuated the callous exploitation of the elderly, allowing people like Dorothea to operate all over the country, in communities large and small.

This is the story of a particularly gruesome event that illustrates the disturbing conditions now thriving in an increasingly uncaring nation. It is an account of shame and loss of conscience, of a major failing in the American system of social care that few have acknowledged and even fewer have attempted to correct.

This story is both sensational and spellbinding. It is also very alarming, because the incidents described could not have occurred or continued without having been sanctioned by layer after layer of government regulation.

The reader will note that this work's publication occurs prior to any trial proceedings involving the charges presently lodged against Dorothea. But through her own actions over many years, she has emerged as a principal character in the ensuing tragic drama.

In fairness, and not for the purpose of disclaimer, it should be emphasized at the very beginning: The objective of this investigative report is not to prejudge Dorothea's guilt or prove her innocent of the murder charges. Dorothea has entered a "not guilty" plea to murder, and her version of this sad and sordid tale may, indeed, in the end, present a reasonable doubt to any future jury.

An important part of this story, however, is on the public record, the verdict already in: America is guilty of gross neglect and an appalling refusal to correct an intolerable but rectifiable problem.

This is the startling story of the human harvest.

DISCOVERY

"Well, ma'am, it seems we might have a human body buried in your yard here."

1

The grin on the lawman's face froze as the sharp point of his shovel struck a hard object underground. A sudden, sickening lurch in the pit of his stomach told him with clarity what he most likely had found. Carefully, he slid the shovel blade a few inches into the shallow hole and pressed it once more into the rich black soil. He tilted the tool's handle back and peered down, not really wanting to, upon the object that he had unearthed: the sole of a tennis shoe and, protruding from the shoe itself, a human bone. Tattered, mud-encrusted wool hung from it like a grisly afterthought, and the putrid odor of decay announced its discovery.

Federal parole agent Jim Wilson arrived at his downtown Sacramento office early on the morning of November 11, 1988. It was Veteran's Day, a state and federal holiday. Wilson, a tall spare man whose intense eyes peered from behind horn-rimmed glasses, often worked these kinds of occasions. Today he had agreed to meet several people early at the Sacramento police department, just down the block from the federal building where Wilson's office was located.

Wilson walked the short distance and entered the office of Detective John A. Cabrera shortly before 8 A.M. The two men shook hands for the very first time.

A sergeant with fifteen years on the force, Cabrera had been in charge of missing persons and homicide for the Sacramento Police Department since 1982. Not a physically large man, he was, nevertheless, a presence of ample authority and reflected a confidence born of experience. He had a gentle and persuasive manner when dealing with people. A neatly trimmed brown moustache adorned his upper lip. He worked hard (by his own assertion and that of fellow officers) and he thought he did a good job with the usual limited resources.

Cabrera introduced Wilson to two women present, Judy Harper Moise and Beth Valentine. Both were social workers for the Volunteers of America (VOA).

The subject of that morning's meeting was a man, one of a large transient population that frequented the area and thought by the two women to be missing. Cabrera was reasonably certain that the fellow had simply drifted on down the road, following the same half-baked wandering instincts that had guided him to the riverfront city in the first place. Cabrera voiced his opinion to the small gathering.

Moise and Valentine, however, insisted with more than a hint of frenzy in their voices that the man about whom they were concerned was more likely just a few blocks away, at a local boarding home run by Dorothea Puente. The two social workers had spent the past two months on an increasingly anxious search for Alvaro (Bert) Montoya, a mildly retarded man whom they had placed as a tenant in Puente's boarding home only seven months earlier, and who subsequently had disappeared without a trace. Recently, they had heard disquieting rumors about dead bodies buried at the residence and, fearing the worst for their friend, were requesting that the police investigate.

Cabrera had decided that he wasn't going to dig up downtown Sacramento just because these bothersome social workers kept insisting upon it. But now he wasn't so sure of himself. The more he thought about it, as a matter of fact, and the more information he gathered, the better the notion sounded.

Sitting in the Spartan surroundings of the department's Detective Division offices, Cabrera, fellow detective Terry Brown, agent Wilson, and the two social workers discussed all of the ramifications of the action advocated by the women.

Brown had been Cabrera's senior partner for four years. Quiet, soft-spoken, his hair graying at forty-three, Brown was a reputed stickler for detail, often to the point of being nitpicky. During their time together in the field, he and Cabrera had developed strong personal and professional bonds, each placing great faith in the other's abilities and judgment. Brown provided a quiet, cautious balance to Cabrera's open, aggressive style, and they worked well together.

It was almost by coincidence, though, that Wilson had been included in the morning's discussion. Among the caseload of felons to whom he was appointed was a parolee named Dorothea Puente Montalvo, who in 1978 had been convicted on federal charges of forging a U.S. Treasury check. At the time, she had been placed on five years' probation, but because of a state felony conviction in 1982, her federal parole had been revoked. Her file had been assigned to a succession of federal agents, finally landing on Wilson's desk. He had received it only two weeks earlier and had met her only once, and then briefly.

The information provided by Wilson regarding Dorothea's criminal history was critical to Cabrera, for until he had talked with Wilson, the detective had no specific knowledge of Dorothea's federal jail and parole details. Nor did he know that she was on high-risk supervision. This information now triggered in Cabrera's mind some flashing red lights of suspicion.

That Dorothea was operating a boarding home, however, was a revelation to Wilson, who had been invited by Cabrera to this meeting just the previous day. Dorothea, with her status as a furloughed felon and under the rules of her parole, was not supposed to be operating a boarding house—largely because that enterprise had been a key factor in her prior legal transgressions.

Wilson had brought Dorothea's parole files with him, and he now produced them from his briefcase. Scanning the records, he informed the group that four different federal parole agents before him had been assigned to Dorothea since her release from state prison in 1985, and had visited her house on fourteen separate occasions. At no time did any of them take note of ample evidence that Dorothea was renting out rooms to tenants. It had appeared to them that she was simply renting her own apartment at the house, just like the residence's other occupants.

This knowledge, coupled with the concerns of Moise and Valentine, prompted Wilson's subsequent decision that he had sufficient grounds to revoke Dorothea's parole, and he said as much. At the very least, Dorothea had incurred a violation by failing to disclose truthfully all sources of her income. Even the slightest violation could result in parole revocation, at the agent's sole discretion. But, Wilson added, it would take at least a week to process the required papers, and he reminded Cabrera that federal parole officers do not possess search and seizure powers.

Cabrera was not concerned. "*I* do," he said, but he worried aloud that no search warrant had yet been obtained that would authorize any law enforcement officer to enter Dorothea's property without her permission. And it seemed highly unlikely to the veteran cop that anyone would allow the digging up of a lovely and well-maintained yard without court-mandated cooperation, whether or not there was anything to hide.

"Well, what the hell," he thought, "it won't hurt to drive over and see the woman." Moise and Valentine's persistence, and a patrol officer's disturbing missing-person report which Cabrera had seen just the previous evening, had piqued his gumshoe curiosity. That report, too, contained allegations about Dorothea and her boarding house . . . and buried bodies.

Cabrera excused himself, asking Moise, Valentine, and Wilson to wait, and gestured for Detective Brown to follow him. The two went straight to the equipment room, requisitioned two short-handled shovels and bright orange coveralls, and returned to Cabrera's office.

It appeared, at least to Moise, that the two cops were still far from convinced that they were embarking on a mission of any real consequence. She thought they seemed dubious, even light-hearted.

Cabrera and Brown got in their standard unmarked four-door Ford Tempo, adding the shovels and coveralls to the high rubber boots already in the trunk. A few minutes later, the caravan was ready to depart, Cabrera and Brown leading the way, Moise and Valentine trailing in their white Toyota van, and Wilson bringing up the rear in his own blue Plymouth Torismo.

The rooming house to which they traveled was situated in a section of downtown Sacramento dominated even now by early twentieth-century, middle-class houses, some restored and well-kept, others in the final throes of disrepair. The two-story, gingerbread-adorned Victorian occupied by Dorothea and her boarders was one of the former, neatly enclosed along with two neighboring houses by a brick and wrought-iron fence, the yards of all three groomed and trimmed. Characterless, boxlike apartment complexes were clustered several doors down. An old-style barber shop with the traditional revolving red stripe pole occupied one end of the block, Joe's Corner bar the other.

Like most other mornings, it was quiet on the 1400 block of F Street, the holiday contributing to traffic being even lighter than usual. A biting wind from the north, quite predictable this late in November, danced dead leaves across the sidewalks; angry black clouds bunched against one another and contributed an appropriate measure of gloom.

The cars containing the two police officers and Wilson pulled to a stop in front of the blue and white house at 10 A.M. Moise and Valentine had decided en route to stay away from Dorothea's, more fearful than the officers about what might be found. Via their car telephone, the pair would remain in close touch with police officials throughout what was to become a day marked by horror.

Leaving the shovels and other equipment in the detectives' car, the three men climbed thirteen steps to Dorothea's second-floor apartment and stood on the front porch. Halloween-colored strips of crepe paper still were festooned over the entrance, and a pumpkin-adorned wreath hung on the door from a rusted nail. Two plastic jack-o'-lanterns grinned eerily at the visitors.

Cabrera knocked.

After a moment, a white-haired, bespectacled woman peered through the white lace curtains. She then opened the door to them, a smile with just a touch of puzzlement on her face, and a friendly salutation on her lips.

"Whatever can I do for you gentlemen?" she asked.

"Hi, Dorothea," Cabrera said, and introduced himself and his companions. Dorothea seemed to take a long look at Wilson. This, after all, was her new parole agent, and she had met him only recently. "Like to talk with you, if you don't mind," said Cabrera, "and maybe to some of your boarders."

"Certainly," Dorothea said, and invited them in from the cold with a gracious offer of coffee. Politely declining, Cabrera told her they were there to follow up on a missing-person report and asked her the whereabouts of Bert Montoya. She said he was in Utah, with relatives, and that the people in the house could verify that. The detectives and the parole agent listened to her story, faces void of expression.

Cabrera asked her about her prior felony convictions, and she answered candidly: "Yes," she was on parole, and "yes," she had been convicted of drugging and robbing people, but that was some time ago, and, "Oh, my, what is this all about?"

A keen judge of character, parole agent Wilson closely watched the exchange between cop and landlady. This was Wilson's first close look at Dorothea, and he was as uncertain as anyone about what lay ahead. He later recalled Cabrera's "masterful job" of engaging Dorothea in conversation. It was a critical moment, because each man knew that at any time Dorothea could ask them to leave, and they would be required to do so. But Cabrera's comfortable manner seemed reassuring to the woman, and she warmed to him and made an effort to be cooperative.

Cabrera thought her receptivity to him might have been the result of something she perceived as a common bond: "Maybe it was because of my Hispanic surname," he later surmised.

Cabrera had seen some bizarre crimes during his seven years in homicide, and one thing he had learned was to keep an open mind. Another was that when interviewing people it helped to assume the attitude that they would be very willing to talk. And Cabrera had learned to listen . . . closely.

Wilson, too, was listening. He wanted to let Cabrera do the

talking for the moment. After all, he was thinking, this matter at hand—rumors of buried bodies—is much more pressing than any parole violation. This was no place, he realized, for a good-cop, bad-cop routine.

But Dorothea was being very cooperative, and she seemed candid in her responses. At a moment he thought appropriate, Wilson broke into the conversation and confronted Dorothea about operating a boarding house for aged people and failing to disclose her means of income in an accurate and truthful manner—both violations of her parole requirements. She shrugged and readily confessed to these transgressions. Then Wilson informed her that he intended to revoke her parole as soon as the proper forms could be filed. Dorothea said nothing, just frowned and nodded somberly.

In the meantime, Cabrera and Brown singled out several of her tenants and began questioning them in a different part of the house, out of sight and earshot of Dorothea. For nearly an hour, Cabrera and Brown interviewed several of Dorothea's residents. Then they returned to the living room where she and Wilson sat, and Cabrera asked Dorothea if she would mind if they looked around the house. Again she agreed, trailing the investigators as they perused the interior of each room, first upstairs, then down. Ten minutes later, as if drawn by some unseen force, the small group gathered outside in the windblown backyard.

Cabrera's curiosity about Bert, the missing tenant, was far from satisfied. In fact, he was finding several responses to his questions from Dorothea's boarders rather alarming, and her own version of Bert's apparent disappearance very unconvincing.

The cop tugged his overcoat tightly around himself in a vain effort to stymie the wind, and walked silently around the yard.

He could feel it.

Cabrera decided to take a big, but calculated, risk. Gently, so as not to frighten her, he asked Dorothea if she would mind if he dug a couple of small holes in the yard. If she was agreeable, he had concluded, she probably wasn't concealing anything and he doubted he would find anything. If she refused and demanded a search warrant, Cabrera's request might panic her into flight before the investigators could return. Did he have strong enough suspicions to warrant putting a tail on her in the interim? Could he even get a search warrant based on the limited information he possessed?

Dorothea's unhesitatingly quick approval was a mild surprise. Cabrera walked to the parked Ford, opened its trunk, removed the coveralls and struggled into them, and slipped into his rubber boots. He grabbed two shovels, returned to the clustered group in the yard, and handed one shovel to Wilson. The men then scanned the yard, commenting to one another about the freshly dug character of much of the soil. But rather than looking suspicious because of it, the yard looked very much like any other yard that saw a lot of care.

"It's almost too nice to dig up," Cabrera told Brown. Dorothea heard the comment, and gushed, "Oh, please, go right ahead, feel free."

Cabrera glanced at Brown, who said. "Why not? We're here, we might as well do something."

Cabrera stood where he could observe the entire property. He pointed to three spots where they might logically begin their dirty search for the missing tenant. Each man began to prod with his shovel in bare soil near a wooden fence, where the earth appeared to have been recently cultivated. They dug down several feet, found only more dirt, and covered the holes.

As they dug, Dorothea walked down the steps and watched the

work proceeding. Cabrera's eyes scanned her face, trying to detect in her the smallest hint of emotion. Not a flicker. She stood quietly observing, calm, cool, and collected, arms folded over her ample bosom.

The officers labored on, their efforts at first revealing nothing but shovelful after shovelful of heavy, black, fertile Sacramento Valley soil. Then, finding nothing, they refilled each hole.

Wilson began to wonder just what he was doing. At the day's start, he had thought perhaps something was amiss; there were too many strange circumstances, too many reasons for suspicion. The whole area did seem to have been well tilled, the ground very loose, but its appearance not really extraordinary.

Now, after an hour of digging, he wasn't sure about much of anything. He and Brown exchanged sheepish grins.

Wilson walked a few steps south, to the edge of a flower bed near the backyard fence, and once again pushed his shovel blade into the dirt. As he did so, an unpleasant question kept crowding back into his head: What the hell am I going to do if I do find a body?

He was barely eighteen inches deep when he turned up something that got his immediate attention.

"Hey, wait a minute, there's some kind of white powder down here," he called out to his companions. He reached down and took some on his fingertips, then held it to his nose for a whiff. "That's really strange," he thought. "It's lime." What would lime be doing in the soil of a garden? Lime is caustic—it kills plants and contaminates soil. It also speeds the decomposition of flesh.

Wilson leaned on his shovel, contemplating this odd new development. He was about to begin digging once again when Dorothea's top-floor roommate, Mervin John McCauley, appeared at his side and told him, "You're going to find a lot of garbage down there, we've been burying a lot of garbage there."

"What kind of garbage?" Wilson asked.

"Just trash," said McCauley.

Why, Wilson wondered, would these people bury trash in the garden when all they had to do was put it out front for the city's sanitation department to handle?

Then his shovel uncovered a piece of woolen cloth. Lime covered it, but Wilson noted that the cloth had not decomposed.

"I kind of stopped, and then put the shovel back, more around the cloth to get at it," Wilson said later. "I was wondering, why would someone be burying cloth like this?"

Then, under the cloth, the steel of his shovel's blade contacted something hard. Despite his doubts, he felt the hair on the back of his neck prickle.

"I still wasn't in the mood to think this might be a body. I thought it might be a tree root," Wilson recalled. "Whatever it was, it was pretty big, pretty unwieldy. It was hard to tell much of anything, because at this point the thing in the ground was still pretty indistinguishable."

Wilson's heart started hammering and he fought off a momentary rush of nausea. He glanced at Cabrera and Brown before continuing; both cops' features hardened, and they walked slowly to Wilson's side.

Moments later, using his shovel as cautiously as a surgeon's scalpel, Wilson coaxed a dirty white object from under the soil and into view. Shredded remnants of clothing and a tennis shoe clung to the object, but the three men didn't need those clues to deduce what it was they had found.

These were cops. They all had seen human leg bones before.

Standing off to one side, Dorothea put her hands to her face in a gesture of horror. Cabrera approached her. He asked her again if she knew anything about the disappearance of Bert Montoya.

"He's not dead," she said.

"Well, ma'am, it seems we might have a human body buried in your yard here."

Cabrera told her that he was convinced that if the officers continued to dig in her yard, they would find more bodies. What did she think of that?

"Sir, I have never killed anybody," Dorothea insisted.

She told Cabrera that she would be willing to take a lie detector test to corroborate her statements, "But not until Monday when I can settle my nerves." Repeating her earlier claims that she had nothing to hide, she invited the officer and his companions to continue their search of the yard and her house if he thought it would be fruitful.

Cabrera felt no reason to question Dorothea further for the moment; she was being very cooperative, that was certain. Brown returned to the detectives' vehicle and radioed for legal advice from the district attorney's office, and for more police assistance. He also requested several pieces of heavy equipment the cops figured would be needed to search underneath several recently poured concrete pads. Some freshly planted fruitless mulberry trees would have to be removed, he had already observed. So, too, would a newly constructed six-foot-square aluminum work shed, also resting on a concrete slab foundation.

They didn't know it yet, but Detectives Cabrera and Brown and parole agent Wilson had embarked on the strangest experience of their careers, one that would deeply and personally affect each man and alter forever the direction of his life. The next few days would wreak havoc on the careers of every man in the police investigative field unit.

One of the first back-up cops to arrive on the scene was Sgt. Jim Jorgenson, Cabrera's and Brown's immediate supervisor. A tall man with a bearlike stature, the sergeant was briefed about the morning's meeting with the two social workers, the subsequent visit to Dorothea's house, the gist of the discussion between her and Cabrera, the digging, and the discovery.

Because the detectives knew only that they had found a human bone and had absolutely no idea how long it had been in the ground, they decided at this point to "freeze" the scene and call for expert and technical help.

The area was restricted to the public; uniformed police guards circled the site as they waited for the familiar, bright-yellow strips of plastic ribbon to cordon it off as a crime scene.

At 11:47 A.M., coroner's investigator Edward Smith responded to the detectives' call, bringing with him Gary A. Stuart and Robert M. Anthony, both forensic pathologists.

Jorgenson was informed by Brown and Cabrera that Bert Montoya had been missing for about ninety days—if he was missing at all—and that the bone couldn't belong to Montoya's body; it could not have decomposed so rapidly. This was just a bone. Who knew how long it had been there?

The detectives immediately got in touch with Dep. Dist. Atty. Tim Frawley. Confident, sharply attired, articulate to the point of glibness, Frawley would be the man who would ultimately determine the correct course of action in the absence of a search warrant. These discussions would be conducted frequently during the next three or four days, establishing a direct line between the cops and the lawyers.

Sgt. Jorgenson mentioned that numerous people at the location might be suspects, including the landlady. Frawley tried to grasp the situation: Dorothea Montalvo Puente was thought to be a respected pillar of the community. She had political friends and solid ties to social services, she seemed well liked in the neighborhood . . . all in all, she appeared to Frawley to be an upright citizen. (For the moment, unfortunately, it completely slipped Frawley's mind that he had prosecuted Dorothea in 1982.)

Frawley carefully weighed Cabrera's good rapport with Dorothea. "Let's continue the way we're going," he suggested, "and see where it takes us. Let's not jump the gun."

Cabrera and Brown agreed. If they arrested Dorothea on suspicion of murder, and the bone turned out to be that of a long-dead transient, the police would really be crucified by the public, the media, and God knows who else. These cops planned on doing this right, going by the book all the way.

The problem was, there was no book on what they were about to encounter.

2

The first thing the interrogators needed was a more detailed discussion with Dorothea. Cabrera ordered her taken downtown to his office.

The unmarked police car bearing Dorothea pulled away from the curb, parole agent Wilson watching as it disappeared around the corner. He then stood aside from the commotion as gray Ford station wagons bearing coroner's deputies, more police vehicles, and the tractor-powered backhoe equipment arrived. Wilson looked at the sky, thinking about how dry the past year had been, and how now it looked like rain. Even as the thought went through his head, a steady and chilly drizzle began falling. He walked to his car, his job for the day completed. That evening he would tell his family about the events of his day, and his daughter would observe that Dad's job was, well, unique.

As the rain fell harder, investigators erected a waterproof canopy over the newly located gravesite. Floodlights were brought in to illuminate the work, but not much more could be accomplished before the murky darkness of the night had completely enveloped the scene.

Posting round-the-clock, armed and uniformed guards on every perimeter of the premises, the investigators departed for the night. They would be back in force early in the morning to resume the search for Bert Montoya, and to complete excavation of the bone that had been unearthed.

Cabrera and Brown questioned Dorothea for three hours. Then they conferred with deputy district attorney Tim Frawley and his associate, George Williamson. They all agreed there was insufficient evidence on which to detain her, and her explanations at the time seemed believable. Having no other alternatives, Cabrera and Brown drove Dorothea back to the house on F Street. The glaring lights of television cameras dispatched from several local TV stations illuminated the street like a large movie set. The steady hum of power generators and the babble of spectators created an air of vitality, a distinct carnival atmosphere. Dorothea smiled at the cops, walked up the stairs leading to her apartment, and closed the door . . . never looking back.

Later that night, she confided to her roommate, Mervin John McCauley, that she was frightened, both by what was happening in her yard and by the police interview. She was not looking forward to the morning. She felt panicky and told McCauley that she should be getting out of there. She knew the police were going to get her, no matter what.

She made more than the usual number of trips during the late hours to the nice oak buffet in her dining room, the one that held the liquor supply. She mixed stout vodka shots with her grapefruit juice, one after the other. She and McCauley got pretty drunk, but she still didn't get much sleep.

* * *

Saturday, November 12, 1988, 8 A.M. The cops returned in full force. Word of the discovery of a human bone had spread throughout the neighborhood and beyond, and a small but aggressive crowd of curious onlookers had gathered behind police lines. Newspaper, radio, and television reporters from all over the state were beginning to arrive, drawn by the increasingly ghoulish tales that a larger cache of bodies might be buried in Dorothea's backyard.

As she had done the previous day, Dorothea remained stoic, arms serenely folded, surveying the growing clamor in her yard through her fashionable bent-arm eyeglasses. Part of the time, she stood right next to the spot where police were digging, as an excruciatingly careful excavation of the hole containing the bone and tennis shoe was conducted.

Dorothea's tenants either stayed fearfully in their rooms or wandered the premises. Several even talked to reporters. But all seven of them were trying to figure out their next move.

Coroner's deputies, police investigators, and the forensic anthropologists used small gardening tools to scrape away piles of dirt from around the emerging skeletal remains, a fine-mesh screen to filter the soil, and one-inch-wide paintbrushes to sweep away the residue from sections of the decaying bone itself.

In short order, investigators had unearthed enough of the body to make several deductions, even though the corpse had decomposed almost entirely, the result of time and of the effect of the lime. The opinion of the two forensic pathologists was passed on by Lieutenant Joe Enloe, the police spokesman who stood within feet of the makeshift grave as he talked to reporters. Enloe clutched a raincoat around his girth, the garment's light color exaggerating the flush on his round face. A fine mist of rain fell on his balding pate and cascaded down the short-cropped gray hair over his ears.

Enloe told the reporters that the body had been in the ground since about April; it was probably that of a "gray-haired, rather petite, elderly female, and was found approximately three feet underground." He added that the body was "lying in a fetal position" but he had no ready explanation for that, nor would he comment on whether he thought the position had any special significance.

Cabrera, watching the scene, felt the same slight confusion and gnawing concern that had prevailed the previous day: He was there to look for a missing *male*. Now this female was found. What was going on?

The digging proceeded. A little less than an hour after the workday began, at 8:50 A.M., Dorothea appeared on her porch and called to Cabrera, just as he was about to start digging in a new spot. Cabrera later wrote in his report of the day's activities that she told him she wanted to walk to the nearby Clarion Hotel to visit her nephew and she was just kind of wondering if she was under arrest.

She hadn't been arrested, so legally she could not be detained. Cabrera's black rubber boots left a trail of mud as he escorted her through police lines and away from the constant, intense glare of media-operated floodlights. Dorothea left the scene wearing a bright red wool coat, pink dress, and purple high-heeled shoes, carrying a purple handbag and pink umbrella.

The small, yellow Clark backhoe, its diesel engine's chug-chug easily overpowering the softer sound of probing shovels, was now wedged into the small side yard adjoining the Victorian. For fifteen or so minutes, the backhoe's operator gently swung the machine's big claw at a thick slab of recently poured concrete, oddly positioned (it suddenly seemed to the searchers) adjacent to the junction of the side and back fences. Only shortly after Dorothea's departure, Cabrera learned that the concrete had been poured about forty-five days earlier, at Dorothea's request, by a pair of local contractors. With a tightening in his stomach, Cabrera watched as the slab was broken at its edges, making it possible for the detective's shovel blade to peel away, ever so carefully, layer by thin layer of the rain-soaked soil.

There, two feet under the wet soil, was the second corpse. It was at the exact spot where Cabrera had been about to dig when Dorothea hailed him to ask if she was under arrest.

The new find was painstakingly brought to the earth's surface. Appearing to be wrapped in cloth (it was later described as "mummified"), the body possessed a torso significantly larger than the first, suggesting that this second victim might be a male.

News of the find electrified the milling crowd of spectators, which by this time was aching for action. Television and newspaper cameras had recorded the departure of Dorothea through police lines, so that by the time this second body was found, in a hole right next to the site where the first had been uncovered, the murmur of public criticism had grown to a roar.

Sergeant Jorgenson sped to the Clarion Hotel's coffee shop, where his hopes of finding Dorothea were rudely doused. Police issued an all-points bulletin for the immediate arrest of their new prime suspect.

Meanwhile, back at the crime scene, forensic anthropologists Rodger Heglar of San Diego and Chuck Cecil of San Francisco had begun overseeing the work that remained to carefully excavate the first body and complete the time-consuming, tedious task of identification. A large, stiff piece of five-ply plywood, four feet wide and eight feet long, was carried from a police utility vehicle and slowly worked under the skeleton. Every attempt was made to leave the bones in the position in which they were found. When the dark task was finished, coroner's deputies slipped a white canvas bag around the body itself and carried the board to a waiting van that would transport it to the coroner's office on V Street, three miles away, where an autopsy would be done.

As the ongoing excavation continued, a curious phenomenon began to occur. Ever since the first bones had been found the day before, the small field team of detectives had been trying to get some specific direction from their superior officers at police headquarters. But supervisory officers, from the assistant chief down to captains, chose, in the words of one incredulous cop months later, "to hide." The supervisors would appear on the site, tell the members of the investigating field unit that they were doing just fine, that they should stay with procedure and keep up the good work. Then they would disappear. The brass shucked their responsibility like a down vest in Death Valley.

At no time was supervisory assistance more necessary. The field cops were required to work at the scene of a newly discovered crime and to keep an eye on several people who might be suspects—all under the watchful eye of newspaper photographers and television cameras. As a van bearing the NBC peacock logo came into view, Lieutenant Enloe knew that the macabre event on F Street had blossomed far beyond anything he had ever seen or been involved with.

The gathering of media personnel was expanding tremendously, now featuring representatives of the national television networks, the wire services, and major newspaper chains. They appeared to have annointed themselves the supreme critics of police procedure, and shouted questions at the working police officers. The field unit members applied again for supervisory help, but there was none forthcoming. They were opening Pandora's box and there was no one telling them not to. Like shipwrecked sailors, they were on their own, even as the sky around them darkened.

* * *

The third body was found at 2:30 P.M. Saturday under a newly planted sapling. Like the first body, this one was in a curled fetal position. It had been wrapped in several layers of a sheeting material, then bound from head to toe with a thin piece of white cotton rope.

The report of coroner's deputy Laura Synhorst was straightforward, chilling:

> We unearthed a large bundle wrapped in a greenish-colored blanket. There were pieces of a light pinkish material attached to the middle portion of the bundle. The body was lying in an east/west alignment with the appearance of the head end to the west.

Synhorst, Cecil, and Dr. Stuart finished their excavation and fully exposed the bundle at 3:30 P.M. They summoned J. Morris and Sons Mortuary Transportation Service. The body was removed to the coroner's office, there to join the previously discovered two in preparation for autopsy.

Next, the investigators began to dig under a new aluminum storage shed situated in the middle of the side yard. Piece by piece, the shed was dismantled and reduced to a pile of sheet metal; then shovels started biting into the soil that had been hidden beneath.

Shortly before dark on the second day of the excavation, it appeared that a fourth body had been found. Dorothea had walked away from the scene just nine hours earlier.

As search efforts for additional bodies were suspended for the night, police spokesman Enloe fully recapped the day's events for excited journalists. It had, indeed, been a day filled with drama for both the media and the officers, beginning with the televised departure of Dorothea through police lines. Possibly, Lieutenant Enloe's enthusiasm for providing an extremely detailed scenario to a hungry press was stimulated by the sting of public criticism he and his fellow cops were absorbing for allowing Dorothea to simply walk away without a tether.

To make matters even stickier, the media was now moving ahead of the cops in the information-gathering process, discovering the identities of Dorothea's tenants and heralding her criminal history. As a result, the media was providing to police almost all of the important data about the circumstances leading up to the disappearance of Bert Montoya. Small wonder the cops were ready to name names regarding prime suspects, and to dangle lofty and colorful theories in front of the newspeople.

Enloe continued his report to the press: None of the bodies found so far showed any signs of beatings, gunshot or knife wounds, or any other evidence of violent death. "We don't expect [violence] was the case," Enloe commented wryly to the assembled reporters. This was the first of numerous implications he and other officers would make regarding the manner of the deaths and the identity of the person they already believed was responsible for murder.

Enloe also offered a motive for the burials, which he surmised from his knowledge of Dorothea's past as a felon: larceny. "It's very possible that there was an attempt to cash Social Security and other checks," he suggested. He hinted at a possible accomplice and added that none of the corpses appeared to be that of the missing Bert Montoya.

"The first body was found under earth. We think that body had been there [about seven months], and Montoya has not been missing that long. The second body was completely wrapped like a mummy, and was found under concrete, so it's hard to determine how long it's been there."

Enloe also confirmed that police were now certain there was "probable cause" to pursue one particular suspect, that an all-points bulletin had been issued for Dorothea Gray Johanson Montalvo Puente. A nationwide dragnet for her was also under way, he said, and an arrest was imminent.

Sunday, November 13, 1988. When police arrived back at Dorothea's house, this time at 7 A.M., word was circulating that the fourth body supposedly found at quitting time the night before was not a body, after all. But about the time everyone on the street had digested that story, the cops *did* find the fourth, again near the backyard fence. It was wrapped in several dark-green plastic trash bags, and lay on its side with its arms down and its legs curled.

"We don't know what we have here yet," Lieutenant Enloe told reporters. "We may have to search for dental records, medical records, and other things in order to find out exactly who these people are."

Cabrera telephoned Moise and Valentine, now at home, and several other social workers and asked them to provide him with a list of people placed by their agencies during the last year into Dorothea's house. He was particularly interested in knowing if any of these people had been reported missing, and asked that some attempt be made to locate those who could be found.

By now, the streets were blocked off on every intersection, creating a large area for people to gather . . . and despite the cold rain, gather they did. The square block was packed with an estimated crowd of more than six hundred gawkers and reporters.

The air throbbed with the sound of cranked-up generators powering the lights and cameras of the media horde and the relentless rattle of the backhoe chewing up Dorothea's yard. Neighbors were recalling Dorothea-related incidents as fast as the television camera operators could focus on their faces.

For police there was a new development, one that seemed to cast suspicion on someone who had not left town. Two of the bodies thus far had been found under newly laid concrete, a fact that Dorothea's very close friend and roommate Mervin John McCauley had difficulty corroborating when questioned by police. McCauley's conflicting stories cast suspicion on him. So did a telephone call from the missing Dorothea allegedly received the night before, a call reported to police by another tenant in the house.

Madder than hell about what was happening, McCauley was questioned at about noon on Sunday and then arrested. He was taken to the Sacramento County Jail and booked on charges of being an accessory to murder.

"He [McCauley] was a confidant of Dorothea's," Enloe told reporters, "but we do not believe he was involved in the hands-on work involving the bodies."

Enloe then hinted that another male, not McCauley, may have assisted in the "actual homicides" that he, Enloe, seemed certain had occurred. "We're making the assumption that it would be pretty hard for a woman of her small size to carry those bodies," he said. The media people dutifully recorded Enloe's comments and speculated on the implications.

Hours later, just before the searchers shut off the backhoe for the night, the fifth body—a male—was found, curled three feet under the surface. It was in a direct line with the fourth body, next to a white porcelain toilet commode that had been turned into an ivy planter.

* * *

Monday, November 14, 1988. Morning brought a hint of sunlight, slightly warmer temperatures . . . and a sixth body. It was pulled up from a spot only inches from bodies four and five. At 4:00 P.M. body number seven was found, this time in the front yard in a small, grassy space under the watchful gaze of a three-foot carved wooden statue of St. Francis of Assisi.

Throughout the digging, Cabrera had been conferring by telephone with the district attorney, social workers Moise and Valentine, and coroner's deputies. The coroner's people were insisting at this point that despite a lack of positive identification on any of the bodies, none seemed to resemble the physical descriptions of the missing Bert Montoya.

This bothered Cabrera, since without the connection of locating Bert Montoya's body in the yard, there existed numerous legal impediments to Dorothea's potential prosecution.

By dark, however, the forensic anthropologists were certain that the third body to have been discovered was that of Bert Montoya. This information provided police with their link between the bodies and the missing landlady that would convince a judge to allow them to search her home. That evening, they took their evidence to Superior Court Judge Marcus Albright and he signed the search warrant authorizing police to enter and probe Dorothea's boarding home the following morning.

While the remaining tenants departed to other residences, police pledged to "dig up every square inch" of Dorothea's yard until they were certain that no other bodies were buried there.

Tuesday, November 15, 1988. Investigators ended the morning's search convinced that there were no more bodies to be found on Dorothea's rented property.

There was, however, another spot that aroused the interest of

Detectives Cabrera and Brown. They had their eyes on a large empty lot across the street from the F Street house—a lot that looked suspiciously like a possible graveyard.

A woman living in the neighborhood reported that she had seen a woman fitting Dorothea's description digging in the field not very long ago, at midnight. There was a hole, and the woman with the shovel who looked like Dorothea was burying something.

Cabrera and Brown, the ranking investigators on the scene, thought that the woman's tip was relevant and should be pursued. Cabrera was able to dig a small trench that measured four feet wide by six feet long, and just a couple of feet deep, before the arrival of Capt. Michael O'Kane, their commanding officer, responding to a radio summons from Brown. O'Kane's handsome Irish face was tense, his manner abrupt, as usual.

The detectives expressed their belief that they should continue, perhaps even expand and intensify, their digging in this new spot. "We still have the backhoe across the street," they told O'Kane. "Why not bring it over and do this thing right?" The two detectives suggested a 20-by-60-foot excavation, or larger.

O'Kane, however, wasn't listening.

"Why not?" the detectives asked.

"I'll tell you why not," O'Kane replied. "Because I say forget it."

The field detectives were astounded. Where had O'Kane been when they needed him? Now, he was taking command? Cabrera and Brown tried to reason with the captain, only to get "pushed against the wall." They stopped talking about the empty lot, but they didn't stop speculating about what the property might hold.

As they left the scene, both were thinking that the lot across the street from Dorothea's was the biggest mystery of all. (As this book goes to press, the lot has not been searched further, and plans have been made for construction of a hostel on it.)

Several days later, the police probed with steel rods the grounds at a residence formerly operated by Dorothea a few blocks away, at 2100 F Street. In the meantime they intensified their now desperate search for Dorothea, while the world smirked, perhaps just a little, at Sacramento's finest.

THE SUSPECT

Hers was a complicated lifestyle. For Dorothea was a producer, nothing less. She stole the script of life and rewrote it to her own satisfaction.

3

In a very few days, Dorothea had achieved international, albeit notorious, recognition. Even she, with all her style and self-confidence, could not have predicted how quickly her notoriety would spread.

After all, hers was a humble enough beginning. One of seven children born to ex-serviceman Jesse Gray and Trudy Yates, Dorothea Helen Gray came into the world on January 9, 1929, in Redlands, San Bernardino County, California.

The family was Baptist, but since times were tough for the Grays there wasn't a lot of energy for religious activity. Churchgoing took a back seat to survival, even when Dorothea was a very young child.

Jesse Gray died when Dorothea was only four years old, and her mother followed into eternal peace just a year later. Dorothea went to live with an aunt and uncle in Fresno, California. By then, she was a seasoned cotton picker, a trade she began to practice at the tender age of three. She once told a sentencing judge that she also picked potatoes, cucumbers, and chilies, finally climbing into trees to pick fruit.

Life in Fresno was not much different for Dorothea than it had been in Redlands. She was obligated to continue her fruit picking to help her new family get by. From her widely varying accounts, related in later years to a series of psychiatrists and psychologists, Dorothea's childhood was sadly lacking in ordinary comforts and happiness.

(For the last twenty years Dorothea has told a more fanciful story of her birth, one that differs significantly from reality. She falsely claims, in numerous court records and other official documents, that she was the youngest of eighteen children born to Mexican parents in Mexico City.)

Dorothea's story gets mixed up around age thirteen, when she either went to Mexico to live with relatives or married a fellow named Fred McFall back in Riverside. No records exist to verify either version. Again, depending on the slant she wants to give her story, Dorothea's new mate McFall either died two days later, or two years later, of a heart attack. Curiously, he is the only one of Dorothea's known husbands whose name she didn't continue using during different times in her life.

After McFall's death, Dorothea "went back to work," but she has never described her labors of this period. Riverside court records describe her, however, as a felon check forger because of a 1948 incident that occurred when she was just nineteen years old. She was sentenced to a year in county jail, serving only half of it before being paroled. It was her first time behind bars, and it would not be her last.

A year after she was released, Dorothea had a baby girl out of wedlock and immediately gave her up for adoption. The daughter, now forty-one, lives in South Pasadena.

It is interesting to note that Dorothea, in her many public-record statements on the subject, steadfastly claimed that she was unable to have children and had lost several through miscarriage or stillbirth. Her natural daughter located Dorothea in 1987, and the pair had a limited, and very strained, reunion. The daughter reported that conversations with her mother consisted of one-sided monologues by Dorothea relating the tough times of her youth. This, apparently, was a vague and indirect attempt to explain the adoption, despite the fact that the daughter felt no bitterness toward her natural mother. After each of their visits, mother and daughter exchanged a few letters and talked several times on the telephone, but the relationship never got off the ground.

In 1952 Dorothea married a robust Swede named Axel Johanson, and they remained together, at least on the record, for fourteen years, until May 1966. It was during this marriage that Dorothea suffered the first of several miscarriages, and the couple remained childless.

Midway through her union with Johanson, Dorothea was arrested in a Sacramento brothel during a surprise roundup by the police. She claimed she was just visiting a girlfriend, but the judge was not listening. She spent ninety days in the county jail, and the next five years on summary probation. Johanson apparently was indifferent to his wife's choice of companions, because they remained married for six more years.

Late in 1966, the same year of her divorce from Johanson, Dorothea married Roberto Puente. It was a coupling that would last only four years. She later said Roberto was much younger than she, a situation that both found intolerable and that precipitated their eventual separation.

Her fourth marriage was to Pedro Montalvo in Reno, Nevada, in 1976. She described Pedro as a physically abusive man, the kind of fellow who liked a little punch with his whiskey. The following year Dorothea sought, and got, an annulment. But they were soon back together, because Dorothea found herself pregnant. Again, she maintains that the child was stillborn.

Dorothea says it was during this time that she started writing bad checks and doing other criminally fraudulent activities that would earn her lots of future attention from the law. She had been living in Stockton, south of Sacramento, and her parole agent eventually helped her move back to the state capital by placing her meager belongings in the back of his pickup truck and assisting in the transfer himself.

After ridding herself of Pedro, Dorothea apparently decided she needed to alter the nature of her doomed relationships with men. It was hard, apparently, for a man to measure up to Dorothea's expectations, and that would be her last marriage.

She supported herself in a variety of ways during the years she was not married. Actually, none of her mates was very good at providing for Dorothea's financial well-being, so she really did rely on her own resources throughout her life. Her work generally followed the same lines—providing caretaking services for elderly people. She secured these positions by assuring her clients that she was a registered nurse, one of many untruths she told concerning her professional qualifications.

By the time I first encountered Dorothea, in August 1986, she had her routine down pat. She was comfortably into the rhythm of her altruistic lifestyle, her carefully cultivated reputation well established.

At the time, I was running a little news syndication operation called California News Agency with a couple of seasoned newsmen. Mike Williams and Mark Larson helped me provide coverage of state government matters for our newspaper clients all over California. The sliver of an office that served this small but mighty news team was located in a high-rise building across from, and with a great view of, the state capitol. We were in the same building as all of the media giants—Associated Press, United Press International, the big California daily newspapers, and a few remaining television-station camera teams.

An occasional staff retreat was at a convenient, nearby establishment called Henry's Lounge, where coffee is most often accompanied by a shot of Christian Brothers brandy, and where the locals can be found hovering shoulder-to-shoulder over their whiskey-and-beer eye-openers anytime after dawn. A throwback from the fifties, Henry's is nestled in among expensively renovated old office buildings and state offices, almost all of which are occupied predominantly by lawyers, lobbyists plying their trade at the capitol, and employees connected in one way or another to the operations of the legislature.

In the days before random drug testing and intense workplace pressure about personal drinking habits, a considerable number of state employees would nip into Henry's for an occasional midday bracer, but nowadays a man wearing a tie in the joint is an infrequent visitor.

Henry's Lounge attracts its share of society's lesser lights, located right on a busy alley a block from the Greyhound bus station. It was one of Dorothea's hang-outs, too. The tavern's customers were predominantly blue-collar pensioners, mostly men who worked hard all their lives only to find their retirement planning far short of the mark and their means of support scraping the poverty level. The tasteful dress and proper behavior of Dorothea Puente set her slightly above the regulars. And she kept an eye peeled for those who might be her peers.

It wasn't long, then, before Dorothea noticed the newsmen. We were "the guys in ties," and that was all it took to make us remarkable. In her wary, survivalist state of mind, she probably thought we were connected somehow to the law, although very few people knew that Dorothea had been out of state and federal prison for only a little more than a year.

As time went by, Dorothea became more comfortable around me. She claimed to be fascinated by the news business, and that subject became a usual topic of conversation whenever our paths crossed. She was quick to buy a drink or two for those who caught her fancy, and of course she never refused one for herself. She drank vodka and grapefruit juice, in a chimney glass with cracked ice. On more than one occasion, she would buy a round of drinks as she departed, indicating her wish with the flick of a bejeweled wrist at the bartender. She often left cash (sometimes a wad of twenties, just as often a hundred) with the bartender, to pay the cocktail tabs of select patrons who would come in later.

Almost without exception, these "privileged few" were the recipients of various kinds of retirement benefits, older folks, mostly men living alone, spending many of their hours in the emptiness of involuntary solitude.

So to some, she was a welcome sight when she swept in. To others, she was a pain in the tail.

Dorothea is the type that one person might consider a raconteur, another a bald-faced liar. But truth or fiction, hers was a steady line of chatter, some of which could be fascinating. She was current, and she was curious, asking question after question that (were she not so pleasant) might have turned offensive very quickly. Coming from Dorothea, what would have been nosey inquiries, particularly in these shadowy surroundings, had the ring of genuine interest. She would sit with her elbows on the bar, her back straight, a picture of elegance in a rough-edged world, dispensing free information, opinion, and cocktails for those she considered her friends.

I had known Dorothea for only about four months when she told me she had a special favor to ask. She wanted to open a trust account for a nephew who lived in Mexico. The nephew needed to sign bank forms, and he couldn't get to California right now. The mail would be too slow. Of course she was perfectly willing to send him the air fare, that wasn't the problem. You see, he had a job, wife was sick, just couldn't leave now, but if Dorothea didn't open the account by the end of the quarter she would lose some important tax benefits.

I shrugged, not really understanding. What could I do to help solve this problem?

Well, she said, maybe I could just sign a little form that she had at home, and then she could have this friend, a registered notary public, verify the signature for her at a later time, and that would solve her sticky family problem. Everything could proceed easily from that point. She needed a signature that was unmistakably male, and of course the name would be Mexican, otherwise her friend would be reluctant to place his notarizing stamp on the form. Needless to say, Dorothea assured me, she would make it "worth my while."

I might not know a tax dodge from a Studebaker, but I can recognize big-time trouble. I promised Dorothea to think about it. The next time I saw her, she talked vaguely about having me over for dinner some time soon, but she didn't mention the signature matter again, and neither did I.

That incident was, in many respects, typical of the way Dorothea eventually came to operate on a day-to-day basis.

She would have some particular objective in mind, likely a rather complex one that could be accomplished only by getting a number of people to each perform a single small task. If there was a breakdown in the plan, it was only temporary, and hardly disabling, because only one element needed to be fixed to get things moving forward again.

From an emotionless perspective, Dorothea was, for a time, a true artist at her deception. She created, stroke by stroke, the chosen texture and aura of her own life. But, she was also the architect of many of her own problems.

She was prone to intermingle key elements of her autobiography, and could have limited the number of versions of it she spread around. She altered her personal history with increasing regularity as she got older, and of course she acquired, to those frequently exposed to her, the reputation of an addled braggart.

She might have been juggling her facts purposely, strolling through the minefield of persistent prevarication simply to see if she could avoid getting caught or to see how well and how quickly she could escape the trap of her own making. She existed for the edge that she always sought in life, trying to beat and exploit the system.

In her circle, around her neighborhood, Dorothea was street-smart like a feral cat. Providing for the needs of up to thirty people required many kinds of purchases. Some of those commodities, such as color television sets, were rather expensive, particularly so when needed in volume. Color television sets in individual bedrooms were very attractive to prospective tenants, and could help the landlady fill vacancies rather quickly. Tight contact with street people helped fulfill these needs, at costs she could manage. In this way, of course, she could also keep a sharp eye on thieves operating on her turf.

She knew what was happening on the streets and was not reluctant to use the information. There is evidence that she often took advantage of "anonymous tipster" programs, reporting to police the alleged wrongdoings of her perceived enemies.

Hers was a complicated lifestyle. For Dorothea was a producer, nothing less. She stole the script of life and rewrote it to her own satisfaction, and then she hunted down the funds needed to stage her production according to her own budget. She designed the sets, directed, did her own casting, and took for herself the starring role. She was involved in sales, promotions and advertising, community relations, accounts receivable, and collections.

Like every long-running play, however, Dorothea's production eventually fell by the wayside, overtaken by time, suffering from a lack of imaginative adaptation to the nuances of the present. Her portrayals became less convincing even as her audience became more demanding. She was weaving loose threads in a script that threatened to unravel.

And in the end, she blew the final scene, the only really important one.

4

Dorothea began to gain momentum in Sacramento's social-services community during the early 1960s. She first became a private, in-home attendant and caretaker, and her chosen wards were elderly and disabled people.

Then, alternately using the last names of Johanson and Montalvo, she managed room-and-board homes in the downtown Sacramento area. First came the Capitol Guest Home at the corner of Alhambra and Capitol Avenues. Then, in the first months of 1968, she reached her pinnacle by opening the largest residence home she would operate during her career.

Dorothea delighted in telling people that the three-level residence home at 2100 F Street had been built at the turn of the century as a high-class bordello. That was the reason, she said, that it had so many bathrooms—one for each of the sixteen small bedrooms, and a well-appointed one attached to the mistress's private apartment. She would also describe a previous owner as the "20 Mule Team Borax family."

She had a grand air about her, and was prone to wearing lavender and pink chiffons, dressing in a flowing, ostentatious, yet expensive manner. She was the very antithesis of seductive. Her wardrobe came in a much larger size then; she had trouble controlling her weight, was quite portly, and often ballooned to more than two hundred pounds. She wore her bleached blonde hair piled high in curls atop her head, in replication of a faddish 1940s style.

Among the luxuries her house offered were color television sets in every room, which at that time was anything but common, even for people of more independent means.

Tom Richardson was a young social worker in 1968, employed by the county of Sacramento at its Stockton Boulevard hospital. It was part of Richardson's job to talk to the rare person, like Dorothea, who offered some kind of living accommodations for the overflow of society. It had been only six years since John F. Kennedy engineered the deinstitutionalization of mentally ill patients, and local jurisdictions were having trouble keeping up with the flood of mentally disabled people reintroduced into communities across America. When someone like Dorothea came along, it meant roofs and meals for people who might otherwise be on the streets.

Dorothea, for her part, did her level best to have those conversations with people like Richardson as often as she could. Richardson was one of the many social workers who knew Dorothea, part of the crowd that occasionally, at her behest, was allowed to enter into her social sphere.

Richardson and his associates appreciated Dorothea's special brand of hospitality. She would play the generous hostess at lavish Thanksgiving, Christmas, and other holiday buffet dinners, inviting downtrodden transients as well as professional social workers into her home.

Dorothea was perfecting the fine art of public relations. Discovering that the free-dinner concept worked so well, she began to sponsor occasional drop-in buffet dinners for no particular reason and with the social workers as primary invitees. Since she employed a full-time cook (sometimes two) during those days, the sumptuous meals served in her home were often international in flavor and presented in a style rivaling the finest metropolitan restaurants.

She took these occasions to inform the social workers that her tenants ate food prepared just as carefully, because she selected a different international dish for dinner each evening. This, she maintained, helped make her multinational guests feel more at home.

The usual tenant at her establishment was aged and infirm, alone and forgotten, generally receiving the kind of government financial subsidy that Dorothea required in return for providing the basics of room and board. For these people, often fresh from an institution, a room-and-board house of this kind was almost beyond their meager imaginations.

Dorothea would, however, provide only the most essential of services: a room with clean linens, bath facilities, meals. By not offering the specific individualized care required by some potential residents, Dorothea avoided the need to undergo any official, regulatory licensing procedures—and evaded the subsequent scrutiny.

An added inducement for her circle of social workers to place people in her home was an offer that was both unique and very hard to ignore: for every two tenants referred to her who were getting full federally provided Supplemental Security Income (SSI) benefits, she would take in one who received only the monthly General Assistance (GA) checks from the county. County funding was more readily accessible but much more parsimonious than the federal allocations. She would tell people that she had been very fortunate in life, and that this was her way of paying back the community in kind, giving for what she had gotten.

Dorothea's generosity with the GA recipients meant that the many social workers with whom she maintained contact were able to place more people at Dorothea's, simplifying their search for suitable lodging for clients and thus simplifying their jobs. Everyone was just about as happy with the situation as they could be. Social workers wished there were many more people like Dorothea.

T. J. Hossli, a former county mental patient and a tenant of Dorothea's during the late sixties and early seventies, remembers the layout of the huge, turn-of-the-century house at 2100 F Street. On the top level was Dorothea's apartment (she preferred to keep her own residence separate from that of her tenants; she would remodel the home at 1426 F Street in the same way.) On the street level were the neat, separate rooms, each with its own bathroom and color television set, for those tenants who received full SSI benefits. In the basement lived the General Assistance people, in "wretched little cubicles with just curtains separating them, only one bathroom for all the rooms . . . pretty substandard."

Hossli was quite different from Dorothea's usual tenant. He first arrived at her door in 1965 at the age of twenty-five, to begin what would be a decade-long association with her. Hossli, holder of a master's degree in engineering, had suffered brain damage in an automobile accident, but other than occasional, trauma-induced and transitory mental problems, he was a functioning person. And since he was neither an alcoholic nor a severely mentally impaired patient on any kind of prescription drug (Dorothea's usual tenant), he could observe daily events with a relatively clear eye. And he did.

Dorothea's third husband, Roberto Puente, was about twenty

years younger than his bride when they married in Mexico City, also in 1966. When Dorothea departed on this matrimonial venture, she asked Hossli to watch the place, take care of the cooking and distribute the tenants' medication. He said he would do everything but hand out drugs, which he was not licensed to do. That won't be a problem, Dorothea said, because she was licensed. So it would be all right if Hossli did it. He still refused.

Upon Dorothea's return, it was apparent to her tenants that her marriage to the young hombre named Puente was headed for troubled waters.

Dorothea owned a new Pontiac Monte Carlo, but had never gotten her driver's license. Hossli was the only one of thirty-one tenants living in the house at that time who was licensed to drive an automobile, so as a result, whenever Roberto wanted to go anywhere, Hossli would be behind the wheel.

Every time they went out, Roberto wanted to stop somewhere so he could try to pick up a woman. On one occasion, Roberto had directed Hossli to take him to a West Sacramento western bar where, as usual, Roberto began chasing several Caucasian women. He could barely speak English, but this didn't stop him. The atmosphere in the bar began to get tense, and Hossli tried to pretend he didn't know the bold Mexican.

He could see that Roberto was about to get into big trouble, so Hossli decided to leave. In the parking lot, he found the Monte Carlo with four slashed tires. He taxied home.

The next night, Hossli was returning from the local coffee shop and had just walked in the door when he received a tremendous blow to his face, knocking him down and stunning him.

It was Roberto, fresh from a violent, physical argument with Dorothea regarding the matter of the night before. Dorothea had accosted him, accusing him of infidelity, and Roberto incorrectly assumed Hossli had informed on him. The punch to Hossli's face was the hot-blooded Mexican's way of extracting his retribution.

Roberto shouldn't have bothered. From his vantage spot amidst a pool of blood on the floor, Hossli saw Dorothea swing and, with one punch, knock Roberto unconscious. The wayward Latin lover rolled down the stairs in a heap, and the tenants who watched the action figured if Dorothea's right hook didn't kill him, the fall would.

A few moments later, Roberto staggered to his feet and made his way out the basement exit. The house occupants heard him roar away in the Monte Carlo, which had four brand-new tires charged to Dorothea.

Hossli got emergency treatment, eight stitches over his right eye. Upon his return, Dorothea exhibited a great deal of concern. Word of the altercation got back to the social-services community, and soon twenty of the house's residents were removed to another environment.

During 1972, Hossli was friendly with a man named John, who lived in one of the basement apartments. Although John didn't talk much about his past, Hossli learned that he had been a college English professor. That was before the scholar met John Barleycorn, and eventually drank himself into that tiny cubicle at Dorothea's house.

John had developed a revolutionary method of shorthand that simplified and abbreviated its learning process and increased its speed capabilities.

One night, as Hossli and his pal ate a late dinner at the nearby Sambo's restaurant, John pulled an envelope from his pocket. In it was a letter from a New York publisher, discussing a book on the shorthand method and specifying a $25,000 rights fee, a certified check in that amount to follow shortly via registered mail. John was elated.

Upon their return to Dorothea's house, the men said goodnight.

Hossli retired to his upstairs bedroom. He arose at 5:30 A.M. as usual and went downstairs an hour later. By then, John always had coffee going. Always. "Seven days a week," says Hossli. But today there was no John. At 11:00 A.M., Dorothea came downstairs for the first time, and Hossli asked her where John was.

"He moved out," she said.

"When?" Hossli asked.

"During the night," she answered.

Hossli went to John's room. It was spotless; every sign of John was gone, clothing and all.

"I have always thought that was very strange," Hossli recalls. "John was a nice man. He would have told me he was moving. He would have said goodby. At least, he would have sent a note when he got relocated. He did none of these things. He just disappeared."

Hossli also knew the man known only as Chief, who had lived at Dorothea's for many years and had become her groundskeeper. Chief would often dig in the house's dirt basement before it was floored, removing debris with a wheelbarrow to the backyard of a duplex across the street. He was always busy, once tearing down a small garage in the backyard and concreting the ground over for a large patio. Chief himself disappeared, without even a wave of his hand, in 1975.

Her many violent, drunken confrontations in the home notwithstanding, Dorothea showed an apparently boundless propensity for lavishing loving attention on people under her care. If anyone knew she already had a criminal record (and very few did), it would look for all the world like she was now well on her way to total redemption. With the balancing evidence of her newfound conscience, who could care that in 1948 she had forged an acquaintance's check, or that in 1960 she was arrested, convicted, and given ninety days and a suspended sentence for residing in a house of prostitution?

Had it been widely known, that criminal history might have rung some bells with social workers. Dorothea had developed skills quite apart from culinary arts; dubbed the Robin Hood of Welfare by social-welfare professionals, she had robbed the SSI recipients to give to the rest of society's unfortunates. And in doing so, of course, the inevitable "expense" money slipped through the cracks and into Dorothea's apron, allowing her to maintain a style of living to which she became irreversibly accustomed.

She became particularly adept at handling heavy drinkers. She knew them to be consistently productive in relation to her own personal cash flow. At the time of the month when the checks arrived, Dorothea would collect and distribute them. (One of her toughly enforced house rules was that she picked up all the mail, always.) Then, from a fat wad of cash, she would play banker for her tenants.

Those tenants who were known to drink heavily (and that was most of them) were given fifteen or twenty dollars in cash and told to go get a haircut. As soon as they were out of sight of the house, they would head for the local bar, as Dorothea anticipated. Often, they would get picked up by police acting on an anonymous citizen's tip as they staggered down the street toward home, broke but drunk. Thirty days in the county jail, the judge would say, and Dorothea would pocket the cash remaining from their checks.

Her house rules were enforced quite arbitrarily. One morning an old man came to the breakfast table without shaving. Dorothea began to badger him about his appearance, and they got into a loud and unpleasant argument. Without hesitation, Dorothea told him to pack up and leave. The man was crestfallen; he loved the place, and begged her to change her mind and let him stay. No dice, the intractable Dorothea said. He packed and departed, very unwillingly. Three months later his old friends back at the residence house heard a depressing story: The man had leaped to his death from the window of an eighth-story room in the fleabag hotel where he had gone to live.

For almost a decade, Dorothea managed to keep her ample skirts clean and whatever name she might be using off the police blotters. She still had her weight problem, but was considered attractive and was able to maintain her popularity with the various social workers who placed folks in her facilities.

But her freedom from contact with the law was about to end. In 1978, while still managing the 2100 F Street room-and-board home, she was arrested by federal marshals and charged with thirty-four counts of forgery involving checks issued to her boarders. Convicted in December 1978, she was placed on five years' probation and high-risk supervision.

Her parole report described her crime: "For approximately three years, the defendant, while operating a board-and-care facility, secured U.S. Treasury checks for her residents and cashed them [unlawfully]."

A psychiatric report prepared at the time of her parole by Sacramento psychiatrist Thomas E. Doody, M.D., diagnosed her as a chronic schizophrenic, "a very disturbed woman."

Despite all this, Dorothea had but one set of plans, which she set into motion the minute she was free: She went straight back into the business of providing care for older people.

In the fall of 1980, Dorothea (using the last name Montalvo) was employed by a bonded home health-care agency. She was an around-the-clock, live-in caretaker to Esther Bussby, an elderly woman who was being admitted frequently to Sutter General Hospital for unusual and sudden medical problems "of unknown origin." Mrs. Bussby would be stabilized by doctors and released, only to return, often within days, stricken by the same odd, comalike symptoms.

During those hospital stays, Dorothea was almost constantly at Mrs. Bussby's bedside, her concern for her charge's well-being evident to all. Nurses on duty would comment, "Don't we wish every old person had a friend like that." Dorothea frequently asked how much longer Mrs. Bussby would be hospitalized.

The curious circumstances of Mrs. Bussby's medical history were confusing and disturbing to her personal physician, Dr. Jerome Lackner. He contacted Mildred Ballenger, a county social worker who included Mrs. Bussby in her caseload, and the two shared details of their experiences with Mrs. Bussby. Ballenger then telephoned Peggy Rossi, discharge planner at the hospital, to secure additional details about Mrs. Bussby's all-too-regular emergency visits. Rossi informed her caller that Mrs. Bussby's admissions always involved some kind of "acute medical stress" but that usually, after just a few days, she would be well enough to be released.

Rossi couldn't understand, either, why Mrs. Bussby was ill so often. After all, the patient had a new caretaker who was managing the administering of her various prescription drugs.

"Can you tell me the name of this caretaker?" asked Ballenger.

Rossi checked her records: Dorothea Montalvo.

What Ballenger then told Rossi began to frighten both women. Clients had complained about this caretaker to Ballenger and it was the social worker's yet-unconfirmed suspicion—one she had previously voiced to Dr. Lackner—that Dorothea Montalvo, Puente, or whatever name she now used, had either attempted or had succeeded in poisoning two of her previous husbands. Ballenger emphasized to Rossi that this allegation had never been proven, but she wondered if it might provide a clue as to Mrs. Bussby's ongoing afflictions. Still, there was no concrete proof of any wrongdoing.

Following one discharge from the hospital, Mrs. Bussby was placed temporarily in a nursing home, where her prescribed medication was very carefully monitored. Immediately following a visit from Dorothea, who had brought food for the patient from home ("A hamburger, I think," said Lackner), Mrs. Bussby suffered a relapse. Ballenger then met again with Dr. Lackner, and asked if he thought perhaps Mrs. Bussby was being poisoned.

Dr. Lackner, state health director in former California Governor Jerry Brown's administration and now in private family practice in downtown Sacramento, immediately replied, "Oh, my God, that's exactly what's going on!"

It was then, Lackner said, that he learned that Dorothea had been calling Mrs. Bussby's friends and relatives to ask for more money "for her care" and informing them that Mrs. Bussby was suffering from cancer.

"There was no diagnosis of life-threatening cancer," Lackner said. "I knew Dorothea pretty well [through her care of other of his patients] and I began to believe that her 'concern' was simply about how long she could keep living rent-free and spending Esther's money." He began to question his patient about this caretaker of hers, and then told Mrs. Bussby of his suspicions.

"She was very angry," Lackner recalled, and she resolved to immediately fire "Mrs. Montalvo," as she knew her. The plan didn't work.

"By this time, I think Dorothea was afraid I was on to her," Lackner said. The day Mrs. Bussby arrived at home, she again fell ill. Dorothea summoned an ambulance and told the drivers to take the patient to the Medical Center in Sacramento operated by the University of California, Davis, instead of the usual Sutter General, where Dr. Lackner practiced.

Physicians at Medical Center were surprised to note that Mrs. Bussby's condition always worsened after visits from her "attentive, solicitous caretaker." They contacted Dr. Lackner, who was quite surprised to learn that Mrs. Bussby was at Medical Center. He asked to conduct blood tests. An unusually high level of Digoxin, a sedative and relaxant, was found.

A recovering Mrs. Bussby fired Dorothea Puente. Ballenger informed Sacramento County Dep. Dist. Attorney William Wood, but he refused to prosecute, citing insufficient evidence. He did promise, however, to take a closer look at Dorothea's activities.

A few months after the incident, hospital officials at Sutter were puzzled by yet another female patient who was exhibiting the very same symptoms that had plagued Mrs. Bussby. Her physician, Dr. Thomas Coyle, had noted in her medical records that he thought she was being poisoned. Rossi, alerted by the similarity of events, contacted Dr. Coyle and discussed her concerns. Dr. Coyle said his patient was under the care of an attendant hired through a licensed and bonded medical agency, but he couldn't remember her name. The physician said he thought the name might be in an address book on the patient's nightstand. Quickly, they went to the patient's room and examined the book's contents.

Written in ink under *M* was the name Dorothea Montalvo.

Rossi reported this information to the hospital's nursing office, but was told by the administrator that nothing further could be done because there was "no evidence." Rossi made a telephone call to Ballenger and informed the social worker about the second incident involving Montalvo. Quickly, the kindly helpmate was summarily discharged. Again, also quickly, the patient made a full recovery from her symptoms.

By this time, Mildred Ballenger was determined to get to the bottom of this troubling situation, and she compiled a file filled with alarming clues to support her contention that Dorothea

Puente was the harbinger of something very bad. Her file soon included reports that at least four other county-assistance clients had suffered odd health problems while under Dorothea's care. One even complained of having heart attacks shortly after eating food prepared by her "benefactress." Ballenger had also received reports from elderly clients that valuables were disappearing from their homes after Dorothea had been there.

In 1981, three years after her parole-oriented psychiatric examination by Dr. Doody, Dorothea had another session with the psychiatrist who had termed her "schizophrenic" and "very disturbed." He now thought she might be making "some progress in her mental condition, although there have been episodes of anxiety and some depression." In September of that year, she was found unconscious on the floor of the 2100 F Street residence house. She had taken an overdose of Metrobarmate, a barbiturate, an uncommon drug for her. She accused a friend of trying to poison her, denying any attempt at suicide.

Again, Dorothea underwent psychiatric examination, but no sign of serious depression was found and she was sent home. Dr. Doody noted in his report to parole that Dorothea had "multiple physical problems" and he was particularly concerned about her body's inability to regulate its potassium level, which might be an explanation for her "disassociative disorder."

Two years later, an article was published in an issue of *Sacramento* magazine at Ballenger's behest, documenting the social worker's misadventures with Dorothea. An excerpt:

> Several of Ballenger's elderly clients over the years had sought the services of [Dorothea] as a home health attendant. Dorothea was an attractive woman, striking, some would say. She had the countenance of a fairy godmother and Florence Nightingale rolled into one. Her

> silvery hair was perfectly in place, her stylish clothes fit well. She always had a pleasant word for everyone, even though she, poor thing, was suffering from cancer.

Her "cancer" would remain a favorite story of Dorothea's over many years, and she often added the postscript that she didn't have very long to live as a result of the disease's steady progress. She did have skin cancer at one time, but it was minor and had been rectified by local surgery years earlier.

According to the article, Ballenger's clients sometimes reported missing items of jewelry, but none could say they had any particular reason to mistrust the "sweet-faced" Dorothea.

The article cited Ballenger's frustration: "Ballenger would have liked to shout all of her suspicions from the rooftops to warn people. But the [Sacramento] county counsel opined the welfare department 'could not interfere with Dorothea's employment.' "

This would not be the last time the oh-so-cautious county counsel would make a ruling that would be of great help in shielding Dorothea from close official scrutiny.

5

The year 1982 stands out in Dorothea's criminal career. In January, she was arrested by Sacramento police and charged with forgery and grand theft. Arresting officers told her she was suspected of phony penmanship on thirty-four government-issued benefit checks belonging to her tenants, some of whom were no longer living at her house. Out on bail, she was arrested once again in April for grand theft, once again involving county and SSI checks.

By now, a pattern had been established. Each of Dorothea's brushes with the law came with the same slant—her apparent attraction to easy money taken from those with little ability to resist her will. And apart from the occasional snafu, such as the increasingly common arrest, she had polished her act to recital quality.

One morning in May, Malcome McKenzie, a seventy-four-year-old retiree who frequented a downtown Sacramento bar called the

Zebra Club, sat with several of his friends sipping an eye-opener when a well-dressed, older woman entered the bar.

Her physical appearance and elegant manner immediately set her apart from the barflys and hookers who comprised the usual female foot traffic in that particular part of town. Her white hair was nicely coiffed and her fashionable clothing was accented by classy and expensive jewelry. With an air of elegance, she selected her perch.

Ordering a vodka and grapefruit juice with ice in a tall chimney glass, she sat by herself for a short time. Silently, grandly, she occasionally sipped at her cocktail.

Within ten minutes of her arrival, however, she had initiated a wide-ranging discussion with the few patrons of the Zebra (all men at that moment) and was showing a particular interest in McKenzie. Shortly thereafter, the woman and McKenzie departed. The bartender later told investigators he had heard the woman ask questions about McKenzie's apartment. McKenzie then offered to show it to her.

When the pair arrived back at McKenzie's small, one-bedroom apartment, he sat down in his favorite wingback chair and told the woman to get a beer for herself from the refrigerator if she wanted one. He gestured toward the kitchen. She said nothing, just stood there looking at him. Within moments of sitting down, the man began feeling dizzy. He fell into a stupor, but remained conscious enough to discern what his "new friend" was doing, and it didn't appear to be something he would like.

"I could see, I could hear, but I couldn't move or talk," he recalled years later. "It was kind of funny when you stop and think about it, because I just couldn't move. She . . . she could have killed me."

Completely paralyzed by a substance that likely had been slipped into his drink while he was still at the Zebra Club,

McKenzie watched through slitted eyes as the classy woman packed his red suitcase with a few of his belongings, including most of a rare penny collection. Then she walked determinedly to the chair where he lay slumped. Without so much as a how-dee-do, she zeroed in on a small diamond pinky ring that he wore and slipped it right off his finger.

"She was a sharp dresser, sharp in her ways. She knew what she was doing. She could have fooled anybody." McKenzie remembers his brush with the nicely packaged woman with a wry smile, but icy fear is what he feels.

The official report of the pensioner's mugging was routed to social worker Ballenger by a contact at the police department. Because there was an important linking witness—the bartender had actually seen the victim in the company of the woman who now had been identified as Dorothea—Ballenger saw the opportunity she had been awaiting. She dashed to police investigators with her file, and she found a receptive audience.

Ballenger told the cops that one of Dorothea's favorite gimmicks to gain the confidence of older people was to introduce herself as a registered nurse and an official representative of the "Sacramento Medical Association." There was no such group, of course, but few elders ever bothered to check on her story. Instead, they willingly, often anxiously, opened their doors to her.

Investigators sought a warrant for Dorothea's arrest by convincing a judge that they had evidence that Dorothea was taking advantage of her position of trust to exploit her hapless victims. Police alleged that "the planning and sophistication with which the crimes are carried out, and other facts indicate [the suspect's] premeditation."

Although Dorothea claimed she was just going to the store when she was apprehended hailing a cab on the morning of May 18, arresting officers found a first-class airplane ticket to Mexico City in her purse. She was also carrying two stolen credit cards and enough cash to have a pretty good time for a while.

Prosecutors added charges implicating her in felony theft and the drugging of another elderly woman named Dorothy Osborne, whom she was caretaking. Admitting she drugged Mrs. Osborne, Dorothea professed to be unable to recall the specific substance she had used. She admitted she stole McKenzie's penny collection, but later recanted that story with the claim that the alleged victim had given her the coins and asked her to buy beer.

The interviewing parole agent interpreted these varying stories to mean that Dorothea felt none of the remorse she so vociferously expressed throughout the sessions. She had even cried and carried on, to no avail.

On August 18, Dorothea pleaded guilty to three felonies. Her parole officer's report listed her crimes, in addition to those related to the McKenzie case: "While in a position of trust [nursing care] she proceeded to take advantage of an 83-year-old lady by forging several of her personal checks and stealing personal property worth $3,800."

In a third, parallel, prosecution, Dorothea was accused of stealing an eighty-two-year-old, bedridden woman's thousand-dollar diamond ring, an heirloom emerald ring, a supply of sleeping pills, and a department-store credit card that soon bore Dorothea's forged signature. It had been used for purchases of more than eight hundred dollars before she was arrested and brought into court.

While she was awaiting sentencing, Dorothea had tried to turn her charms on the presiding jurist, Judge Roger Warren. From her jail cell, she had sent two handwritten letters, the first arriving at the court on June 8:

"Dear Judge Warren: I have been in front of you two times, and soon to be in front of you again, if not this month, then next . . .

you only know by what you read on the paper in front of you about me." She then went on to outline her "difficult" early life and her efforts to be a good citizen as an adult. She cited her numerous civic activities and the contributions she had made to political candidates—"out of clean money," she thought it necessary to add.

"I admit I'm a forger," she wrote, making an admission that in later years would become almost a motto for her.

The second letter, dated July 25 and also addressed to Judge Warren, began with the observation that she was uncertain "if we as prisoners are supposed to write to you or not, but I'm going to take a chance."

Dorothea had heard through the ever-active prison grapevine that the judge would be giving heavy consideration at her sentencing to the plane ticket found in her purse at the time of her arrest. This indicated to Judge Warren that a flight to avoid prosecution was occurring when Dorothea had been caught, and that she was likely to flee again, given the opportunity.

She attempted to explain away the plane ticket by saying she was headed to Mexico because a sister had died the day before. She noted that another brother, for whom she provided sole support, had died in Mexico since her incarceration.

"Please," she wrote,

> just give me please the least [prison time] you can so I can send [the rest of her family in Mexico] money to buy meat, eggs, milk, since my [remaining] brothers and sisters are so old. I don't mind if I have to report each day or what.
>
> I know I have done wrong. These months [in jail] have been terrible on me. But worse on my family, as I have not been able to send them any money. I feel so terrible for the poor people I did wrong to.

Her old acquaintances at state parole were not buying any attempt at straight probation. In a tersely written report to the court, parole officials made it crystal clear that the court should not be taken in by her hard-luck stories. The report noted that Dorothea told them at the time of her arrest that she felt great remorse for the people who lost their personal possessions because of her crimes. She "could see that they were either needy or old people who had a right to continue to possess their property."

Dorothea stressed that she had not taken any of the stolen property from her residence, and admitted forging two checks. She had made restitution, she said, and was at a loss to explain her actions "since she didn't really need the money that badly."

Her parole officer, Robert F. Keldgord, said that in his opinion,

> [Dorothea's] expression of remorse was diluted by her attempts to manipulate the interview. While she appeared distraught throughout the interview, it was apparent that she was extremely observant of the notes that were being made, and at one point asked for an explanation of a particular word. She read upside down the notes as she sat on the opposite side of the interview booth.

As his recommendation, the parole officer wrote:

> The defendant is seen as undeserving of probation as she has [usually] concentrated her criminal efforts on a segment of the community that is the most vulnerable, the ill and the elderly. Her criminal acts, therefore, are callous and unconscionable.

Unmoved by her repeated pleas for "her family's welfare," on August 18, 1982, Judge Warren handed Dorothea the maximum for each count, a total of four years and four months, and off she went to California Institute for Women in Frontera.

By the fall of 1983 Dorothea had adjusted fairly well to prison life and had been moved to the "campus," where the main prison population was housed. She had a job, a "pay slot" in Prison Industries, handling not cash but redeemable printed credits used to pay prisoners for their work. She frequently worked overtime, causing no waves.

All this soon would change. On October 6, a young inmate named Maureen McGlorin was transferred to the campus. McGlorin had first encountered Dorothea in the Frontera reception center at the time of their initial processing. Dorothea must have been her charming old self during that meeting, because before it was over she had won a good, new friend in McGlorin. McGlorin remembered Dorothea as being "an extremely decent person, kind and considerate." This, according to McGlorin, was an opinion shared by "officers and inmates alike."

A week or so after Dorothea's incarceration, an incident occurred that cost her dearly. McGlorin was walking with another woman on the afternoon of her second day on campus when she was attacked by three other women who blindsided her from the rear. She was beaten with a pipe and managed to break away from them in the nick of time: "They intended to use their knives on me." She said her companion "ran away and didn't summon help." Bystanders either ignored the commotion or stood by laughing, and of course no one came forward to identify the attackers.

Until Dorothea, that is. Dorothea had overheard a conversation after the beating in which the identities of the attackers were mentioned. Without hesitation, she took that information to her jailers. McGlorin says Dorothea did this "knowing the danger to herself."

Dorothea's altruistic action quickly backfired on her.

McGlorin was recuperating from her emergency treatment when, a week later, Dorothea was wheeled in strapped to a gurney. She, too, had been beaten. When the women first glimpsed one another, they both broke into tears. Feeling responsible, McGlorin was sickened by what she saw.

Later, Dorothea told McGlorin the story of her assault. She had reported earlier that day to her job, and had gone into the restroom when she was confronted by five angry women, their features distorted by nylon stockings pulled over their faces. One of the attackers held her around the neck from behind, a blanket was thrown over her head, and she was knocked down, kicked, and stabbed twice with a pair of scissors. The masked women accused Dorothea of being a snitch in the McGlorin incident and this, they gloated, was their way of expressing their extreme displeasure.

Because of her sudden status as an informer within the general prison population—a position that required protection from further physical harm—Dorothea was placed in isolation.

McGlorin recalled that:

> Dorothea was put in a dismal, dark, and airless cell with nothing but a toilet and a bed, in a place called "Deep Six." But she didn't remain there long. Illness forced her back to the infirmary. I didn't see her again for almost six months. When I did, she had lost a great deal of weight. She had had a heart attack. I later heard it was two.

McGlorin's letter to Judge Warren was a sincere attempt to get a reduction in Dorothea's sentence. She wrote:

> I feel such sorrow at being the [unwitting] cause of this tragedy, a heart attack, irrevocably affecting her health,

> her selflessness and courage on my behalf, a virtual stranger has lost her her job, the money from which she so sorely needed. She no longer qualifies for the Inmate Work Time Program [because of her illnesses and long infirmary stays]. Your Honor, her punishment has exceeded what you intended it to be. I beg you to consider a modification in her sentence.

McGlorin said Dorothea was "afraid to go anywhere, and well she might be." In relating the dangers of prison, McGlorin told the judge, "One girl was found beaten unconscious with socks containing bars of soap, and [with] a pencil sticking out of her ear. Another woman carries the scars from boiling water."

The young inmate concluded with a vote of confidence for Dorothea, hardly prophetic: "If she were put on probation I'm certain Dorothea would do nothing to jeopardize her freedom and return her to this place."

Dorothea's parole officers were quick to respond to the attempt at a sentence reduction or modification. Robert E. Ghiglieri, senior deputy probation officer for Sacramento County, and agent Keldgord, wrote to the judge that they believed the matter would best be handled by either a transfer to another institution or protective custody. They had already seen the kindlier side of the prisoner, and they had not been impressed.

Part of their letter said; "Because of the very serious nature of the offenses committed by the defendant, it is not felt that the court should take any action in resentencing the defendant."

The court heard the arguments and concurred with parole. Dorothea served out her full term. When she was released more than three years later, she looked like a new woman. She had lost seventy-three pounds.

6

Upon her release from federal custody on September 9, 1985, Dorothea had no real home to which she could go. In addition to her jailhouse blues, all the furniture and other belongings she had left behind had been plundered.

It was to the unique world known as Alkali Flat that Dorothea now turned. Alkali Flat lies on Sacramento's northern edge, scant blocks from the polished opulence of the restored state capitol building. As in much of the downtown area, the houses are an eclectic mix of old and new, but here—unlike many of downtown's upwardly mobile neighborhoods—the ambiance is dominated by creeping structural decay rather than renovation. Blight seems to be winning the war with time; only occasionally does a residence reflect regular maintenance.

"The Flat" is populated by more renters then homeowners, and boasts a small grocery store or two, a six-dollar barber shop, several liquor stores, a restaurant with heavy wrought iron covering its windows, the now-famous Joe's Corner bar, and assorted other business establishments. Its regular occupants coexist with another, more transient, clientele. Vagrants, drifters, and other street folk mosey over from the nearby American River and the adjacent railroad tracks to occupy the various vacant buildings, empty, weed-choked lots, and gravel alleys.

These people are the overflow—some would say effluent—of society. They are the rejects, the down-and-out, the hopeless. Bums are not popular with the permanent residents of Alkali Flat.

In neighborhood parlance, these are "the pukes."

That may be the prevailing local attitude, but it is not necessarily the reality. As often as not, the kinds of people who find themselves on the hostile streets are incapacitated, alone, unable to care for themselves, virtually helpless on the most cutthroat edge of civilization. Many of these derelicts are prevented by mental or other disabling deficiencies from taking the few steps necessary to find some sort of governmental assistance. They are the ones who have fallen through the cracks, lost amidst humanity, stepped on and around, the ones whom life passes by without so much as a disdainful glance.

Dorothea knew she would find an abundance of society's castaways in this downtown Sacramento neighborhood, and she, of course, believed herself to be particularly well suited to her self-assigned task of sheltering and feeding these unfortunates. She moved easily and comfortably in her adopted environment.

She may have been down upon her release from incarceration, but Dorothea was far from out. She still had several thousand dollars in a bank account. She still knew how to talk to people. Soon she had ferreted out a family friend, Ricardo Ordorica, whom she had met in 1974 at Joe's Corner where each had gone to hear a group of Mexican singers. Ordorica would later recall that first encounter: "She bought me a beer and had it sent over. She was like a movie star. She was with her 'husband,' a bodyguard, and her chauffeur."

Dorothea was so taken by her newfound friend that she virtually adopted Ordorica, referring to him as her nephew for years thereafter. She would visit his family and always, always brought an armful of gifts. His daughters called her Tia (Aunt) Dorothea.

Ordorica owned a large house in the downtown area, a neatly maintained blue and white Victorian located at 1426 F Street. In September 1985, Dorothea paid Ordorica two hundred dollars in cash for the first month's rent of a small room at the end of the lower-floor corridor.

It was Dorothea's intention to go back to the room-and-board business, despite requirements of her parole that she avoid that profession. Instructions accompanying her parole precluded her from "working with the elderly, and . . . handling government checks of any kind issued to others."

She began to telephone and visit her former associates in the social-welfare business, letting them know that she was back in town and soon would be ready to receive guests.

To those social workers who knew only that Dorothea had been gone for a while, she told the story that she had been helping relatives in Mexico during a lengthy crisis; to those who correctly ascertained that she had been doing prison time, she told the story of her "innocence and exoneration" and her noble return to Sacramento to pick up the pieces of her life.

During her first months of freedom, Dorothea scouted for a residential location that would satisfy her particular needs, and tried at the same time to polish her public image. She told Tom Richardson, the county social worker, that she had been falsely accused of the crimes in 1982, had proved the charges false, and had been completely cleared of all wrongdoing. She expected to get her city license very soon. She wouldn't need a state license, she noted, because her operation was not going to be large enough.

She talked about her plans to lease the old Franklin Hotel (since demolished) for the purpose of establishing a residential home. These plans would not come to fruition, because she was unable to show sufficient credit to swing the lease.

After deciding she wasn't going to find the type of building she thought she needed, Dorothea went to her good friend Ordorica with a proposal that made him very happy: She wanted to rent his house at 1426 F Street, the *whole house*, and could pay him six hundred dollars a month for it.

Ordorica, a short, slightly built man and a Mexican immigrant, had arrived in the capital city in 1966, and had considered himself lucky to land his first job as a janitor at the old Mansion Inn (since renovated and renamed the Clarion Hotel). He had become chief gardener at the same establishment, was fifty years old, and—other than buying his house—had yet to make his first investment. Now he had big, American-sized ambitions. He wanted to move his wife Veronica and their children from downtown into the suburbs, while retaining ownership of the F Street house. Here was the manner by which his goal could be accomplished. Veronica shared his glee and together they went shopping for their dream house in the suburbs.

Dorothea said she wanted to open a boarding house for the poor and elderly; her monthly rental payments would more than cover the mortgage. Her proposal was very pleasing to Ordorica, because now he could get ahead financially and at the same time help do something good for others.

The soon-to-be landlady forked over the first month's rent and took possession of the residence.

Dorothea began her search for "clients" in earnest. In telephone calls to as many social workers as she could locate, including county employee Richardson, she outlined the "many advantages" of making referrals to her. She reminded Richardson, "Of course, you already know how good my cuisine is."

Richardson, unaware that Dorothea's most recent absence was prison-related, simply acknowledged her reappearance without fanfare. His file card from 1986 has the following notations: "Dorothea Puente (Johanson), 1426 F Street, 3-bedroom apartment, 443-4496. $250.00 and $275.00; close to Consilio; city license; has cat. Quality care. Speaks Swedish, Norwegian, Danish, Italian, Spanish, Portuguese, Greek." Of all the languages, Dorothea only spoke limited Spanish.

At the time, Richardson perceived Dorothea as "a gentlewoman, very businesslike. She tended to be skeptical of most people, somewhat paranoid that people around her were out to get her." She told Richardson he was "one of the few people" she could trust. She added, for good measure, that cancer would abbreviate her life.

Richardson thought she was a bit unusual, a woman with a good heart who seemed to mean well and was just a little bumbling in her efforts. She was among the best available in an imperfect system, but her price and her offer seemed right.

For her part, Dorothea worked hard at perfecting the social graces that were becoming such an integral part of her business. Every day she made the rounds of places she considered most likely to be professionally productive.

During the work day, she would frequent the various local neighborhood self-help and assistance organizations. In the evening and at night, she might be found in any one of the numerous blue-collar bars dotting downtown Sacramento's landscape.

At each place, she would locate the kind of people she was seeking, the pensioned elderly.

Dorothea seemed a popular figure wherever she went. She

joined every Mexican organization and association she could find, even serving on the boards of directors of several. She backed Mexican political candidates with cash donations. She became a member in good standing of the Sacramento Metropolitan Chamber of Commerce, of organizations such as the Consilio and Comite Patrico. She helped give a fund-raising dinner for Merv Dymally, an ex–lieutenant governor of California; attended political functions for Congressman Robert Matsui and State Assembly Speaker Willie Brown; and, in a letter to one judge, called former California Supreme Court Justice Cruz Reynoso "my good friend" (Reynoso can't remember ever meeting her).

All her favorite organizations, causes, and politicians got regular donations from Dorothea, always in cash. She never asked for a receipt for these tax-exempt contributions.

Her professed circle of influence had grown enormously during her time in prison; she bragged to friends that she had personal connections to the Shah of Iran, the King of Jordan, and the Pope.

Dorothea also claimed a "close friendship" with Joe Serna, at the time an official of the neighborhood group Consilio and now a Sacramento city councilman.

Serna remembers Dorothea always showing up for Mexican community fund-raisers:

> She was more of a social type; she never really did any kind of volunteer work. She was quite a welcome person in those days, because the Chicano movement was really just getting off the ground, and she was a supporter. She made a lot of campaign contributions, and she asked me once if she could sponsor a fund-raising dinner for me. I was starting to get a little street-wise myself by then, and she didn't seem quite right, so I just said no.

But Dorothea's preferred form of socializing was in her favorite bars. There were three: the nearby Joe's Corner, with a primarily Latino clientele; Henry's Lounge in midtown, generally frequented by a mixed crowd of pension-aged men; and the upscale Clarion Hotel, an inn catering to middle- and upper-income traveling executives with expense accounts. At the Clarion (which she reached by walking through her backyard, down the alley, then two blocks right) Dorothea would introduce herself as either "Mrs. Johanson" or "Mrs. Montalvo," depending on the nationality she wished to portray. At this and other upscale establishments, she would make certain that people understood the Montalvo surname was Spanish rather than Mexican.

Over a three-year acquaintanceship with Dorothea, Jan Simone, the hotel's afternoon-shift bartender, developed memories of her that are not at all pleasant. "The woman was a phony, plainly and simply," she says. "But she wasn't fooling anybody around here with all her stories. She lied every time she opened her mouth."

To be sure, Dorothea had her share of detractors at Henry's Lounge, too, but she also counted numerous friends. Henry's was a place where she would engage any nearby man in conversation that almost always led to a discussion of his means of support. She had a very gentle way of getting to the subject of money, but she got there.

Many of the men to whom she talked were lonely pensioners. Their entire social world centered around places like Henry's, where a beer and a casual conversation could last for hours. Opportunities to talk to a woman in such a place were infrequent, particularly a woman who knew things like Dorothea seemed to know. And she seemed so *concerned* about everyone.

The subject of the conversations was most often kept close to the vest by these men, members of a generation of Americans who considered money issues a very private matter. As a result, few of the men realized until after her sensational arrest for murder that they had been just one of many sources of data for Dorothea, that she chatted up the same topic to everyone in pants. Did she recognize, and exploit, the common male penchant for privacy regarding income?

Locked in her memory were all of the key numbers pertaining to Social Security benefits, and all her information was current. As often as not she could point out to her enthralled new male acquaintance various ways of increasing the amount of his own monthly check. To this day, some of the older men around Henry's will cackle and recall the names of some of those who got increased benefits because of a well-placed tip from Dorothea, and are still around to tell their tale.

The drinking establishment's two female bartenders, Mitch and Nancy, heard these conversations far too often to remain complacent in their feelings about Dorothea. They were as worldly-wise as she, and the women recognized Dorothea's dialogue as opportunistic, and nothing more.

But at places like Joe's Corner, the run-down, rambling neighborhood bar just steps from her residence, the woman known as Missus Puente was always welcome. Dorothea would swirl in like Mexican royalty, an instant focus of attention. Here was a lady with class, with style. She would greet everyone in Spanish but would revert quickly to English. She was generous in her frequent sponsorship of cocktails for the house. Dorothea had her favorite cocktail waitresses at Joe's, to whom she would give expensive perfumes as presents. Her checks were always welcome, too (personal or endorsed), because the management considered her credit beyond reproach. Also, upon her departure, the tips she would leave were almost as impressive as her presence.

And, ah, the stories she could tell.

She was a former surgeon, forced to retire several years earlier when she began losing her hand-to-eye coordination. She was a registered nurse, had served as a young front-line navy nurse in the Pacific theater during World War II. She had survived the infamous Bataan Death March and beatings by Japanese soldiers en route, and as a result now had a metal plate substituting for the roof of her mouth. She had cancer, probably didn't have long to live, but what the heck, don't anyone give it a second thought. That cancer, of course, originated with her exposure to radioactivity in Hiroshima, where (as an American war nurse/prisoner of war) she happened to be when the Enola Gay dropped its atomic payload. She had all these nephews and nieces living in Mexico, all of whom depended upon her for total financial support . . . but everything would work out all right.

Her gift for kindly blarney served her well; she became all things to all people, just what one wanted, a sympathetic ear, full of wise suggestions. In a world populated by desperate, lonely people, a helping hand like the one offered by Dorothea was as good as gold. She was the closest thing to an earth mother some of these folks would ever find.

The deceptive demeanor she displayed for the public at large often slopped over into her home life. Former tenants remember a woman with many sides, one who would take in every stray cat that happened onto her doorstep, then evict without notice a tenant who displeased her. She fit the classic *Dr. Jekyll and Mr. Hyde* persona. But her frequent benevolence to her tenants tended to offset in their minds her widely perceived mean streak.

To John Sharp, a sixty-four-year-old retired cook, Dorothea gave a substantial break in the rent upon his release from the hospital after back surgery, when he had no place to sleep. She arranged for installation of cable television into Sharp's room, and paid the cost for him. One evening, Dorothea arrived unannounced at his door with a surprise gift: a comfortably upholstered rocker-recliner to help ease his back discomfort. Sitting alone later in his new chair, watching cable TV, he felt so good about his benefactress that a few tears coursed down his tough, grizzled cheek.

The dark side of Dorothea always lurked near the surface, however. She had a reputation for being physically tough. She would get howling drunk and have knock-down, drag-out fistfights with her upstairs roommates, including Mervin John McCauley. Any handy household item might be thrown with deadly intent. One night a small refrigerator was pressed into duty as a missile, and it crashed loudly through a door and down the rear stairway.

She was methodical in her search for those who could help populate her boarding house, because she almost always needed new tenants. Turnover, the old bugaboo of landlords everywhere, was particularly high in the kind of establishment run by Dorothea. The folks would come and they would go, booted out or just hitting the road, and often enough without a word of goodby. Because this happened with regularity, the occasional disappearance of someone was hardly a notable event.

Such was not to be the case with Ben Fink. Fink was a local, a 1950 Sacramento High School graduate who misplaced his zeal for life early and replaced it with the kind of fire in the belly one can buy in a bottle. Fink had been drinking heavily since he was seventeen. He didn't range far from home, just kind of stayed in town getting plastered. His family never knew exactly why he drank so much. A brother, Robert, recalled years later that Ben "had to have an escape from, I guess, being who he was—just being Ben."

Fink tried a couple of times, somewhat halfheartedly, to beat his personal demons. He's check himself into a treatment facility and cultivate a new, if temporary, attitude. But as soon as he'd hit the road, as bad luck always had it, he'd encounter his muse, the open saloon. One sniff of liquor and Fink would fall off the wagon again. He tried to live with relatives, and for a while he'd be just fine, pleasant, polite. Then the liquor would grab him. He'd get nasty with everyone; soon no one could stand being around him, and boom, he was back out on the streets.

Late one night in January 1988, Fink got a mighty heat on and raised an unholy commotion that extended Dorothea's patience to the limit. He was throwing chairs and tables, breaking windows in his bedroom, and pounding raucously on the hallway walls until everyone in the house was awake.

Dorothea, her bathrobe cinched resolutely around her waist, soothed Fink as best she could. She talked Fink into accompanying her to her apartment, telling him that she would "make him feel all better."

Fink didn't make the slightest trouble after that. In fact, the next time anybody saw him, he was stretched out on the coroner's slab.

It was with Fink's disappearance that Dorothea's carefully fabricated world began to fall apart. Some of her tenants, after all, still had their wits about them. When Fink dropped from sight, there was cause to wonder. When the ripe odor of death permeated Dorothea's upstairs apartment days later, there was cause to wonder. When Dorothea tried thirteen times to shampoo the smell and the stain out of the upstairs spare bedroom's rug, there was cause to wonder. Meanwhile, Dorothea explained the smell by citing a faulty sewer in the backyard, and volunteered that Ben Fink "had gone up north."

But who knew anything for certain? There was confusion around the household. Who of the tenants wanted to risk the only home he or she knew? Eviction would be imminent if Dorothea had done no wrong. And who wanted to be *living* there if (horror of all horrors) the darkest of thoughts proved true?

Some neighbors, though, found the foul air unacceptable, and complained to authorities. On June 1, 1988, a man from the Sacramento County Health Department showed up. Assistant Sanitarian Richard Estrada didn't find any apparent problem.

"Obviously," he later insisted, "if there had been a problem, we would have given a written notice of violation. There was no notice given. Usually, the source of the odor is something out in the open. If not, we don't go digging up people's yards."

At the time of the Fink episode, Dorothea had fine-tuned her method of operation by tapping into every available government-supported program that she could, orchestrating like a maestro. The more competent she became at manipulation, the farther she would push her limits. It was the kind of thing she had done all her life, playing on the outer edge of everything, going for the gusto in her own crooked way.

She thought she had it all figured out.

SOCIAL WELFARE

This landlady knew the ropes. She could relate to her prospective tenants. She cooked great meals . . . canned her own vegetables. And she kept a gorgeously maintained garden.

7

By not licensing her boarding home at 1426 F Street, Dorothea avoided contact with pesty bureaucrats and their silly regulations.

She didn't know it at the time, of course, but by the simple action of establishing this boarding home, she would set into motion a sequence of events that would someday produce a virtual mountain of red tape within the governmental bureaucracy. The success of her business endeavors would also help to illustrate the abundant and befuddling deficiencies in various agencies' social-services systems.

Dorothea had sensed, then taken full advantage of, the opportunity to design anew the personal reputation she desired. And her top priority was distancing herself from the reality of her prison term.

It hadn't taken too long for the Sacramento social-welfare machine's personnel to grow comfortable with Dorothea. By 1986, several different social-welfare agencies had steered more than twenty-two people to her for stays of varying duration.

Circumstances of fate helped Dorothea accomplish her public-relations coup.

Her old nemesis Mildred Ballenger, the tenacious county case-worker who compiled the damning record on Dorothea back in 1982, had retired from the service of the county. Also retired was William Wood, the Sacramento County deputy district attorney who was a key part of the successful prosecution team that nailed Dorothea for the Zebra Club drugging and theft.

As a result of these important missing links in the official chain of information, the significance of Dorothea's reemergence into the old-folks community was diminished in the eyes of the brand-new generation of social workers now manning the controls of local, city, county, and state welfare entities.

Simultaneously, computers began to replace field-assigned social workers, resulting in fewer people who might have any professional interest in abuses of the elderly.

What all this would translate into at a later date was an informational vacuum, one into which many solid clues about Dorothea's "other side" entered, never to emerge again.

Dorothea's activities in the community were common coin to many employed in government social work, but she was able to keep the entities and the individuals well separated, and as a result she became the official concern of no one. With no interference from any source, Dorothea flourished.

She had established her modus operandi. Insisting on being able to dictate the physical appearance of her residence home, she set house rules that limited tenants in their wanderings. Often they would simply sit in their rooms, doors closed, watching television, sleeping, or just staring at the ceiling. To the casual observer, the Victorian could have been a quiet, single-residence home.

Additionally, Dorothea operated her business almost exclusively on a cash basis, probably to reduce any paper trail that could be created by dealing with banks and other financial institutions.

This practice also made it possible for her to cash her tenants' checks easily, an activity that gave her access to large amounts of cash at certain times of the month. After collecting the checks, she would cash them, quite lawfully, through a prearrangement with a friendly barkeep or neighborhood grocer. As usual, Dorothea would make their cooperation worth the effort.

The importance of controlling her environment was something Dorothea had learned about, the hard way, at Frontera.

Probably the first place where the tides of fate could have changed, offering resistance to Dorothea's progress, was from within the offices of her federal probation and state parole agents. But she engineered her relationship with a variety of these agents during the first two years following her prison release in 1985 with expert manipulation.

Dorothea remained on dual supervision until the end of March 1986, when her state parole concluded. Federal parole officers stayed in regular touch with her, since she was on high-risk supervision. The federal officers now report a total of seventy-eight contacts with Dorothea during the thirty-two months following her release from custody, thirty-five face-to-face, either at her house or the agent's office, and forty-three by telephone.

The face-to-face visits take on special significance in reexamining the events on F Street. Twenty-one of these prescribed visits occurred at the federal parole office in downtown Sacramento. The encounters generally took place on the occasion of Dorothea's monthly report, which she prepared and delivered. The fourteen home visits almost always were initiated by Dorothea herself, by telephoning one of four different parole officers assigned to her and offering the suggestion that "perhaps I can stop by your office tomorrow" to set a time for the next home visit. This practice allowed Dorothea to avoid the usual surprise visits that parole agents employ, the kind of spontaneity that might have led to discovery of the fact that she was running a boarding house and had as many as ten people at a time renting rooms from her.

She was supervising her own parole agents, manipulating while appearing cooperative. She was doing such a bang-up job that not one of the professional lie detectors even noticed her handiwork.

The few times that her agents did check on her at the Victorian, they saw a physical layout that was perfect for the kind of deception she needed to practice.

The building's two stories were divided into two flats, the upper ostensibly separated from the several apartments below. But by simply walking around Dorothea's own residence, the stairway to the lower apartments would have been easy to detect. That discovery, in turn, would have proved suspicious only if agents had thought to talk to the renters of the street-level units.

After a while the parole officers became lulled into complacency by Dorothea's apparent willingness to cooperate; she made herself into one of the friendlier components of her busy agents' schedules.

She also adopted the unusual habit of gardening at very odd hours, 4:00 and 5:00 A.M., which had as one advantage the elimination of any risk that her parole agent might show up and see her (supposedly only a tenant at the house) taking care of the grounds—a task that might require an explanation and that might call unnecessary attention to herself.

The agents believed they were only trying to protect Dorothea's rights of privacy. They did not often involve other people in the examination of parolees' conduct, because to do so might serve to inform others, unnecessarily, about the felon's status. That can disrupt the smooth integration of the parolee into the community—which, after all, is the main goal of the parole program.

Perhaps it was because of the constant reassignment of agents and their rapidly rotating and bulging caseloads that Dorothea was allowed to perfect her own unique entrepreneurial endeavors. Perhaps it was simply a cut-and-dried instance of professionals going through the motions of doing their job, rather than diligently working at it.

From what her numerous assigned agents now say, Dorothea was deceptive in the appearance she presented to them. No one figured out that she was running an old folks' room-and-board establishment out of her house. Dorothea made certain of that.

8

The tenants who lived at Dorothea's boarding home arrived at her doorstep from a variety of sources, but one particular organization—in fact, one social worker—would prove to be a most dependable supplier of the ever-shifting stream of clients that required constant replenishing.

St. Paul's Senior Center, the oldest congregation in downtown Sacramento, is part of the Episcopal Church's Community Services program, Northern California diocese. When a large segment of the church's membership moved away to the suburbs, St. Paul's became a mission and began to administer assistance to the disadvantaged, the disabled, and the elderly. Some of the mission's activities included home visiting, counseling, telephone reassurance to the homebound elderly, and other volunteer services.

In 1986, St. Paul's formalized a pact with the Sacramento County Division of Mental Health whereby the county would fund a new set of services for homeless and elderly mentally disabled people. St. Paul's would administer the service by hiring a full-time social worker. The objective of this new employee, according to the contract, would be

> to support the elderly in maintaining independent living status; to link the elderly, mentally ill, homeless or near homeless persons to mental health services, diagnosis, and treatment housing [sic] as well as extensive intervention advocacy and ongoing support to gain or maintain independent living in a stable home setting.

The staff of St. Paul's new component worked with more than three hundred clients annually, and was reponsible for following up on numerous clients who had been released from jail, prison, or an inpatient psychiatric facility.

When the contract with the county was won, St. Paul's hired Peggy Nickerson, then thirty-seven, as its social worker, paying her a salary of $18,500 a year. A small woman with black hair, sad brown eyes, and a round face fired with compassion, Nickerson's job was to evaluate referrals of elderly mentally disabled people who chose to live in the downtown area for economic reasons. Nickerson also located housing and maximized Social Security benefits for each client, in order to ensure that all appropriate payments were being received.

She delivered a lot of bang for the county's buck. A county evaluation later would praise her efforts, calling her "commendable" and noting in its conclusion that her "motivation and commitment are obvious."

Shortly after Nickerson started her new job, she was visited by a polite, pleasant, white-haired woman. That visit would change Nickerson's life.

The widow introduced herself as Dorothea Montalvo, and she came with a most welcome proposal. She said that she was a widow with a large house, and believed it was her time to give back to the community, to other people. She offered rooms at her house for anyone who needed help.

Nickerson at first was somewhat skeptical: This woman, despite her rough edges, looked a little too sweet, a little too nice, to handle the kinds of people who would be parading in and out of her home. Nickerson told Montalvo that she would be dealing with people who had little or no self-discipline, who would be drunk and fighting with one another as soon as the Social Security checks arrived each month. They would vomit all over her nice house. They might become abusive and vulgar, hallucinate and call police about secret rays coming through their bedroom walls. There would be junkies, drunks, stinking street people—"very difficult clients," as Nickerson described them.

"No problem," said Dorothea. "I can handle those folks, no problem." They talked further. Nickerson began to perceive several primary traits in Dorothea: She appeared friendly enough, willing to help in any way, but very tough too, and could curse like a trooper.

"I saw that, before the end of that first visit. She laced her sentences with curse words. She said she liked to have a drink," Nickerson recalls.

Nickerson had to revise her early concept of softness. *This* landlady knew the ropes. She could relate to her prospective tenants. She cooked great meals, a typical breakfast being bacon, eggs, pancakes, and cereal. She canned her own vegetables. And she kept a gorgeously maintained garden.

All things considered, Dorothea was quite a discovery, and Nickerson was elated. Sacramento, not unlike any other big city around the country, has an ever-dwindling supply of rooms and shelters for the aged, poor, mentally impaired, and homeless. The resulting squeeze forces people to take what they can get, which often is next to nothing.

During the following three years Nickerson placed more than 350 needy people in potentially permanent homes. And on thirteen occasions she drove clients the short distance from her office to give them the chance to live in a tidy, pretty Victorian with the fair-faced and foul-mouthed woman named Dorothea.

During almost exactly the same period that Nickerson and Dorothea were cultivating their mutually agreeable relationship, another friendship was forming on the other side of town. This special bond, between two social workers and a mentally handicapped man, would become paramount in the sad and sickening drama that would unfold on F Street.

Several miles south of Dorothea's house is a small, plain plot of land surrounded by a high Cyclone fence, upon which stand several long, narrow buildings with aluminum roofs. On one edge of the property is a high levee bordering the deep and dangerous Sacramento River; opposite it is the old city cemetery.

This is the site of the local alcohol detox center. Every day and night, black and white police vans deliver dozens of sotted passengers to the center. There the inebriates get a minimum four-hour stay and temporary possession of a thin, dirty mattress on the floor, where they can sleep off their latest binge.

The center provides a sobering environment. Basically just two warehouses with cold, concrete floors, it is a fragile buffer between life and death for some of these people, because the winters in Sacramento can be quite frigid. The sleeping area is about one hundred feet long and forty feet wide, just large enough to contain sixty single-sized mattresses placed quite close together. Open showers are at one end, adjacent to the staff's office space. The high windows are covered with dusty, inexpensive blinds that remain open most of the time; only two small, wall-mounted air conditioners are visible to serve the entire building. A nearby Quonset hut serves as the center's mess hall, groceries and supplies for which are provided by a plethora of donors.

People employed at the center, for the most part, exhibit the patience of Job in dealing with the guests, often seeing the same pitiful faces day after day.

It was this same spirit of human kindness that ultimately resulted in Alvaro (Bert) Montoya living at the detox center.

Bert wasn't a drunk like the usual guest at the center, although he did like a belt every now and then. But he was mentally retarded and seemed to have no home, so the detox center's staff adopted him and gave him a place to sleep, an arrangement that lasted for eight years.

While at the center, Bert found love and care. It had been a long time since he had felt welcome anywhere; he had been on the road for many years. Born in Costa Rica on September 8, 1936, Bert was mistreated by his father, a barber, who regularly beat Bert's mother. She eventually moved to New Orleans with her son, by this time a teenager, and a niece and nephew. Bert became a U.S. citizen in 1964, and landed a job at eighteen despite his increasingly obvious mental retardation.

Bert was thirty-two years old when, in the spring of 1968, he suffered what psychiatrists would describe as a sudden psychotic break. He became paranoid, withdrew from people; his entire behavior pattern altered. These "fixed delusions" came complete with auditory hallucinations—that was when the voices first began talking to him. These were Bert's demons, the spirits that would haunt his every waking hour.

His mother, confused and panicky, sought the help of her Baptist minister, but the minister quickly discerned that he was out of his league. He secured help from the mental-health professionals, and their response was typical of the time.

Bert was taken against his will to a psychiatric hospital, where electric shock treatments were freely given but did not help. He was given tranquilizers, and in a confused state of mind mistakenly decided that he could leave. He was tackled near the front door by several burly attendants, wrestled roughly into a straitjacket, and placed in total restraint. It would be several weeks before his mother could arrange for him to be released into her custody.

That experience with a mental institution was all Bert needed to know about the kind of "help" that awaited him in the world outside. He decided to do something to help himself. Immediately upon his arrival at home after being released from the hospital, he packed a few articles of clothing, told his mother that he would never go through such a painful and degrading experience again, kissed her goodby, and hit the road. He didn't tell his mother where he was going, nor did he contact her when he got there, fearing that she, out of concern, might reveal his location to the people that Bert felt would be chasing him.

He headed for Southern California, then to San Francisco. In the late 1970s he was at a board-and-care home in Galt, California, twenty-seven miles south of Sacramento, and in 1981, without any formal announcement, he arrived in Sacramento at 2700 Front Street, the detox center. He was dirty, disheveled, and by now confused and mentally incapable of dealing with daily life. He was readily and warmly received.

Volunteers of America, operator of the detox center, is another private social-welfare agency that has contracts with government for providing care for people unable to provide for themselves. A Sacramento entity since 1911, VOA provides homeless and inebriate shelters, and operates a mobile intervention program called Courtesy Outreach Service for the homeless mentally ill.

The program connects clients with health support, and is funded under contract with the county. VOA's agreement with the county does not specify as a VOA responsibility the securing of either housing or funding for their clients. That formality, though, didn't stop the organization's good-hearted employees from trying to accomplish all that they could.

Judy Harper Moise and Beth Valentine were the outreach social workers selected by VOA to do the in-field, hands-on work of locating, contacting, and helping prospective clients.

Moise, a sturdy woman with features almost too motherly for her line of work, started with the organization as a full-time employee, at $240 weekly, in 1986 when the program was first funded. She had been attracted to the social-welfare business after an unfortunate family experience exposed her to what she viewed as an uncaring social-service bureaucracy. She considered the lack of empathy on the part of the professionals unacceptable, and vowed to help change the situation. That decision altered her life in more ways than one. Her younger associate, Valentine, worked part-time at VOA's downtown temporary housing facility until she joined Moise in the field in 1986.

In order to accomplish the program's stated goal, each woman made two hundred personal contacts each month, attempting to ease the burden of life for as many souls as possible. Pagers worn around their waists were beeping constantly as telephone calls came in almost around the clock.

The work of Moise and Valentine put them in contact with many other social workers, all of whom had similar goals: find decent housing and adequate care for indigent, helpless people.

One of the professionals with whom Moise and Valentine regularly associated was Peggy Nickerson, the very effective St. Paul's

Senior Center caseworker. And naturally Moise and Valentine, by late 1986 an inseparable pair, spent many hours at their own facility, the Front Street detox center.

Like the regular staff at the center, they soon grew extremely fond of their "mascot," the lovable bear of a man named Bert Montoya, who roamed around the premises in nearly constant conversation with his ever-present demons. He was often found warily circling the old cemetery, gesturing with an extended finger to his tormenting spirits, convinced that by this action he could keep them at bay.

In spite of his eccentricities, Bert was a friendly and trusting man, with huge brown eyes that sparkled and sun-weathered skin that wrinkled when he laughed. During the recent past he had grown a full beard, salt-and-pepper, giving him a look that he kind of liked. He didn't communicate with people very often—most of his conversations were reserved for his demons—but when he did talk, it would usually be in guttural Spanish. He spoke some English, but preferred his native tongue.

Moise and Valentine wanted to find a real home for Bert, and during the following two years that objective became a dominant focus of their professional lives. After all, the detox center, despite its affectionate personnel, could not provide the homey atmosphere that everyone agreed Bert needed.

But locating a permanent domicile for Bert proved a difficult task. Despite his cuddly reputation around the center, Bert could be very stubborn. He was a bit of a free spirit himself, especially after he had resisted taking his prescribed tranquilizers, which was most of the time. This trait probably resulted from memories of the very unpleasant treatment he had endured years earlier at the psychiatric hospital.

Because of his lack of cooperation in the matter of medication, he would often slide into a mild psychotic state, disappearing for days without a trace, only to return disoriented and grubby.

Complicating his physical health was a severe case of psoriasis on his head—thick, white, and scaly. He had suffered for years from the affliction, but he steadfastly refused to allow anyone to medicate it.

He also had a red-tape problem: at some time in his past he had scrambled in his mind the figures in his own Social Security number, so his caretakers had been unable to secure governmental assistance, the kinds of funds that would make him much more welcome at many different locations. Moise and Valentine were cautious about their inquiries regarding Bert's situation, because they worried—knowing so little about his past—that he might be in the United States illegally, an undocumented alien. And his deportation was something his friends greatly feared.

Nevertheless, Moise and Valentine, undaunted by Bert's lack of finances, were determined to succeed in their self-appointed mission. By the beginning of 1988, they had inquired into twenty-eight different possible boarding homes and agencies where they hoped Bert might be welcome. At each the answer was. Sorry, no room at the inn. But the duo persisted, and finally solved the mystery of Bert's Social Security status: He simply had transposed several of his assigned numbers, an easily correctable situation. He was a U.S. citizen after all! Soon Bert was receiving full monthly benefits, and Moise and Valentine felt greatly encouraged.

Now they could find him a decent place to live.

9

While Moise and Valentine searched for a new guardian angel for their Bert (with their tracks heading inexorably toward Dorothea's house), the landlady was fielding a few problems of her own. Unbeknownst to the social workers, accusations of theft around Dorothea's establishment were beginning to circulate in official government circles. A woman named Brenda Trujillo was being particularly vocal.

Trujillo, recently released from federal prison, was living at Dorothea's. The two women had met five years earlier, in the Sacramento County Jail, en route to the Federal Prison for Women, Frontera. It was to Dorothea that Trujillo immediately turned upon her parole when she needed a place to live.

A Social Security "report of contact" from May 15, 1987, written when Trujillo sought benefits, noted that Dorothea "owns a house on F Street. She has several rooms she rents for a flat fee of $150 a month. She allows [tenants] access to a refrigerator, but [they] do not have access to her kitchen and are not allowed to cook. She [Dorothea] agreed to allow claimant [Trujillo] to live at her rooming house rent-free until claimant could get on General Assistance [GA] and pay rent."

At the start Dorothea had been very helpful to Trujillo, first encouraging her to apply for, then aiding her in the acquisition of, her full complement of allowable SSI benefits.

Then Trujillo's luck started to sour.

On April 5, 1988, she was arrested on suspicion of murder and booked into county jail by police detectives Terry Brown and John Cabrera. While she was being processed, Trujillo made claims to the detectives that Dorothea "had bodies" at her house, implying that death had occurred at 1426 F Street. But her credibility was dubious, as far as the cops were concerned, because she waited until the end of her interview and booking processes to make the allegations.

Thus, the charges Trujillo made fell on unreceptive ears. Cabrera, working her case in the murder of a Sacramento man named Charles Nash, believed Trujillo was simply trying to throw him off the track by tossing out false leads. Trujillo's comments regarding Dorothea, recorded on videotape by police, were brief and nonspecific. But to be on the safe side, Cabrera forwarded the tape to the district attorney for his scrutiny.

Trujillo was subsequently cleared of suspicion in the Nash murder, and the district attorney eventually decided that her claims about cadavers at the F Street house warranted no further investigation.

Two parole violations caused Trujillo relatively short periods of incarceration. Both arrests were at the behest of her parole officer, who received anonymous tips from an unidentified woman. This sub-rosa informer whispered that Trujillo was using alcohol and taking drugs, both in violation of her terms of parole.

During her brief first jailing in June, Trujillo told a story to which no one listened. She said she had been drugged by Dorothea, who had then called the parole officer to report Trujillo's "violation" of parole terms.

In mid-1987, upon her release from this first parole-violation jail term, Trujillo moved in with her mother and continued her litany of accusations against Dorothea. Trujillo swore to anyone who would listen that the landlady had been stealing her SSI checks, which had continued going to the F Street address during Trujillo's repeated trips to prison. Trujillo expressed her suspicion that $4,300 had been improperly appropriated by Dorothea, who had also tried to poison her.

She told this to a court-appointed state psychologist, Dr. Angela Curiale. A physically compact, no-nonsense professional who had heard the best of stories from the best of liars, Dr. Curiale had short-cropped hair that was dark and beginning to gray. She was fond of blue jeans, casual shirts, and large earrings. Gallic eyes, big, brown, soft, belied needle-sharp perception honed by the perverse skills of her adversaries, the countless phonies she had encountered during twenty-two years in the analysis business.

After her session with Trujillo, Dr. Curiale walked across the hall of her office building to repeat the curious story to Mark Fischbein, Trujillo's parole agent.

Fischbein put little stock in what he was hearing. He did not believe Trujillo, thinking instead that the parole violator was merely trying to improve her precarious legal position and shorten her pending prison term by casting aspersions upon Dorothea. Fischbein responded to the psychologist's fears by saying that Trujillo might actually be the threat and that he had more concern for Dorothea's safety than Trujillo's. He suggested that Dr. Curiale conduct an in-custody psychiatric examination of Trujillo.

Fischbein later said that at this time he was under the impression that Dorothea was acting as an advocate in assisting Trujillo with drug and alcohol rehabilitation. At times Dorothea would complain to him that Trujillo lied to and stole from her, and brought friends to the home against Dorothea's wishes. But Dr. Curiale was convinced that Trujillo's complaint had, at the very least, some merit.

At this time, in June 1987, Dorothea was no longer on dual supervision, her state parole having ended several months earlier. Dr. Curiale was therefore placed in the position of having to prove to her supervisors that her suspicions were correct, and then convincing federal authorities to initiate investigative and remedial action. Neither objective was easy to achieve.

During her second 1987 parole-violation prison stay in September (also for forbidden drug use, also initiated by an anonymous call from a woman), Trujillo continued to complain to Dr. Curiale about the theft of her checks and about the alleged drugging.

This prompted Dorothea to write a letter to Trujillo in prison:

> Brenda,
> I think you better call Mr. Fischbein and tell him you're making a mistake, then we can see each other again. I will find a room for you before you get out, if only you'll give me a few days' notice.

Naturally, Trujillo was not about to live at Dorothea's again. But her complaints did not deter Fischbein and his fellow agents from proceeding with their plans to refer yet another parolee, named Jose, to Dorothea's boarding house. Wanting to expedite that referral, Dorothea wrote another letter to the incarcerated Trujillo:

> Brenda:
> Jose's parole officer came today to investigate the room, he was the one who arrested you [last time] . . . you had

> told them that I kept you locked up and forced drugs on you. . . . Anyhow, they approved of Jose . . . I think you should call Mr. Fischbein and apologize. I think you owe me that much.

Trujillo's allegations were largely ignored. The parole people and the arresting police detectives, Terry Brown and John Cabrera, discounted her claims about Dorothea.

Dr. Curiale, though, proved to be a much more sympathetic listener when Trujillo squawked. After all, she had been Dorothea's court-appointed parole psychologist for several years. The psychologist couldn't foresee it, of course, but her pending involvement with this matter would become a protracted, frustrating, and fruitless clash with an immobile bureaucracy.

Dr. Curiale talked to her associate, state agent Fischbein, suggesting that they "tell the Feds" about the alleged theft of SSI checks from Trujillo. Fischbein said he wasn't prepared to do that with the skimpy information he had been given. He felt that Dr. Curiale was asking for something well out of the range of state parole's responsibility, all on the basis of her unsubstantiated "feelings." He also believed that more evidence would be requested, evidence he couldn't supply.

Dr. Curiale then checked with Social Security and discovered that, indeed, $4,300 had been sent to Trujillo at 1426 F Street, and that the checks had been cashed, but that was the extent of Social Security's knowledge or responsibility. Two months later, she inquired again: Yes, the checks were still being sent to F Street. Yes, they were being cashed. Trujillo, of course, was still in prison.

At the psychologist's suggestion, Trujillo wrote a letter to the Social Security Administration (SSA), in which she said that Dorothea "has never told me the checks were coming . . . the woman is on federal parole for the same offense."

SSA apparently received, and filed, the letter. There is no existing evidence of a subsequent SSA investigation into Trujillo's series of allegations.

Dr. Curiale was convinced that Trujillo was telling the truth about her problems with Dorothea. She also suspected Dorothea was toying with the dosages of prescription drugs being taken by her tenants. Dr. Curiale's thinking was that if Dorothea was drugging Brenda Trujillo, then she was doing it to others. And since she knew details of Dorothea's felonious past, she felt her logic was based on fact, not pure speculation.

She requested a meeting with Dorothea to discuss the Trujillo issue. Always the cooperative soul, Dorothea sat chatting with her old friend Dr. Curiale on July 6, 1987.

It was during this session that a chilling thought occurred to Dr. Curiale. She remembers:

> I was looking at Dorothea sitting there across from me, so well dressed, and that jewelry she was wearing . . . those stones are real, that watch is genuine platinum, with diamonds. *Platinum,* for God's sake. Do you know what a platinum wristwatch costs? How in the world does she afford that kind of quality, with her jail time and all? How?
>
> And then it hit me. I remember thinking, "This woman is killing people." I felt no surprise, no shock, there was no feeling of gee whiz . . . just this sudden realization that, yes, that is exactly what's happening.

She wrote a report on the matter, incorporating all of her suspicions. A copy with a cover letter was mailed to Dorothea's federal parole agents. In part of the report, Dr. Curiale made her most dramatic official charge: "This is more than fraud—this is the killing of people by poisoning them."

Federal agents deny receiving any such report.

The weeks and months that followed were unpleasant for Dr. Curiale. In her decades of working with criminal mentalities, she knew that the murderer who kills for money, successfully, likely will kill again.

The psychologist's support from her contemporaries, if indeed she ever had any, was fading fast. She began stopping people in the halls to tell them, "We have a problem here, Dorothea's killing people. What are we going to do about it?" And it wasn't too long before her coworkers didn't want to see her coming, because they knew only too well what she would start in on.

As for Dr. Curiale, the answer now seemed rather simple: Some agency of the law, perhaps even state parole, should put someone undercover into Dorothea's house to find out once and for all if murder and mayhem were being committed there. That suggestion, also, met with stony silence from her peers.

Her efforts were taking a toll, both on her and on her associates at parole. Tension was high, because Dr. Curiale had reached a point where she simply did not understand ("still don't, to this day") why no one cared.

In late September 1987, extremely dissatisfied with the reaction she had received thus far, Dr. Curiale says she called the Sacramento Police Department and spoke to an officer in the detective division.

The psychologist outlined a harrowing tale of poisoning and theft of checks. According to Dr. Curiale: "[The officer] listened to my whole story. Then he asked me what evidence I had." He was pleasant, but told her that without more evidence he really could not file a report. He would, however, "keep [Curiale's comments] in mind."

Police Chief John Kearns would later explain his difficulty in substantiating Dr. Curiale's claim: "Dr. Curiale did not document the call, and we [police] have been unable to locate anyone who received such a call."

With no apparent police interest in her story, Dr. Curiale turned her efforts toward a place closer to home, where certainly she could get action. Her hope was that someone in Internal Affairs—a special-services unit in the state Department of Corrections' parole division responsible for investigating cases such as the one reported by Dr. Curiale—might be able to help determine if odd things were actually happening at Dorothea's residence home.

Dr. Curiale wrote two reports in September, one citing the subject's surname as Puente and the other as Montalvo to help alleviate any confusion, and sent both to agent Todd Johnson. Johnson filed the reports without taking any immediate action—the most official attention they would ever get. (The records were misplaced when the unit moved to different quarters shortly thereafter, and eventually surfaced in January 1989—too late to help any of the seven people found in Dorothea's yard, and just in time to embarrass the special-services unit in the chaotic aftermath of the F Street discovery.)

Dr. Curiale asked her secretary, Lucy Bettanini, to check all available state and county records to determine if Dorothea was using any aliases of which she was not aware. None turned up.

Even as her detractors attempted in various ways to implicate her in felonious activities, Dorothea continued to correspond with Trujillo in prison, often sending her care packages filled with toiletries and other sundries. At about the same time, her boarder Eugene Gamel died.

Gamel was fifty-eight. He had been found in his bed, comatose. He died before help could be summoned, the apparent victim of an overdose of amitriptyline and ethanol.

When police officer Michael Dubray and coroner's deputy Donna O'Ray-King arrived at the F Street house, they were told by Dorothea that Gamel "was known to have a history of numerous suicide attempts in the past." With no reason to suspect anything else, the police and coroner reports officially listed Eugene Gamel's death as self-inflicted.

Gamel's sister later reported to authorities that Dorothea apparently had obtained Gamel's power of attorney and was controlling his Social Security checks even after his death, but no official investigation of this report was undertaken, and no action was initiated.

This, then, was the existing situation at Dorothea's house when Judy Moise and Beth Valentine intensified their citywide search for a suitable new home for Bert Montoya. Because of their earlier successful efforts, Bert was now receiving his full monthly allotment, $556, from Social Security. Also, a request had been made for supplemental benefits, and there was every reason to believe that he would get the additional monthly payment.

Early in January 1988, when Moise and Valentine were talking to Peggy Nickerson, the social worker at St. Paul's Senior Center, Nickerson suggested they might want to consider contacting "this great woman" named Dorothea who provided housing for people like Bert. Nickerson explained to her colleagues the downside of the landlady: her salty language and her volatile personality.

Moise and Valentine were not too concerned about Dorothea's reputed hard edge, because they were familiar with the sort of strong, unyielding personality needed to control the kinds of people they were assisting. They decided as they stood there that they would visit Dorothea soon.

They contacted her by telephone to make arrangements for an

interview, and Dorothea impressed them as being cooperative and encouraging.

Shortly thereafter, Moise and Valentine bundled Bert into the back seat of their dirt-streaked white van and drove him to the house on F Street to meet Dorothea. He was not the least bit apprehensive: his friends had told him that if he didn't like what he saw, he was free to go back to the detox shelter with them at the end of the meeting.

Dorothea greeted them warmly and exuberantly at her front door, welcoming Moise and Valentine in articulate English, and speaking what seemed to be fluent Spanish to Bert. His eyes lit up, and he jabbered back at her, a sudden smile on his face. She *understood* him. The landlady and Bert seemed to have immediate rapport. Moise and Valentine exchanged secret, happy smiles.

After they had entered the house, Dorothea told Bert that she would cook Mexican meals for him. "I make the world's best tamale," she boasted. Taking Moise and Valentine aside, she informed them that she was a registered nurse, and that she would be able to manage the treatment for Bert's stubborn case of psoriasis. Dorothea told the pair that she also believed she would be able to gently prod Bert into taking a more active role in his own affairs, and said she would introduce him socially into his new community.

Dorothea then took Bert down the hall to show him his own bedroom. This was truly the best he'd ever had. And there was a thirteen-inch RCA television set, right next to his very own twin bed. It was all his!

Turning to business, Dorothea told the social workers that she served as substitute payee for several other residents in the house (she did not), and it would be most convenient if she performed the same function for Bert. Moise and Valentine thought that was just fine, because the job demanded someone who was close to Bert on a daily basis.

Bert agreed; he told Moise and Valentine that he would like to live with his new friend Dorothea. He had seen all he needed. He had found a home at last.

Moise and Valentine left Dorothea's room-and-board home that Valentine's Day with their prayers answered. They had done their job. Dorothea could now take over.

THE SEARCH

Moise and Valentine felt nauseated. Until that moment, they had been able to convince themselves that Bert really was lost in Mexico and would soon return. They now knew that was not going to happen. Beyond any reasonable doubt, Bert was home already.

10

Those first few months at Dorothea's house truly were the best of times for Bert Montoya. His little bedroom at the end of the hall, with framed pictures on the wall and curtains at the windows, became a magic world filled with a kind of wonder that until now had been missing in his difficult life.

In addition to the obvious improvements to his environment, Bert enjoyed another long-absent quality of life: privacy. After years of having at least sixty roommates, he now had a door with which he could shut out everyone else in the world any time he wanted.

From the very beginning of his stay, Dorothea lavished him with attention and apparent affection. He got his promised Mexican dinners, and he had someone to talk to who actually listened to him. Dorothea involved Bert in household matters, helping him to contribute to his own steady, albeit slow, assimilation into the real world around him.

The first really visible indication of Bert's metamorphosis was the almost-overnight cure of the psoriasis on his head. For years Bert had been very uncooperative with any attempts to treat his condition. The end result of its neglect was a very serious case, but Dorothea was not deterred. She had kindly but firmly insisted that she apply the prescribed medicinal ointment twice daily, rubbing it gently, slowly, directly onto his skin. This was something that even his longtime friends at the detox center had been unable to accomplish.

"That was amazing," recalled Judy Moise a year later. "She cleared up that terrible, terrible case of psoriasis in just a couple of weeks, and did it by putting that medicine on his head herself. She just wouldn't take no for an answer."

Even more amazing, perhaps, was Bert's emerging socialization. One day Moise made one of her routine telephone calls to the house to talk to Dorothea. A man answered, speaking English. Moise hesitated, then asked, "Is that you, Bert?" Moise was floored by the ensuing conversation, because Bert not only had answered the phone in a proper manner but had then conversed easily with her for several minutes, mostly in English, before summoning his landlady. These were behaviors that even his friends rarely saw, and they rejoiced in Bert's newfound confidence.

But it wasn't all for Bert's benefit; Dorothea also had gained something from the new friendship. Some long-buried instinct in her had been revived.

In Bert, Dorothea had found a project, and she spared neither time nor expense in her pursuit. She babied him, providing food and other luxuries that only he, of all his fellow tenants, received. The other members of the household were jealous at the attention that Bert was getting, but that certainly didn't bother him. This was just about right, he thought. He was exactly where he wanted to be.

But almost from the beginning there were problems brewing between Bert and Dorothea, serious differences that were much less visible than Bert's numerous physical and emotional improvements.

The voices in Bert's head remained an extremely important part of his life. Simply moving into Dorothea's house did not stop nor quiet them, which pleased Bert. He had grown quite comfortable with the voices and had, in fact, almost developed a fondness for them.

Bert also discovered, on his frequent forays around the block in Dorothea's tree-lined neighborhood, that the spirits from the graveyard near the detox center had accompanied him to his new residence. This could not be taken lightly. He found it necessary to continue both his conversations with them and the extended-finger gestures that he had found so effective in the past. He conducted these monologues in quite an agitated manner, and—it seemed to Dorothea—always smack dab in front of her rooming house.

Dorothea found Bert's conduct a little embarrassing. He was much more visible than she thought he should be, or needed to be; his conduct not only was unseemly, it called attention to the kind of people staying at her house—those who required some kind of care and assistance in order to successfully negotiate their day-to-day activities.

This was a particularly serious issue for Dorothea. She could avoid the need to secure any type of government-issued license to operate her rooming house only by limiting her services, ostensibly, to room rentals and meals. Even her humanitarianism in the persistent treatment of Bert's psoriasis would have been considered "providing care" in the most technical of senses, if anyone in the licensing bureaucracy had ever placed themselves in a position to notice.

And because of the flavor of Dorothea's peculiar personal criminal history, even this limited care might have been enough to ring bells regarding her licensing inadequacies. A license application, of course, would have required inclusion of information regarding her felony convictions and likely would have resulted in denial of the license.

From an economic standpoint, Dorothea couldn't risk losing her boarding house operation; her living expenses came exclusively from fees she was able to glean from her tenants' monthly assistance checks. Also, she was forbidden (again, because of her felony convictions) to work for any bonded health-care agency, so her professional options were very limited. By her own doing, she had placed herself in a very, very difficult position.

It was April 1988. Bert was getting used to his new room at the F Street house, and to Dorothea's tender loving care. Dorothea's kindly demeanor, a facade she presented to the many social workers in the capital city's circle of volunteers and professionals, was an affectation she could assume whenever it was needed. During those times when she was in more private surroundings, she could be tough, cunning, and streetwise—a woman with a lethal tongue who was more than capable of fending for herself.

Neighbors would later recall her wild mood swings. On one occasion she would be friendly and chatty, just a nice little lady who was a pleasant addition to the neighborhood. Then, without warning, she would lash out at a passerby, cursing and threatening for some past slight—a boisterous party, perhaps, or a phonograph played too loudly.

Oddly, it was Dorothea's uncontrollable penchant for gutter talk that finally started getting her the kind of notice she had labored so long to avoid.

During the early part of 1988, the Volunteers of America social workers, Moise and Valentine, had been waxing eloquent to anyone who would listen about their "find," the marvelous, lovable Mrs. Dorothea Puente. One of their listeners was a county-employed psychiatric social worker named Mary Ellen Howard.

The mere mention of Dorothea's name stopped Howard in her tracks. Howard had just been interviewing one of her male clients, who had told her about getting tossed out of his boarding house. His landlady had demanded that he apply for General Assistance, and he had been evicted, locked out of the house, when he refused.

The telephone call she made on behalf of the client was not an official part of Howard's duties; she knew, however, that sometimes these clients of hers inflated their problems. This specific problem probably was not as insolvable as it seemed, and Howard thought perhaps a friendly call to the landlady could get things back on track.

As she would later recount, Howard was "stunned" when the operator of the room-and-board home, who identified herself as Dorothea, lambasted her with a barrage of cursing. The ferocity of the verbal attack left an indelible impression on Howard, who found herself wondering how a woman could sound like that and still provide warm and tender care for helpless old people. There would be no resolution of her client's housing problem with Dorothea, either.

Howard did a slow burn about the rude phone call for days before finally making a call of her own, this one to Moise and Valentine. Howard inquired as to whether this particular landlady might be the same person about whom they earlier had been so complimentary.

She was indeed.

Howard related her recent experience and how it had affected her opinion of Dorothea, then suggested to Moise and Valentine that it was her feeling that perhaps they might want to give second thoughts before attempting to place any more people in Dorothea's home.

This was a startling suggestion to Moise and Valentine. The Dorothea they had come to know was very different from the woman that Howard now described. They thought of Bert, and his surprising but very welcome improvements, all at the hands of this woman now being defiled.

After listening politely to the story Howard told, the two social workers chose to dismiss it. Dealing with a woman's bad temper was a small price to pay for Bert's having a home of his own, one that appeared to come fully equipped with love and caring.

Meanwhile, Howard had begun some informal inquiries of her own. She learned from retired county social worker Mildred Ballenger of the odd circumstances surrounding Dorothea's history as a caretaker for elderly people.

Howard also contacted Sharon Cadigan, a sheriff's deputy stationed at the California Department of Social Services. Howard asked Cadigan to run a check on Dorothea's criminal records. Deputy Cadigan soon reported that Dorothea was on parole for actions against property and for passing bogus checks.

Howard asked if there were any charges against Dorothea for mistreating people. "No," was the answer. Howard told the deputy that Dorothea was running a boarding house, and was told in return that the landlady had a right to have a business license, and they had no right to interfere.

Howard did not report her findings to her supervisor, knowing that already she was far afield from the duties outlined in her job description. She felt that her boss would be more concerned about that deviation from duty than he would be about any supposed problems with someone in the private sector.

She was right in her assessment. In a subsequent interview with investigators, Howard's supervisor expressed the belief that Howard was off base in her actions, which, if known, would have resulted in the imposition of formal disciplinary measures.

At about the same time that Howard was beginning to sound her warnings about Dorothea, another incident was unfolding that easily could have triggered an official red flag in the social-welfare community.

Polly Spring, a veteran social worker employed by the adult protective unit of the Sacramento County Department of Social Services, was having a routine conversation with Peggy Nickerson of St. Paul's Senior Center. Spring's job, to provide information and referrals for clients, required close contact with Nickerson, and Spring often called upon her for help.

Nickerson mentioned having placed numerous people in Dorothea's house. Bells went off in Spring's head; she remembered something about this Dorothea. Spring had been a friend and professional associate of Mildred Ballenger, the retired social worker whose persistence had helped result in Dorothea's 1982 conviction.

The exact version of their discussion that April day varies. However, both women generally agree that Spring issued a warning of sorts to Nickerson—along the lines of "that woman is crazy as a hoot"—and informed Nickerson that Dorothea had been in trouble with the law.

To Nickerson, the warnings made no sense. She had heard directly from clients that Dorothea's house was a fine place and that her treatment of her tenants was good. Secure in that knowledge, Nickerson continued to think of Dorothea as a valuable aide to the poor, and thus her impression of the landlady remained favorable.

Nickerson also had experienced personality clashes with Spring in the past, a factor that bolstered Nickerson's decision to ignore Spring's advice. If she couldn't deal with Spring on the small things, how could she take her recommendation on a matter of such importance as a home for clients?

Spring tempered her concern about Dorothea by reassuring herself that, from what she knew, the woman was simply providing room and board, not care and supervision, for her tenants. Consequently, Spring had no *official* reason to be concerned.

Shortly afterward, Mary Ellen Howard and Polly Spring had a discussion in which Howard mentioned Dorothea's name. By this time Spring had talked at length with the retired Mildred Ballenger about the landlady on F Street. In the interim, she also located the *Sacramento* magazine article describing the confrontation between Dorothea and Ballenger (using a pseudonym for Dorothea) and outlining the very exploitable loopholes existing in Social Security law regarding substitute payees. She gave a copy of the article to Howard.

After sharing this information, Howard and Spring met with Moise and Valentine and expressed considerable concern for the people rooming at Dorothea's—including Bert.

Howard revealed her uneasy feelings about Dorothea since the profanity-laced telephone call. Spring related the experiences of her former associate Ballenger—documented in the *Sacramento* magazine article—and also suggested that Dorothea had been involved in "some kind of homicide" in the past.

But Moise and Valentine would hear no evil about Dorothea. As far as they were concerned, Dorothea had performed a veritable miracle with Bert, and that was not something to be taken lightly. In fact, Bert's progress had intensified. Both Moise and Valentine were witnessing in Bert a significant rise in self-esteem that was reflected in his sudden attention to his grooming—the result of Dorothea's efforts. Even if Dorothea did the things of which she was being accused, she must have changed. She was different now . . . there must be some mistake.

Moise and Valentine could not suspend their fervent belief in Dorothea, although both now contend they heard no mention of homicide from Howard and Spring.

"Well, where should we put Bert?" Valentine asked Spring.

Spring suggested a place called The White House.

Valentine snorted derisively and looked at her partner. The pair felt slapped in the face. They had firsthand experience with *that* establishment, having once placed a client with cerebral palsy there. The client was forced to live in virtual squalor in a room strewn with garbage; he was neglected and suffered from numerous open, untreated sores on his body. It had been very difficult to get Adult Protective Services, Spring's employer and the proper county government agency, to even open a case for investigation.

This newest suggestion from Spring deepened Moise's and Valentine's suspicions that the county employee was not only overreacting, but, lacking their depth of field experience, was unable to see things in a clear light. They dismissed the accusations.

Without direction, Spring floundered. She was well beyond the bounds of her job right now, she knew, but this seemed an issue that she couldn't put behind her and still sleep at night. A week later, on June 9, 1988, she wrote a memorandum to her immediate supervisor, Phil Goldvarg.

> Re: Dorothea Johanson AKA Dorothea Puente.
>
> Ms. Puente has surfaced again in the community furnishing housing and tender, loving, but streetwise care to vulnerable clients. She is used by Case Management Services and by Peggy Nickerson [of St. Paul's Senior Center]. Since neither referring agency is aware of Ms.

> Puente's history, each is enthusiastic about her not requiring money up front and running a good unlicensed facility.
>
> Ms. Puente, as this department is aware, poses some dangers to helpless clients, however, and I wonder what our responsibility is. I knew Dorothea as Ms. Johanson in the sixties and seventies, [when she ran a boarding house] located at 2100 F Street. Her facility was ultimately closed and she was sent to prison then for misusing clients' funds. Informally, Judy Moise and Peggy Nickerson have been informed of [Dorothea's] history as far as I remember it.

The memo ended with a question: "Is anything more required?"

Goldvarg was curious about the level of care Dorothea was providing for her clients. If there was too much physical care, then she needed a license, which she didn't have, and at that point—not before—the matter would become a concern to him. He did, however, call Peggy Nickerson to ask about Dorothea, and during that call he says he mentioned hearing rumors that Dorothea had placed "knock-out drops" in people's drinks in bars. What was Nickerson's opinion of the landlady?

"No problems at all," said Nickerson. Today, Nickerson disputes that Goldvarg mentioned anything even remotely like "knock-out drops" during the call.

The day he received the memo, Goldvarg discussed it with his supervisor, Fran Alberghini, who in turn went to her boss, Charlene Silva. At this time, Alberghini was under the impression that Dorothea was providing only room and board, and this was the opinion shared by all of her coworkers in Adult Services. From that meeting, Silva says, she gleaned the facts that "Dorothea had been found guilty of drugging clients, and that the Department [of Social

Services] had been told only that Dorothea was operating a rooming home."

Silva was "very concerned" about what she heard, but her first impulse was defensive: How far could she go to inform people? After all, she had no current facts, nor had any real allegations of neglect or abuse been made. And, very importantly, no client of the county was lodging with Dorothea. So was it Adult Services' concern? She then suggested that Alberghini first contact the county counsel regarding the degree to which they could share information about Dorothea with any outside agency, based on their present information. Then, she offered, Dorothea should be reported to the California Department of Social Services, which could investigate the possibility of a license violation.

As requested, Alberghini contacted Michelle Bach, deputy county counsel. Bach was very cautious. Did Alberghini have any indications that Dorothea was doing something she shouldn't be doing? No. Did she have a client at Dorothea's? No. Then stay away from all this, Bach said, vociferously discouraging any sharing of information about Dorothea with the general social-services community. Bach's concern was singular: to protect the county from any future litigation that a wrongly accused and righteously indignant Dorothea might initiate.

The whole affair frustrated Alberghini, because she was as aware as anyone of the vast "gray area" in the laws applying to privately operated boarding homes. She later observed, "There's zillions of them [boarding homes] in any community, and if you don't have a specific complaint about something happening to people, I don't know that anybody . . . you, me . . . has a responsibility to go to law enforcement."

Silva instructed Goldvarg to contact the state's board-and-care licensing investigators about a license violation. He called the Community Care Licensing Division of the state of California, which grants licenses to a variety of facilities if requirements can be met. He was connected with Kathleen Stadler, a licensing program analyst.

Stadler's notes about that phone conversation reflected Goldvarg's contention that he thought Dorothea was running a room-and-board home only. Goldvarg then related the concerns of his department about Dorothea and her "possible criminal past," including allegations of homicide. He got Stadler to agree to look into his complaint, and then asked if it were possible for him to remain anonymous throughout the inquiry. "Certainly," she said.

Ten days later, on June 20, Stadler showed up unannounced at Dorothea's for a half-hour visit that would have future implications much larger than the state analyst ever imagined. Her intention was to determine if Dorothea was providing "care" for her tenants rather than simply room and board. According to the strictest interpretation of Stadler's job description, she was required to determine *only* if Dorothea's particular operation incorporated any activities that required a license *per state statute*, and she looked for indications that a violation was occurring. The very narrowly focused interview that Stadler conducted with Dorothea was, in retrospect, quite understandable. She went by the book because she was looking for licensing infractions and not for missing persons. No one had instructed her otherwise.

Specifically, Stadler's investigation followed licensing standards and was limited to whether or not one or more of the following activities were occurring at Dorothea's:

- Providing assistance in dressing, grooming, bathing, and other personal hygiene
- Providing assistance with taking medication
- Storing and/or distribution of medication
- Arranging and assisting in medical and dental care

- Maintaining house rules for the protection of tenants
- Supervising tenant schedules and activities
- Maintaining and supervising tenants' cash resources or property
- Monitoring food intake or special diets
- Providing other basic services an independent person ordinarily provides for himself

Dorothea was doing all of these things.

As Stadler talked to Dorothea, a paunchy, Hispanic man with a salt-and-pepper beard watched silently from the background. Stadler had no reason to think that Bert Montoya or anyone else in the house had received medical assistance of any kind from the landlady. Bert, of course, was not questioned and said nothing that would arouse Stadler's suspicions.

In the report that she subsequently wrote (disdaining a typewriter and penning the report entirely in longhand), Stadler suggested, incorrectly, that she "toured" the entire structure. In fact, she had no real chance to do so. In order to get to Dorothea's front door, she mounted the steps to the second-floor entrance, where she was met by a friendly and very cooperative woman who said yes, she was Dorothea (Puente, this time), and yes, please come in. Once inside that second-story flat, there was little reason to think it was connected to the lower level. All of the tenants lived downstairs, and Stadler's tour did not uncover the physical layout of the back of Dorothea's flat, where a covered breezeway with stairs connected the top and bottom floors.

Stadler asked Dorothea if anyone lived with her. Dorothea said yes, and took Stadler into the kitchen, where roommate Mervin John McCauley was sitting. Dorothea introduced McCauley as her cousin, and the pair casually insisted that no one else lived with Dorothea, whom they claimed owned the house. Stadler seems to have exhibited no curiosity about the first floor and its use, and Dorothea expertly kept her unwelcome visitor on the move, in the direction she desired, which was out the door as fast as possible.

For a few moments, Stadler wondered if maybe Dorothea was providing the forbidden care and supervision for this McCauley fellow, and she trotted him through a verbal checklist in order to make an evaluation of this possibility. The state analyst decided she believed him. There was nothing dramatically out of whack that Stadler could detect.

Before Stadler departed, she had Dorothea sign her report, on which was noted Stadler's conclusion that no licensing violation could be found and that the complaint Goldvarg had generated "cannot be substantiated." Dorothea got a carbon copy of Stadler's report right then, and saw her guest to the door.

When Stadler got back to her office, she wrote her full report. Her belief that she had accomplished her purpose is reflected in this excerpt:

> [Dorothea] states she owns the building. Lives in it with her cousin Mervin McCauley, who does not require care and supervision. He rents a room and goes out for most of his meals. Once in a while she will take someone in for the night from St. Paul's Church. Receives no payments. This being when someone has bet or blown an SSI check or has been kicked out of their place. A young man did stay one time for 24 days. Had been in a car wreck, was on crutches. Stayed for free. No money exchanged. The man was evicted because he did not follow house rules.

It is now clear from Dorothea's responses during Stadler's interview that she feared her questioner might already have information about people staying for periods longer than a few days, that some of her guests were somehow incapacitated, and that people were paying her for their lodging.

On the off chance that Stadler might even know about the young man kicked out of the house, for the apparent reason of failing to apply for General Assistance funds from the county, Dorothea included the caveat about no money changing hands. By saying this, Dorothea was covering herself: Money dealings with tenants would have been a clear indication that the landlady was not telling the truth.

Stadler called Peggy Nickerson, who had been identified by Goldvarg as one of two sources of placements at Dorothea's house. Stadler wrote about that conversation:

> Nickerson stated [that] approximately two years ago Dorothea called to offer her home as a temporary shelter. A little less than once a month, Dorothea takes in people who have run out of money. They stay for one to five days. Dorothea provides food and shelter for free. The people she takes in are independent but have just run out of money.

Much of the data Nickerson gave to the state employee was misinformation, and the exchange would later haunt the social worker. But Nickerson harbored serious doubts about the bureaucracy's ability to function in an effective, humane way. She had witnessed the results of far too many unwise decisions made by individuals employed by the state and county—people who didn't even work in the field, as she did. So she purposely misled Stadler, telling her that Dorothea offered only free and temporary care. This specific information was vital to the conclusions drawn by

Stadler: that Dorothea was not running a board-and-care home, and therefore had no need for a state license.

Stadler's investigation was completed. Her boss, Joseph Lopez, reviewed her report and wrote on it, "No further evaluation or follow-up needed." He was satisfied that all of the correct procedures had been followed by his subordinate. Stadler then called Goldvarg to tell him that no substantiation of his allegations could be found. Goldvarg had "no further comments," according to Stadler's report.

By the end of June 1988, any real degree of curiosity about Dorothea by the social-service agencies had begun to peter out.

At about the same time, Peggy Nickerson paid an unannounced visit to Dorothea's house, just to say hello to her client who lived there. When no one answered her knock at the door, she entered. It was then that she unexpectedly witnessed Dorothea verbally abusing an elderly tenant. Suddenly, Nickerson thought she saw something unpleasant in the landlady, and was uncomfortable with the thought of sending more referrals to the F Street house.

She would not do it again.

The house at 1426 F Street, where police investigators discovered seven bodies buried in the front and back yards. *(Dan Blackburn)*

Dorothea Gray Johanson Montalvo Puente is accused of murder in the deaths of nine elderly and disabled welfare recipients. *(Owen Brewer, Sacramento Bee)*

Jim Wilson, Dorothea Puente's federal parole agent, dug up the first body. *(Dan Blackburn)*

Coroner's deputies examine gravesite on the second day of excavation. *(David Morris)*

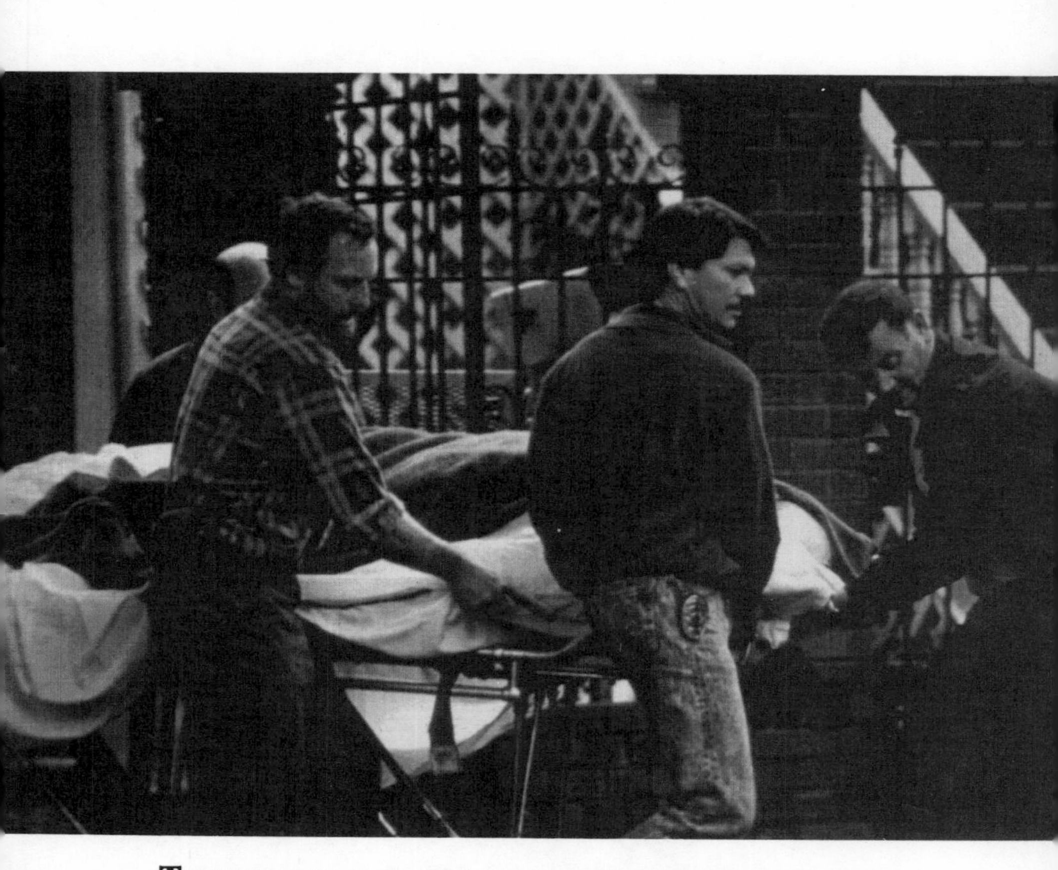

The body of Benjamin Fink is removed by police and coroner's deputies. Fink was last seen after being told by Dorothea that she'd "make him feel better." *(Genaro Molina, Sacramento Bee)*

Two curious onlookers, Shirley Gish, left, and Katherine Phelps, were part of a large crowd that gathered on F Street during the excavation. *(Dick Schmidt, Sacramento Bee)*

Det. John Cabrera, right, escorts an angry Mervin John McCauley from the F Street house after his arrest as a possible accessory. McCauley was released within hours. *(Genaro Molina, Sacramento Bee)*

A coroner's deputy removes dirt from the seventh gravesite where the body of Betty Palmer was found. *(David Morris)*

Police Sgt. Bob Burns, in front of a sea of microphones, answers questions from reporters following Dorothea Puente's departure from the scene. *(David Morris)*

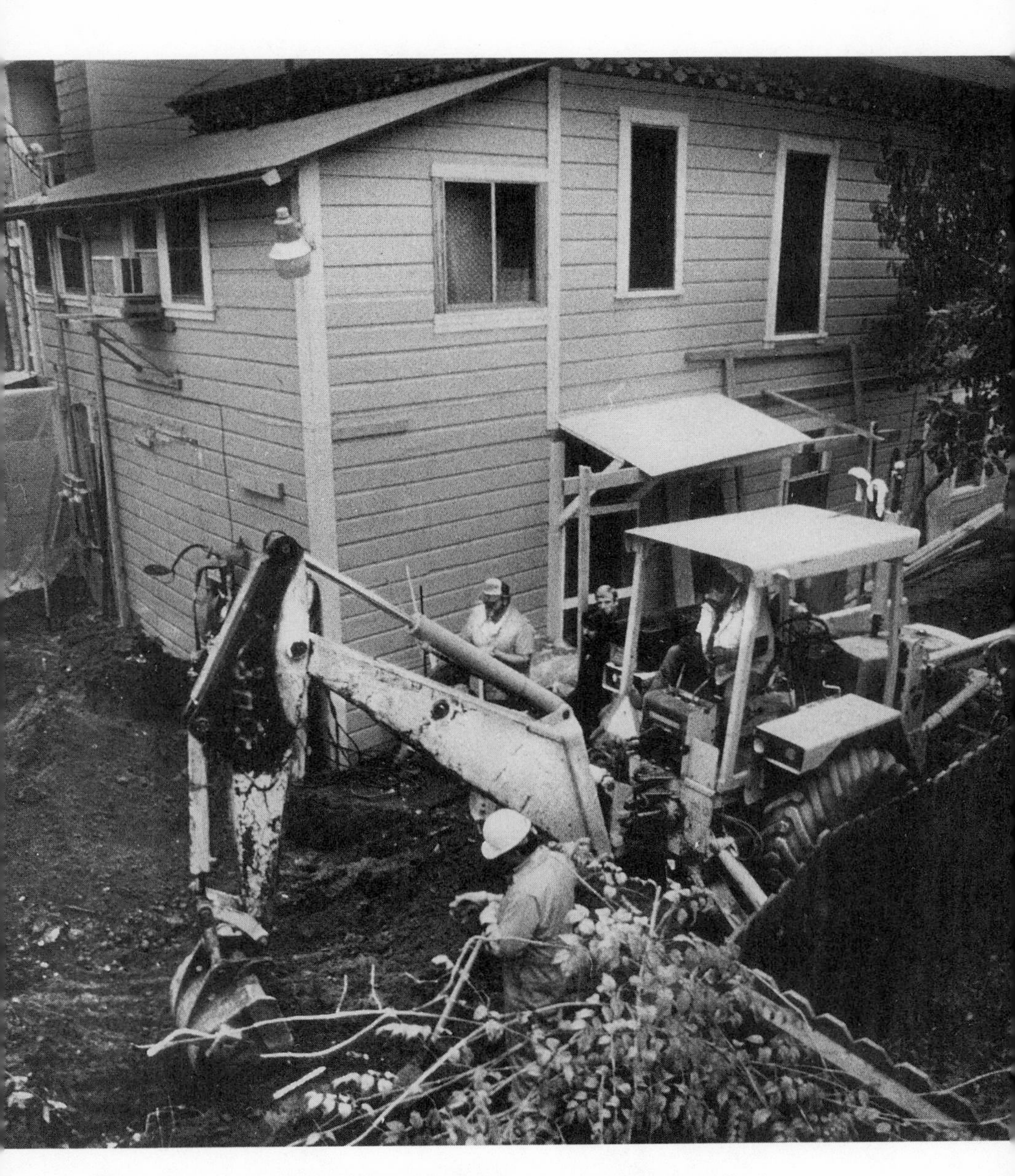

Backhoe operator carefully scrapes earth in the backyard of Dorothea's house while police, coroner's deputies, and workers watch. *(David Morris)*

Veronica Ordorico, foreground, and her husband, Ricardo, first befriended Dorothea, then rented their residence to her for use as a board-and-care home. *(Dick Schmidt, Sacramento Bee)*

Joe's Corner bar, across the street from the 1426 F Street house, which Dorothea frequented and where she first met homeowner Ricardo Ordorico. *(Dan Blackburn)*

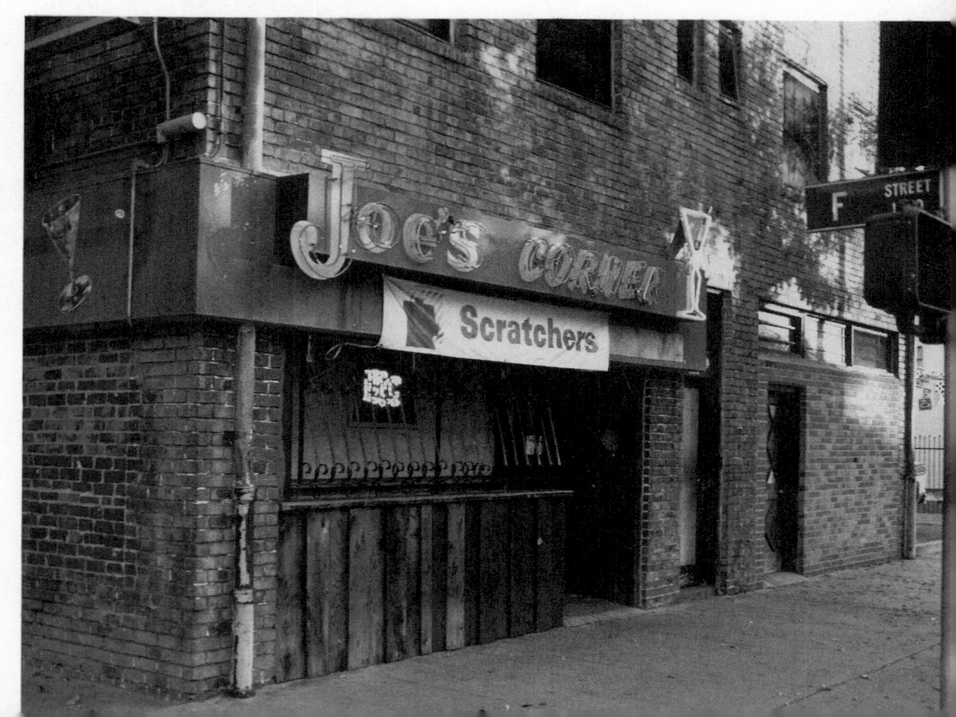

Dorothea's "showplace" boarding home at 1400 F Street, where she brought Roberto Puente following their 1966 wedding. While she lived here, she was charged with forging thirty-four checks belonging to tenants, and subsequently was convicted. *(Dan Blackburn)*

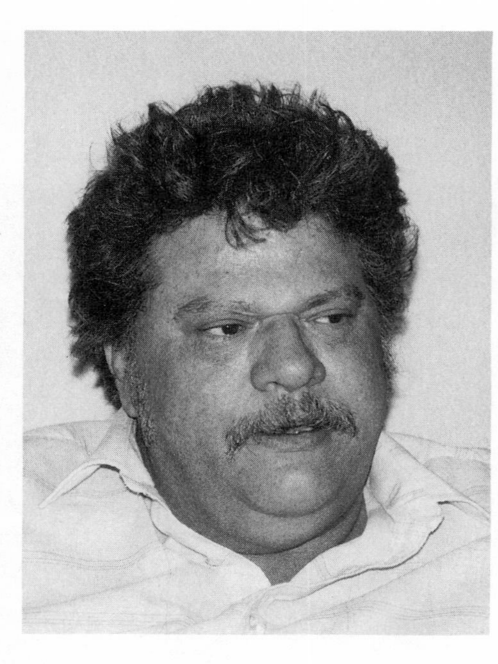

A former resident at the 1400 F Street house, T. J. Hossli was slugged by Roberto Puente during the latter's angry marital rift with Dorothea. *(Dan Blackburn)*

Bill Johnson was the last social worker to see his good friend, Bert Montoya, alive at Dorothea's house. *(Dan Blackburn)*

Peggy Nickerson, the social worker who "discovered" Dorothea Puente's boarding home. *(David Morris)*

State parole psychologist Angela Curiale was unsuccessful in convincing her associates that suspicious activities were occurring at Dorothea's house. *(Percy D. Ledbetter)*

Judy Moise's search for Bert Montoya prompted the Sacramento police investigation that led to the discovery of the seven bodies in Dorothea's yard. *(Dan Blackburn)*

Social worker Tom Richardson knew Dorothea from the mid-1960s. *(Dan Blackburn)*

The Royal Viking Motel and the T.G. Express restaurant, where Dorothea spent much of her time while hiding in Los Angeles. *(Dan Blackburn)*

Det. John Cabrera and Jim Jorgenson, at right, escort Dorothea to Burbank International Airport, where the KCRA-TV Lear jet was waiting. *(Dick Schmidt, Sacramento Bee)*

Cabrera and Dorothea on the controversial media-initiated flight home from Los Angeles. *(Dick Schmidt, Sacramento Bee)*

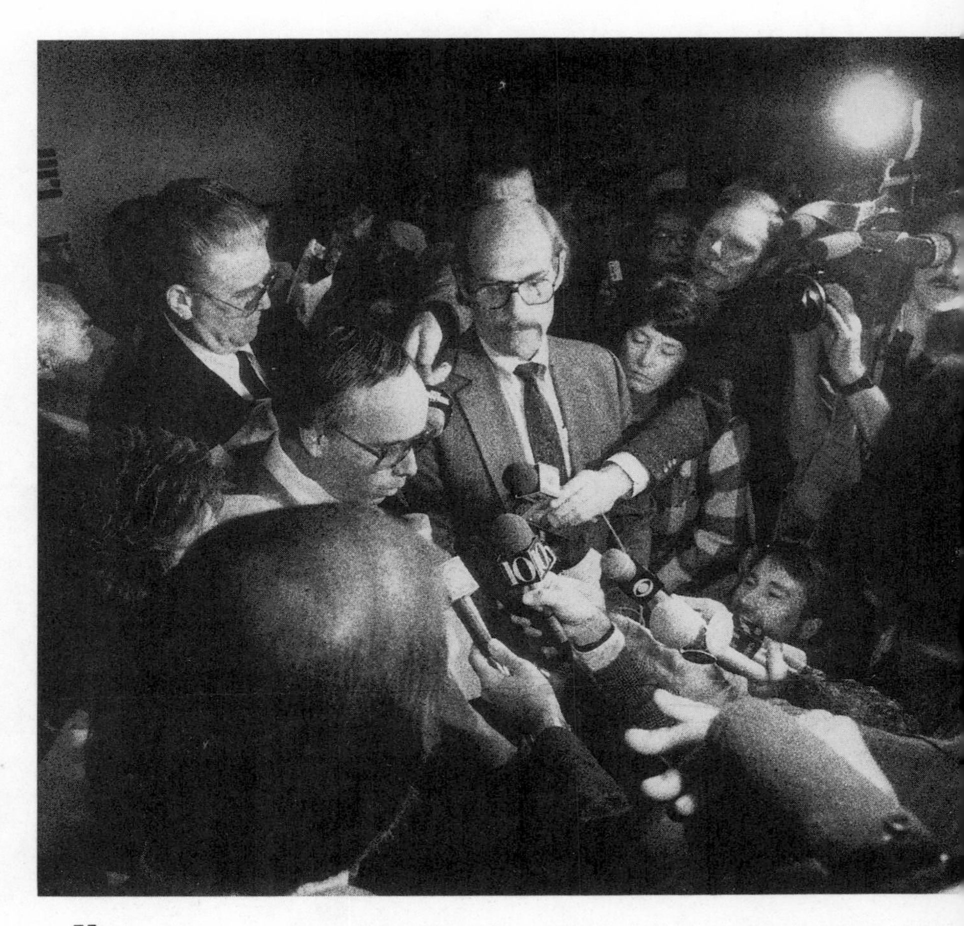

Kevin Clymo, wearing glasses and facing camera, listens to associate Peter Vlautin address the media following Dorothea's capture. *(David Morris)*

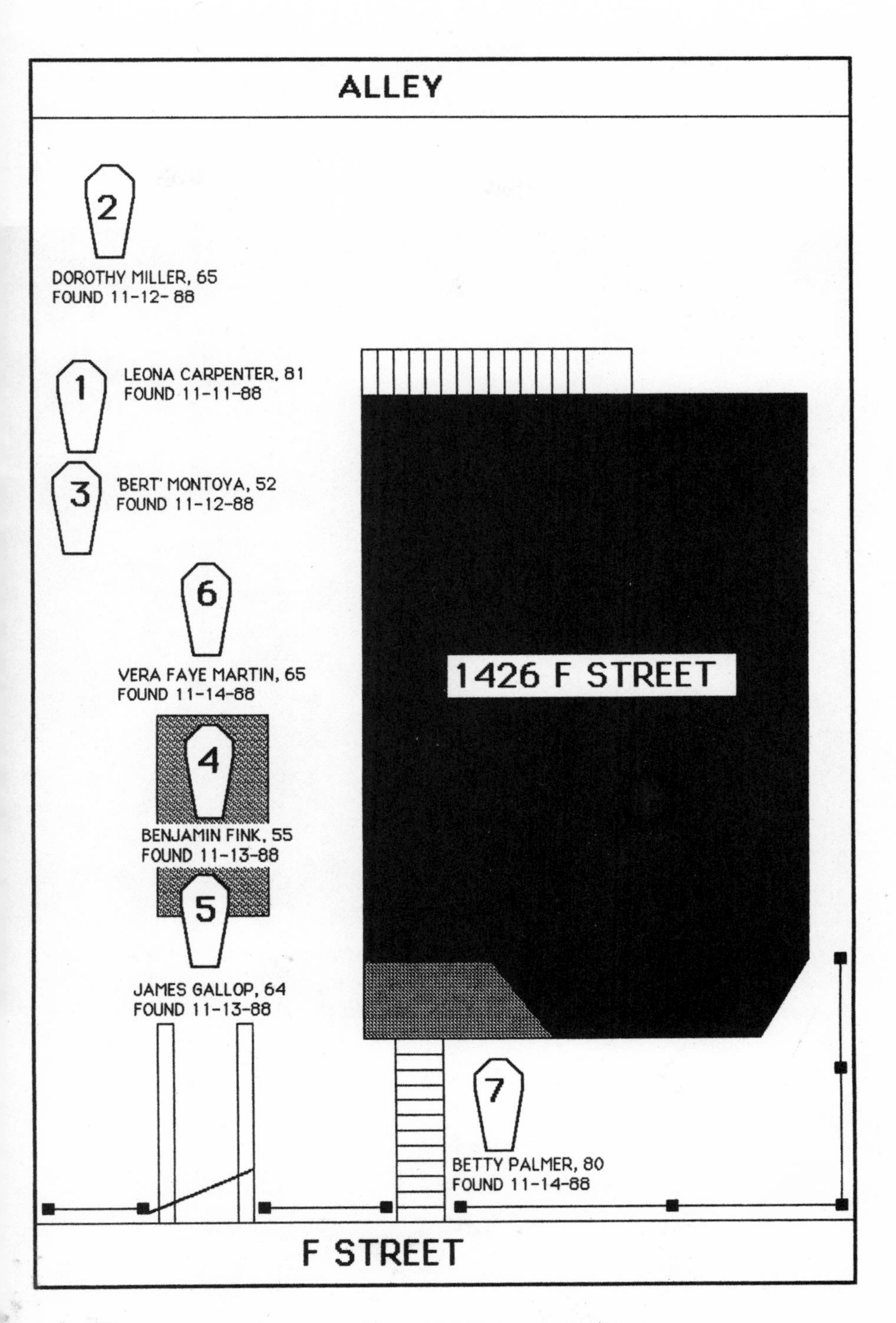

Locations of the seven bodies discovered at 1426 F Street. *(Mark Mitchell)*

Alvaro "Bert" Montoya's disappearance was not ignored by his social worker friends. His was the third body to be found. This rare photo of Bert was taken from a video frame. *(Judy Moise)*

11

A little more than a month later, Bert Montoya showed up back at the detox center. His enthusiasm for living at Dorothea's had dimmed. He went straight to one of his good friends, detox staffer Bill Johnson, and insisted that he did not want to go back to the house on F Street.

Bert's primary complaint was that Dorothea did not like his conversations with the spirits and she was making him take his prescribed medicines—the tranquilizers that made him less concerned about placating those voices in his head. But he also tried to make it very clear that his dissatisfaction went deeper. Unfortunately, Bert was much less eloquent on these matters, and his efforts to raise concern were doomed to failure.

Johnson had toured Dorothea's house before Bert moved in, and at that time found everything all right, on the surface. But Johnson, unlike his associates Moise and Valentine, harbored real doubts about Dorothea. He didn't trust most board-and-care operators, believing them all to "be in it for the money." He didn't think Dorothea was any different.

"My feeling wasn't necessarily personal," Johnson recalled later. "It's just that in my years of working [at the detox center] I have learned that many of these board-and-care homes exist only to rip off older people."

Johnson also had heard dark stories about Dorothea from Lucy Yakato, a county chest-clinic nurse who made regular forays to the house to medicate Bert for a nearly eradicated case of tuberculosis. Yakato did not like Dorothea at all, and apparently the feeling was mutual.

Johnson, though, had been pleased by Bert's continuing personal progress since his residency with Dorothea, and he knew that Bert was happier with himself, too. Johnson told Bert that the two of them would go back to Dorothea's and they'd all get this straightened out.

Bert trustingly went along, assured by his buddy that if he didn't want to stay with Dorothea after the three-way discussion, he could get right back into the van and return with Johnson to the detox center.

Upon their arrival, Johnson explained the situation to Dorothea: Bert was unhappy because she was "forcing" him to take his medication. Johnson wanted to hear Dorothea's answer, but Bert broke in, offering new information. He often awakened Dorothea at night, Bert told Johnson, so she could medicate him. That didn't make sense to Johnson in view of Bert's earlier comments, and he decided then that maybe the medication issue wasn't what was really bothering Bert.

"Looking back," Johnson said,

> I can see how she was intimidating him, controlling him. He wouldn't have awakened her for the medication if she

> wasn't having that effect on him. [At the time,] I took that as a sign that Bert really wanted his medication, but it wasn't, and it should have alarmed me.
>
> I wasn't smart enough to see it. Bert just didn't like to make waves, and he didn't want to then.

Johnson then told Dorothea that he generally distrusted people who operate board-and-care homes.

"If," answered Dorothea grandly, "I was in it for the money—which I am not—I would have kept the bigger place." She was referring to the house with all the bedrooms at 2100 F Street. Johnson didn't know, and she didn't volunteer, that she actually had lost that residence because she had been arrested, convicted, and imprisoned for, among other things, her criminal acquisition of other people's money.

Johnson's thoughts kept bouncing around in his head. His instincts were telling him to put Bert in the van and leave. But his logic kept interfering:

> The difference was roast beef with Dorothea, sandwiches and soup with us. Also, Bert didn't have priority at the detox center, he didn't have a guaranteed bed. If we filled up, Bert would have to go. With only a few more months until winter, I didn't like the idea of my favorite person sleeping in the rain just because I made him leave Dorothea's.

Dorothea then told Johnson that she had grown tired "of all these people coming around all the time," referring to the social workers Moise and Valentine and to nurse Yakato. Johnson could take Bert or leave him, but "this heavy foot traffic has got to stop."

Dorothea sealed the issue by saying to Bert, "You can leave if you want, you don't have to stay here."

Johnson lowered his defenses when she said that, and so did Bert, who by this time had started thinking about the roast beef and potato dinner baking in Dorothea's oven.

Johnson remembers sadly,

> I see now that Bert was just confused, maybe didn't know what he wanted. I let her play around with me right then. I shouldn't have let Bert talk at all, because all of a sudden she had him saying that he wanted to stay there, after all. He shouldn't have been saying a word. I should have forced the issue. He was my friend. If I had told him to get into the van, he would have done it.

In the end, Bert decided to stay. It was 3:30 P.M. on August 11, 1988, and it was to be the last time that Bill Johnson, or any of his many other friends at the detox center, would see Bert alive.

In September, Judy Moise tried several times to reach Bert. Each time Dorothea would report that Bert was not there. At first, this was not alarming to Moise and Valentine, because each time Dorothea's explanation seemed somewhat plausible.

But soon the social workers were getting edgy. After informing Dorothea that she was running out of patience, Moise was told "the most amazing story."

Bert, said Dorothea, was in Mexico with her relatives. All of the house residents had gone on a field trip south of the border, hosted by Dorothea herself. While the group had been visiting Dorothea's sister and brother-in-law, Bert had so impressed his new friends that they had invited him to stay on for a while, as their special guest.

"That stopped me cold," recalled Moise.

> Bert was a nice guy, and we loved him and all that, but he wasn't really the kind of person that would turn out to be so much fun that you'd want to single him out of a crowd and beg him to stay with you. Something sounded very wrong.
>
> Also, Bert was not really capable of getting around by himself, and here he is somewhere in a foreign country. I was really afraid that he would get lost down there. In fact, the more I thought about it, the more I believed that he had gotten lost, and that Dorothea was afraid to tell anyone for fear she would be held responsible.

Moise requested Dorothea to have Bert telephone Moise from Mexico so she could speak directly to him. Dorothea promised to have Bert call.

In the early part of October, Moise called again. Dorothea took the call with a smile in her voice. Bert had called *her* "several times" and he was just fine, thanks, and wanted Dorothea to pass that on to Moise, Valentine, and anyone else who might be expressing concern.

Moise and Valentine paid a surprise visit to Dorothea early on the morning of November 1. Upon their arrival at 6:00 A.M., they found her wide awake, fully dressed, sitting on the front steps. She was "drawn and ashen and looking ill," as the social workers later described her. When Moise and Valentine informed Dorothea that they were there to make other living arrangements for Bert, big tears rolled down her cheeks, and for a few moments she found it hard to find her voice. She had already bought his Christmas present, she said in a quivering voice, so please, please let him stay . . . at least until after the holidays.

The women weren't about to allow that, but they decided to let Dorothea think they might. Moise exaggerated her position with her agency, saying she was a case manager with both the authority and the assignment to relocate Bert. That, she added, was the purpose of their visit this morning. They demanded that Dorothea get Bert back to Sacramento immediately.

Dorothea seemed very cooperative. Since there was so much concern—completely unwarranted, she insisted—why, she would just go on down to her sister and brother-in-law's house in Mexico and bring him home herself. They would be back on Saturday, so why didn't Moise make plans to come over that day, and see him for herself?

Moise declined: she had plans for the weekend. But she would check back the following Monday, November 7. "Have Bert here," she said in a threatening tone. "If he isn't, we'll file a missing-person report with the police."

That weekend was filled with anxiety for Moise and Valentine. Neither woman really believed in her heart that Bert was in Mexico, but it was their only thread of hope, because the alternative was potentially so terrible. They wanted desperately to believe Dorothea's story, as foolish as it was beginning to sound. They sensed that something was very wrong, but putting words to the vague feeling was extremely distressing.

Dorothea could easily have said that Bert had wandered off, that he was probably somewhere right around the neighborhood. Indeed, this would have been a much more plausible explanation than his being in Mexico. But she had not said that. Instead, the complexity of her story about Bert's whereabouts triggered foreboding, unspeakable alarms.

Over the weekend, the administrative offices of the Volunteers of America were broken into. A file cabinet was trashed and a note was found on a desk, with a single word typed on it: "murder." Nothing seemed to have been taken, and Moise would always contend (without any supporting evidence) that the objective of the vandalism was the acquisition of her home address. She began to fear for her personal safety, thinking Dorothea's sphere of influence extensive enough to pose a threat.

Moise and Valentine arrived at their office at 8:30 A.M. on Monday, prepared to depart almost immediately for Dorothea's with the hope of seeing Bert. Ten minutes later, the phone rang. Moise answered and identified herself.

A man with a Hispanic accent said: "Hello. I am Michel Obergone, and I am Bert Montoya's brother-in-law." Startled, Moise could say nothing before the man went on: "I'm calling from Utah. I'm on a business trip and I went through Sacramento on Saturday." He said that he had stopped by the house on F Street and surprised Dorothea, who had just arrived back from Mexico with Bert in tow. He had been in contact with Bert for more than a year, Obergone said, and he had been wanting to see him again "after all these years." Overruling Dorothea's polite objections, Obergone claimed to have taken Bert along with him on a sales trip to Utah.

"Let me talk to Bert," Moise insisted. Obergone replied that Bert was "under the weather" and had stayed in the motel room, across the street, while this phone call was being made.

The man went on to say even more surprising things, while Moise listened, her mouth hanging open in amazement.

"Because in our culture we don't take charity," he said he was going to cancel Bert's monthly Social Security checks. (Bert had never, never voiced any such cultural concern, probably couldn't even understand such an esoteric nuance, and had often expressed happiness at having the monthly financial assistance.)

Dorothea had given Bert six hundred dollars for the trip, Obergone continued. (Where in the world would she get that kind of money?)

Then Obergone said he had Bert's Medi-Cal card in case of any emergency while they were on the road. *That* was particularly confusing. If Dorothea had not wanted Bert to go somewhere, why would she be so cooperative as to give this man Bert's Medi-Cal card? Moise's cynicism was growing stronger by the minute.

Assuring them that "everything is all right," the man calling himself Obergone then hung up, leaving two very shaken social workers looking at one another in confusion.

Shortly thereafter, Moise picked up messages that had been left for her on her pager. One in particular caught her attention.

Another man's voice, this one devoid of any discernible accent, said, "Hello. This is Don Anthony . . . I mean, Miguel Obergone-Michel, and I am calling from Utah." He then proceeded to relate much the same message as the earlier caller had.

Now the social workers panicked: Their pager had a very limited twenty-mile range. The telephone call could not have been placed from Utah!

Without hesitation, Moise dialed Dorothea, who picked up the phone and answered with saccharine sweetness, "Hel-lo?"

Ignoring any introduction, Moise asked point-blank, "Who is Don Anthony?" There was a long, long silence. Moise reminded the landlady of the date, Monday, November 7, the deadline for producing Bert. Then Dorothea proceeded to tell the same story they had just heard from the man who had claimed to be Obergone.

"No dice," Moise said. "We are going to the police to report Bert as a missing person."

"Please wait until 3:00 P.M. today," begged Dorothea. Astounded by this latest request, Moise, her voice shaking with fear and anger, reiterated her intent to contact police officials without any further delay. (There has been considerable speculation as to the motive behind Dorothea's odd plea, ranging from her awaiting the delivery of the afternoon mail to a possible plan for sudden departure. To Moise, however, it meant only one thing: hurry.)

When she hung up, Moise called Peggy Nickerson at St. Paul's to ask if Nickerson could help her locate one of Dorothea's current tenants, a man named John Sharp, because she thought he might be able to provide key information about the goings-on inside Dorothea's rooming house. During the same phone call, Nickerson told Moise for the first time that she had become disenchanted with Dorothea and did not plan to send her any other clients.

When she hung up, Moise swallowed her pride and dialed Polly Spring, the county social worker whose words of caution Moise had ignored earlier. She needed more information, she told Spring, and divulged the occurrences of the past few weeks. Spring told Moise that she had good reason to be concerned, and that her plan to call police into the matter was a good one.

Moise then phoned in the missing-person report.

Only an hour or so later, Officer Richard Ewing responded to the report for an initial routine inquiry, and was greeted by Dorothea in her most friendly and accommodating manner. She expressed her belief that no real problem existed, that the social workers were simply overreacting to Bert's trip to Utah. She said yes, she was operating a rooming house, and of course he could look around the place all he wanted. She repeated Michel Obergone's story as she escorted Ewing around her upstairs apartment, which she carefully noted was separated from the downstairs area. They walked around down there, too, and then Ewing talked to several of the other tenants, one a man who identified himself as Mervin John McCauley. All backed Dorothea's story, in simpler terms.

Ewing was fairly satisfied that nothing was amiss and was preparing to depart when one of the house's residents, a short man with wispy strands of gray hair and horn-rim glasses whom he had interviewed earlier, surreptitiously slipped him a folded piece of paper. The officer pocketed the note until he could read it without being conspicuous a few minutes later.

There were just four words, but they prickled the hair on the back of Ewing's neck: "She's making me lie."

Ewing slowly walked back to where the little man stood, and subtly indicated with his eyes that he would meet him down the street as soon as possible.

When they were a block away from the house, the man, John Sharp, told Ewing that Dorothea had asked him to support her version of Bert's disappearance and had added that "she would make it worth his effort." Sharp insisted to the cop that there was more going on at Dorothea's than could be discerned from casual observation. He told Ewing that "big holes" had been dug in the yard by parolees from the California Department of Corrections. He reported that a resident named Ben Fink had gotten rip-roaring, falling-down drunk recently and had caused a great commotion. Dorothea had asked him up to her apartment, assuring him that she would "make him feel better," and no one had seen Ben Fink again.

As a final comment, Sharp informed the officer (who by now was scribbling furiously on his notepad) about "the odor of death" that had accompanied Fink's sudden disappearance.

That same afternoon, Ewing made a verbal report to the detective in charge of missing persons and homicide, John Cabrera. Cabrera asked Ewing to expedite his written report and to deliver a copy directly to him when it was ready.

At that point, Cabrera informed his two immediate superiors, Sergeant Jorgenson and Lieutenant Enloe, that he was expecting a report on the matter from Officer Ewing very shortly, and that when he received it, he planned to do a little snooping around. Jorgenson and Enloe readily agreed.

When Cabrera did see the report, his eye landed on the address,

1426 F Street. He paused, his mind clicking. Then he remembered! That was the same address where the parolee, Brenda Trujillo, had been living when he had arrested her back in June on suspicion of murder . . . when she had made those vague accusations about her landlady's supposed theft of assistance checks and drugging of tenants.

But Cabrera remained unconvinced about the severity of the immediate situation. He had been on the police force for almost two decades, head of missing persons for five years. In his experience, transients like Bert almost always turned up after a few days. Sometimes, usually informing no one, they just wandered off to settle somewhere new. Nevertheless, Cabrera decided that a closer look was necessary: Officer Ewing's report, coupled with Cabrera's own recollection of parolee Trujillo's complaint, had greatly aroused the investigator's interest in Dorothea and her rooming operation.

While the police were talking among themselves downtown, Moise and Valentine drove to the local Social Security office and took the first steps necessary to suspend the mailing of Bert's regular monthly assistance check to 1426 F Street: They notified the federal agency that Bert was an official missing person.

At about 3:00 P.M., back at the detox center, Moise and Valentine got a message from a contact at the Bannon Street Homeless Shelter. John Sharp had arrived, and was asking to stay. The women jumped into their van and dashed to the shelter. Sharp repeated for them the story he had told Officer Ewing. When he got to the part about the parolees digging the holes in Dorothea's yard, Moise and Valentine felt nauseated. Until that moment, they had been able to convince themselves that Bert really was lost in Mexico and would soon be home.

They now knew that was not going to happen. Beyond any reasonable doubt, Bert was home already.

* * *

What occurred over the next two days remains the subject of intense debate among the people involved. Disagreements exist regarding meetings and phone calls, and specific, documented evidence is lacking. The following sequence of events is the most accurate one that can currently be established.

On the day after her disturbing dialogue with John Sharp, Tuesday, November 8, Moise telephoned Cabrera.

"What are you doing about finding Bert?" she demanded.

Cabrera outlined his sincere doubt that Bert was really missing. He agreed, however, that there were some suspicious circumstances. As a result, he thought the situation warranted an ongoing examination, and he promised to poke around as soon as he was able. He then tried to explain his own heavy work load and priorities. Moise was not in a mood to listen, and soon concluded the conversation.

On Wednesday, Moise was back on the phone. This time, Cabrera was out of the office. He was trying to contact Dorothea's state parole agent, Mark Fischbein, who also was in the field and unavailable.

Since she couldn't find the cop when she needed him, Moise returned to the Social Security office on L Street and asked to talk to Rudy Sanchez, a midlevel official with whom she had previously worked on Bert's earlier claims problems. Moise told Sanchez that one of Dorothea's tenants (who would turn out to be John Sharp) had shown her evidence that at least ten Social Security checks were arriving each month at Dorothea's house. Moise added that she suspected Dorothea was substitute payee on all of the checks, as she was on Bert's.

Sanchez reminded Moise of the morass of regulations and proper procedures with which he had to deal, sighed deeply, and predicted that it would all take time, lots of time, to get any kind of federal investigation under way.

By Thursday, Moise had whipped herself into a bit of a frenzy, fearing simultaneously for Bert's and her own personal safety. She called Cabrera again. He wasn't in his office. No one at the station told Moise, but Cabrera was at the nearby federal office building looking for Dorothea's newly assigned federal parole agent, Jim Wilson. Moise didn't know what was going on, and she was seething; she demanded to be connected to Cabrera's immediate supervisor, Sergeant Jorgenson.

Moise remembers telling the sergeant that she was quite dissatisfied with the police department's efforts on the Montoya case thus far, and she claims to have threatened Jorgenson with contacting the office of the local member of Congress, Rep. Robert Matsui. Jorgenson remembers the conversation his own way, not recalling any mention of the congressman. (In the retelling of her story much later, Moise recanted the so-called congressional threat.) Jorgenson assured her that the case was being looked into and he ended the conversation believing Moise was satisfied with their discussion.

Arriving back at his office that same afternoon, Cabrera called Moise and Valentine to set up a meeting in which they could lay out their entire package of suspicions to him and his senior partner, Det. Terry Brown. They agreed that on the following day, Friday, November 11—Veteran's Day—they would all meet at the Detective Division.

After the women left, Cabrera picked up his telephone and dialed Jim Wilson's number. It was beginning to sound like Wilson was a man who ought to be at this meeting, too.

FLIGHT AND CAPTURE

"In twenty-three years of law enforcement, nothing is beyond the realm of believability."

12

Friday, November 11, was very trying for Dorothea. It was evident to her that the nosey detective with the moustache and the aggravatingly pleasant manners wouldn't be happy until he had poked around her yard with his shovel. The very thought of that happening caused her to feel a disturbing, increasingly heavy weight of apprehension. But she had decided there was no other reasonable option, so she carried on with her charade.

Then the parole agent and the cops found those bones, and she knew it was time to "rabbit"—street talk for "run for your life, keep your head down, and don't look back." And that's what she told her roommate Mervin John McCauley she planned to do, the night before she fled. Earlier, she had spent three hours being questioned by Cabrera and his tall buddy Brown, but she had insisted from the start that she knew nothing about the body buried in her yard and had killed no one. She expressed to Cabrera her sincere intention to be as cooperative as possible in finding the culprit. (It is possible that at some point during the interview Dorothea named another person as the suspect, but Cabrera will neither confirm nor deny this. As this book goes to press, no one else has been charged with any related crime.)

Cabrera knew that he had sufficient reason to take Dorothea into custody for questioning, but since his interrogation had failed to secure the slightest self-incriminating statement from her, he believed that caution would be the safest approach.

It would be imprudent, Cabrera noted in later reports, to hold Dorothea any longer than allowable under the strictest interpretation of the law. Anyway, she would be easy to find if police felt the need to question her further; she had been staying right at the scene of the digging, almost vigilant in her observation.

So the cops let Dorothea go home to F Street that Friday night, driving her back in the rear seat of the unmarked detective's car through a growing sea of people clustered around her domicile.

A platoon of uniformed police guards watchfully ringed her yard where the big hole had been dug—the one containing the skeleton of some little woman.

Dorothea slept fitfully Friday night in her second-story apartment. Floodlights washed her window and she found it impossible to shut out the commotion on the street. The din inside her head was even more bothersome. She talked long into the night with McCauley, often walking to the bedroom window to peek through her lace curtains at the crowd, which steadily dwindled through the night. By morning she had a plan of sorts, and it did not involve sitting around and waiting for the cops to arrest her, as she was certain they intended to do.

She arose well before daybreak, showered at about 6:10 A.M., dressed in her favorite pink wool dress, and slipped into purple high-heeled pumps. Then, ever the lady, she hooked a string of pearls around her neck, slipped on her grandmother's four-carat topaz ring, and dabbed perfume behind her ears. She fixed a breakfast of scrambled eggs and microwaved hash-brown potatoes for herself and McCauley, tossing a little vodka into their tomato juice because it looked like it might be one of those days.

At 7:00 A.M. Saturday, the cop cars pulled up, one after another, until the street in front of her house was packed with black and white cars and those damnable unmarked ones. It looked like a parking lot, and Dorothea by this time was fraught with anxiety, nervously snapping at McCauley and anyone else who ventured too close to her. As the cops got out of their cars, Dorothea pulled on a long, red wool coat, slung her purple purse (containing about $3,600 in cash) over her arm, selected her favorite pink umbrella from the antique stand by the front door, and marched bravely out to greet her somber guests and the maddening crowd.

As it had the day before, a cold, intermittent rain was falling. Dorothea stood Sphinxlike, arms folded, keeping her expressionless face pointed away from the clamoring cameramen who were being held at bay—barely—by a cluster of uniformed cops.

Despite her pleas of innocence, Dorothea correctly figured that the only reason the cops hadn't arrested her already was that the body they had found was that of an unknown woman, badly decomposed and definitely not the body of Bert Montoya, the person being sought. Still, Dorothea *was* the keeper of the grounds, and she guessed that if a suspect was needed she would be the logical first choice.

Dorothea was thinking as police began to dig that Saturday morning—and before they had gotten too far—that "rabbiting" time had arrived. At about 8:50 A.M., she saw Cabrera walk to a different spot to dig. She called to him from the stairs and he went up to meet her. When they were nose to nose she told him that she would like to walk to the nearby Clarion Hotel to visit her nephew and have a cup of coffee. Cabrera agreed, as he was still reluctant to book her. He even took her elbow to escort her through the crowd of gawkers, as news cameras clicked and whirred.

Opening her umbrella, Dorothea walked briskly to the hotel's canopied entrance, but that was as close to her "nephew" as she wanted to get. He was unrelated to her, after all, and in reality was Ricardo Ordorica, the increasingly distressed owner of the house on F Street. She actually met McCauley around the corner and they summoned a taxicab that drove them to Tiny's Lounge, across the Sacramento River in Broderick. Manager Robert Parker, Jr., said later that the pair arrived at 9:15 A.M. and that McCauley was wearing a baseball hat. McCauley drank draft beers and Dorothea had her vodka and grapefruit juice ("about four of them," Parker proudly related).

At just around the time Dorothea and McCauley were arriving at Tiny's Lounge, John Cabrera was peering into his most recently dug hole in her backyard, at the second body. He felt sick, and the sight and smell of this new corpse was only part of the reason. He was the one who had let Dorothea go!

Cops were hastily dispatched to the Clarion, where a quick search of the coffee shop and everywhere else she might be revealed what Cabrera had already guessed: Dorothea was in the midst of a flight to avoid prosecution, and he was about to be subjected to a lot of very close and critical public attention, which he had always hated.

After a final bracer at Tiny's, McCauley called a taxicab for himself. It arrived at 9:54 A.M. McCauley got off at the corner of Fifteenth and H streets, three blocks from the F Street boarding house. At 11:19 A.M. another cab, this one from Capital City Co-op Cab and driven by Don Kent, was called to Tiny's. The female passenger's objective was Stockton, seventy miles to the south. Kent agreed, saying the fare that far would be approximately seventy dollars and he wanted it in advance. He wasn't about to take that ride and have a problem collecting the money. She gave him five twenties and told him to hold it until their arrival, and off they went.

Kent was favorably impressed with his fare and later recalled, "She was a rather comely woman for her age."

At 2:00 P.M. a Greyhound bus pulled out of the Stockton terminal en route nonstop to Los Angeles. One of its twenty-six passengers was the much sought-after woman in the red coat, Dorothea Puente.

Sacramento police thought that she had relatives in Southern California, so they immediately sent bulletins out with her description. They hoped she would blunder into their hands as easily as she had walked away. She didn't show up at any of the residences police knew of, and today they are uncertain as to exactly where she went and what she did.

Dorothea, too, has been mum about her whereabouts during the first night of her journey. She arrived at the Los Angeles bus terminal shortly after 10:00 P.M. on Saturday. The following day, at a little after 11:00 A.M., another cab dropped her off at Third and Alvarado Streets, a predominantly Mexican neighborhood with a classic big-city mix of low-rent commercial and residential buildings.

She checked into room number 31 at the Royal Viking Motel shortly before noon, paying cash for two nights ($73.92 with all taxes included, no receipt needed) and told motel manager Ray Robinson that she probably would keep the room for several more nights after that. She signed the motel's register with the name Dorothy Johanson.

The Royal Viking is comprised of randomly aligned, two-story, stucco-covered wings painted white with yellow trim. Its guests are in search of a bargain and willing to spend the night in Ramparts, one of the city's seedier districts. Dorothea's room was clean and comfortable enough, however, and featured the usual plastic chairs, loudly patterned bedspread, cheap swag lamps, laminated nightstands mounted on the walls, and small kitchenette with stove and refrigerator. Room 31 is directly across from the motel's office and is one of the newer of the Royal Viking's forty-three units.

The weather that day was cool, and Dorothea cranked up the room's thermostat immediately after double-bolting the door behind her, and before removing her long, red wool coat. There was certainly no thought of using the motel's swimming pool, and she easily ignored the televised professional football game between the Los Angeles Raiders and the San Francisco 49ers. Instead, she kicked off her shoes, fell onto the room's king-sized bed, and was soon fast asleep.

As Dorothea dozed, the body count back in Sacramento had risen to five, and the cops were trying, without much luck, to hold their heads high in the gale of public criticism they generated by letting their key suspect walk away unfettered—with their assistance, in fact. Their chief, Jack Kearns, was at a conference for chiefs of police at the Hilton Hotel in downtown Los Angeles, and he didn't see any real reason to go home, despite the fact that the biggest crime story he'd ever be around to witness was unfolding right in his jurisdiction.

Kearns later claimed that he "was keeping in touch by telephone and television" with updated reports of the grisly discoveries of buried human remains on F Street.

In days ahead, the manner of Dorothea's departure would become very controversial for the entire police department, but particularly for its chief. Kearns hadn't yet fully grasped the depth of the tragedy—and the public relations mess—that awaited him at home.

When Kearns finally did return to Sacramento, six days after the first body was found, he was in time for a morning press briefing. But by then all seven bodies had been dug up, and any chance of salvaging the image of the police as super sleuths was long gone. In its place was the widespread public sentiment that the cops had bungled the case badly, in front of the whole world.

At noon on Sunday, as Dorothea was settling into a deep sleep, Mervin John McCauley was arrested in Sacramento by Detective Cabrera on charges of being an accessory to murder. Police announced that McCauley was not suspected of actual murder, but that he was being accused of lying to police on two occasions during the excavation of the bodies—about the date on which the backyard concrete had been poured and the telephone call from Dorothea on Saturday, after she had left Sacramento.

Dorothea awakened at about 6:00 P.M. and walked to T. G. Express, a small restaurant adjoining the Royal Viking Motel complex, whose bright neon sign promised THAI AND CHINESE, GOOD FOOD. Daytime waitress Wenanuch Boonjindasup remembers Dorothea ordering barbeque pork and chop suey to go, along with a couple of Budweiser long-neck beers.

When she departed the restaurant that Sunday night, Dorothea bought a copy of the hefty Sunday *Los Angeles Times*, in which she shared billing with newly elected President Bush and his Florida fishing trip: TWO BODIES UNEARTHED AT BOARDING HOME, MANAGER IS SOUGHT. The story told her she'd better keep a very low profile, and Dorothea swiftly walked back to her room.

Other than her occasional short forays to T. G. Express, Dorothea remained in her room. Each time the maid, Lenore Jones, arrived at the room's door, the occupant would brusquely dismiss her.

"She never opened the door more than a crack," Jones remembered. "She tried to keep her face hidden. She was always dressed with makeup, like she was going out."

By Monday night, the police had found the sixth and seventh bodies and concluded, with help from heat-seeking detection equipment, that no more were buried on the property.

"There are no more bodies at this site," said Sgt. Jim Jorgenson. With the assistance of forensic anthropologists Cecil and Heglar, it had been determined that the third body was that of Alvaro (Bert) Montoya. A Municipal Court judge signed a warrant charging Dorothea Puente with the murder of Montoya, and police officers made plans to search the house thoroughly the next day.

On Tuesday, Dist. Atty. John Dougherty stated that charges against McCauley were being dropped because of insufficient evidence. The suspect had been held in the new Sacramento County Jail just blocks from Dorothea's boarding house. He went home, despite the suggestion in court records that he may have helped dig trenches in Dorothea's yard.

By this time the Sacramento cops were in a code-three panic. They sent out so many bulletins for the missing landlady that other police departments began to get short-tempered. Las Vegas, Nevada, police Sgt. Tom Wilke said he had received conflicting messages from Sacramento: "We got one wire from there that says she's en route to Mexico, another that she's on her way here [to Vegas], another one that she's been spotted in Reno," Wilke told the Associated Press. "I didn't look who signed them because I thought they were all bullshit, anyway."

* * *

For her first three days in Los Angeles, Dorothea's pattern had been the same. After dark, about 8:00 P.M., she would walk to T. G. Express. Her habitual meal of one beer and the soup du jour was noted by night cashier Nina Chung. Then she'd buy two beers to go, and return, after no longer than thirty minutes, to her room.

Dorothea's constant perusal of the Los Angeles newspapers and close monitoring of the color television in her room kept her informed about the progress of the drama unfolding in Sacramento. She was pleased when she read on Tuesday that the charges against her former roommate McCauley had been dropped. That was one less thing she had to worry about. She also read that laborers in orange jumpsuits had begun to fill the big holes in her beautifully landscaped yard.

The cops at home had become handy, if unwilling, targets for frenzied reporters, most of whom seemed satisfied with asking the same question over and over again: "Didn't you make a mistake by allowing Puente to leave?" Police patience with the press was sorely tried; spokesman Bob Burns responded each time he heard that particular query by wondering, "Any other questions?"

Finally, on Wednesday, Police Chief Kearns flew back to Sacramento to attempt a little crisis control.

By that same day, Dorothea had a serious case of cabin fever. She had paid her rent through the following Saturday, but she knew that the Royal Viking, despite its transient atmosphere, was no place for her to be loitering. She had read that by now seven bodies had been found in her yard and that the hunt for her now extended nationwide. She was far too visible, even in this part of town where many are outlaws. Her picture being in the newspapers and on each television newscast made her extremely vulnerable to capture. She decided to venture out, to find more anonymous, and cheaper, digs.

As shadows lengthened on the Royal Viking, Dorothea departed. On foot, she marched straight west down Third Street, past the rambling St. Vincent's Hospital, the Otological Clinic, and the scattering of businesses and stores, many already closed for the night. There weren't too many people on the streets yet, but Dorothea wasn't worried about that. She felt quite comfortable in her surroundings.

Her odyssey landed her in front of a run-down and intimidating little bar called the Monte Carlo I, more than a mile and a half from the Royal Viking. The heels on her purple pumps had been trashed by all the walking she had done, and she needed a place to rest; the tawdry tavern and its occupants posed no threat. She entered confidently, took a stool at the far end of the horseshoe-shaped counter, and surveyed the few customers.

From his vantage spot, retired carpenter Charles Willgues thought Dorothea a sight for sore eyes. The sixty-seven-year-old widower lived alone in a small apartment just two blocks from the Monte Carlo I, which he considered to be his only real hangout. He was a short man, slender, with wispy gray hair and wire-rimmed glasses that accentuated his experienced blue eyes. Worry lines furrowed his ample forehead even when he smiled. He wore the look of a man accustomed to working hard for a living and drinking hard for fun.

Not too often, he found himself thinking as he gazed at Dorothea, does a woman like that wander into this joint. And about that, of course, he was absolutely right. Dorothea ordered a vodka and grapefruit juice, tall, and proceeded to drink it while surveying her counterparts.

"Hello," Willgues called out to the woman in the pink dress. "The fan over there blows right at your back, so why don't you move on down here out of the draft?"

She readily complied, and soon they were talking like old friends. The heels of her shoes were shot, she complained, because she had done a spell of walking.

"No problem," said Willgues, ever the gentleman. "Enjoy your drink and I'll take care of these." He took her shoes and walked across the street to a shoe-repair stand, where for three dollars the heels were replaced. Upon his return, Dorothea reimbursed him and bought him a beer.

During the next ninety minutes, as Dorothea slowly sipped one drink after another, their talk turned personal, and Willgues began to think he might get lucky. A woman patron who was watching all this happen from a few stools down later observed: "She [Dorothea] looked really cute. She had her hair real pretty and her makeup real nice. She did not look fat like the lady on TV" (a mug shot circulated to the media had made Dorothea's face appear somewhat chubby).

For his part, Willgues was captivated by his new friend's tales and her style. Her clothes were well tailored and he thought her "very ladylike." She said her husband had died only a month earlier, in San Francisco, and that she had traveled to Los Angeles for a change of scenery. She said she was fifty years old and was thinking of resettling, finding a new job (maybe as a maid) and a new place to live.

"She didn't know what she was going to do with the rest of her life," Willgues recalled. "She said she had no family, that she was all alone." But there was "no sign of trouble," he added. "The only thing she seemed worried about was finding a job and getting out of that motel."

Dorothea hinted broadly that she was lonely, and that perhaps, if he thought it was all right, she could cook a nice, big turkey with all the trimmings for Thanksgiving dinner, when the holiday rolled around in a week. They could share it. Willgues said he would think about it.

She even wondered aloud if maybe they could move in together.

This was moving much faster than Willgues had dreamed. It wasn't a particularly surprising offer, really, for the streetwise Willgues, who knew that people in his neighborhood looked for many novel ways to share expenses. "It may have seemed weird, but it's normal around here," he noted. Soon the pair's conversation landed on the subject of money.

Dorothea had been seen breaking a couple of twenty-dollar bills, but had made no flashy show of having a purse full of money. Then, almost as though a button had been pushed, she asked Willgues about his income. Willgues told her that he lived on skimpy Social Security disability payments, and that by the time he paid his $367-a-month rent and the light bill, he was broke.

He was a bit surprised that she exhibited considerable understanding about the amounts of money distributed through government pension plans. "I said to her, 'I get $533 a month in disability payments,' and she said, 'Oh, you can get $680.' She seemed to know everything about Social Security."

They made a date for the following day, to go shopping for some new clothes for Dorothea. At 4:30 P.M. Willgues called a cab for her return trip to the Royal Viking Motel. He then warned her about the pimps, pushers, and other low-life who populated the mean streets at night, and bought her a take-out dinner of charcoal-broiled chicken. Before she left, she asked that he telephone her at 8:30 that night, room 31.

Willgues was ecstatic; he went to his small, run-down apartment, stopping for a few minutes at a neighbor's to tell him all about the attractive, exciting new woman he had met and about the date scheduled for the following day.

But even as he settled in to watch the six o'clock news, he felt the same nibbling in his gut that had been troubling him all afternoon . . . ever since the "widow Johanson" had first asked about his means of livelihood and pressed the conversation about Social Security benefits. Willgues had the vague feeling that if he watched the TV news, something might jog his memory.

Back in Sacramento, at just about the same moment, Police Chief Kearns was settling down in his office to watch the news on TV. But unlike Willgues, he knew exactly what he was going to see—and he knew he wouldn't enjoy it. Kearns was being widely criticized by the media for being, in their view, slow to return from his L.A. conference. And this, his first full day back on the job, had not been a good one. The heavyweight dragnet was out for Dorothea, but here at midweek she still hadn't been caught, and every passing day seemed to bring him a new packet of grief.

The chief had been greeted upon his arrival back in town by an editorial in the city's biggest newspaper, the *Sacramento Bee.* The writer wasted no time in getting to the point:

"It's hard to believe it's real . . . police work so inept that the prime suspect is allowed to disappear because the police don't think she'll go anywhere."

It had been necessary, Kearns reasoned, to haul out the biggest guns in his arsenal to fight that kind of embarrassing criticism, and that was why he had called that morning upon the district attorney's office.

Dep. Dist. Atty. Tim Frawley, in a substantial departure from normal office procedure, talked freely in an effort to brush the police work in a more acceptable color. Frawley, the prosecutor who had provided legal advice to the police through the search of Dorothea's yard, said detectives simply were trying to preserve the legality of their search when they let Dorothea walk away Saturday morning.

"The police did not want to restrict her movement and jeopardize her consent to the search," said Frawley. He estimated that the police had been in "that precarious position" for no more than an hour, between the time she walked away and the time the second body was found. Even later, Frawley maintained that "that was the window of her opportunity, and she made her getaway. It was a confusing situation and I can understand how it happened the way it did." He should have understood; it was his advice that the members of the detective field unit were following.

The chief made his mea culpas, too. His police "had acted properly" by not arresting Dorothea when they had the chance, he insisted. There was not "a weight of probable cause." Those are the words he used, and he seemed for the moment to be following the script with which he had coached his lieutenants all week: no probable cause, no arrest.

"Of course," added the chief, "with a crystal ball or Monday-morning quarterbacking, the probable cause possibly could have been stretched, and there may have been an arrest made." It was a bit of a backpedal, and the media began to demand clarification. "Was a mistake made by the police?" The question was asked repeatedly, relentlessly.

And then the chief changed his tactics entirely, landing in the middle of his biggest public relations problem yet. Kearns looked sincerely at the television cameras and announced, "She should have been followed, she should have been tailed very closely. She was a prime suspect in a homicide case and there isn't any excuse, as far as I'm concerned, why the suspect wasn't kept under surveillance. It was a judgment call gone awry. The Sacramento Police Department made an error and as a result of that, we lost the suspect."

None of this would have happened, one is left to surmise, if the chief had been in town. "Any other questions?" Kearns asked. It had not been a good day for the Sacramento men in blue.

At the moment he finished talking, Kearns lost forever the respect of many of his men.

* * *

The answer to one of the big questions that had been dogging Charles Willgues four hundred miles to the south was now taking some shape in his mind. He had seen nothing on the evening news that gave him a solid clue, but still he felt an insistent and growing realization. That little, gray-haired lady, those Social Security discussions . . . it all fit . . . that might just be her, could be the one whose picture had been on Channel 2 that very morning, the landlady from Sacramento . . . even though she had told him she was from San Francisco.

Willgues, playing out his hunch, telephoned Gene Silver, assignment editor for Channel 2 News. That was at 7:40 P.M., and Silver immediately departed for Willgues' apartment, a picture of Dorothea under his arm. Upon his arrival, Silver had Willgues call Dorothea at the Royal Viking, as he had promised he would at 8:30. Willgues asked her if she had eaten her dinner, and Dorothea said, "Yes, some of it." She seemed anxious to get off the phone, so the conversation was very short.

The two men sat and watched the news broadcast at 9:00 P.M., and then Silver called the police.

Detectives went to Willgues' apartment. When it seemed apparent that they were going over to question the woman in the pink dress, Willgues made a plaintive request: Could the cops wait until tomorrow night? He had a date with her the following day and he sure as heck would like to keep it. The detectives smiled wanly and drove off toward the Royal Viking.

In her room, Dorothea had been munching halfheartedly on the charcoal-broiled chicken when Willgues had called, and she didn't feel much like talking. She was thinking about their earlier conversation and wondering if perhaps she hadn't been a little too candid about everything.

Then came a knock at her door. It was Police Sgt. Paul Von

Lutzlow and associates, and the sergeant politely asked Dorothea for some identification. She produced a driver's license with the name Dorothy Johanson. Von Lutzlow's heart thudded: He knew this to be one of the aliases the suspect from Sacramento had been reported to be using. A search of her purse turned up another license, this one bearing the name Dorothea Puente. The L.A. cop informed her that she was under arrest.

Von Lutzlow said she was "calm, cool, and collected, almost as though she was expecting us." Quickly she was cuffed, placed in the back seat of a black-and-white, and whisked off to the nearby Ramparts precinct station, where she was fingerprinted and booked. It was shortly after 11:00 P.M., and Dorothea had been missing for 60 hours.

13

There was much joy at capital city police headquarters when news of the arrest came through. Cabrera and Jorgenson began making plans to fly to Los Angeles. However, there were no commercial flights that late at night, and the Sacramento Police Department does not include a jet airplane in its transportation inventory. For a short time the cops could only ponder their alternatives. They didn't want to waste any more time than necessary in getting to their prize; they had lost her once and they weren't going to let it happen again.

There was another, more technical, problem. If the L.A. cops held Dorothea in their jail for more than five hours, she would have to be arraigned in Los Angeles; if the Sacramento cops could get to her before that, she would be arraigned with pomp and ceremony, on their turf.

Aside from the obvious benefits of returning home triumphantly with their elusive prize, some potentially irritating complications could evolve if they waited until morning. There would be more paperwork, more time required to get Dorothea back, and more time for the media to snipe.

Minutes after the beginning of their nightly newscast, officials at KCRA-TV, Channel 3 (the Sacramento NBC affiliate), made the cops an interesting offer: Space could be shared with them on the Lear jet that the TV station, along with the *Sacramento Bee,* had just chartered. That might help Kearns' guys get Dorothea back to town in a timely fashion. The cops agreed instantly, and off they flew toward Los Angeles.

Dorothea had been transferred from Ramparts to Parker Center, the downtown police headquarters complex, and there the media caught up to her again, at 2:30 A.M., when she began her trip home. She was led out of Parker Center with her arms shackled in front of her. Her head was bowed and she looked frail and tired. She said nothing as she was turned over to Det. John Cabrera and bundled into a police unit for the fifty-minute drive to Burbank International Airport. Waiting for her there was the airplane and the journalists, KCRA-TV reporter Mike Boyd and cameraman Mike Domalaog, and *Sacramento Bee* photographer Dick Schmidt. Before she got on the plane, Dorothea was read her Miranda rights.

In what was to become a point of heated debate in legal circles everywhere, the cops, the cameras, and Dorothea headed back to Sacramento. En route, she made just two statements to the journalists before ending the off-the-cuff interview. She noted, "I used to be a very good person at one time," and then claimed, "I have never killed anyone, I told you that. I have not killed anyone. The checks I cashed, yes."

At 5:00 A.M. on Thursday, November 17, Dorothea was back home. Sergeant Jorgenson, who had accompanied her and Cabrera on the flight back, made a brief statement to reporters who had gathered to wait: "We're glad to get her off the streets." To the question of whether he could "believe" what was happening, he responded, "In twenty-three years of law enforcement, nothing is beyond the realm of believability."

The scene awaiting Dorothea upon her predawn return to the Sacramento Executive Airport was one that neither she nor her captors could have predicted. There were bright lights, television cameras, newspaper photographers, reporters, and local TV anchors—enough to satisfy even the most demanding movie star. Legions of uniformed police assigned to help guard the prisoner contributed to a colorful atmosphere of high excitement.

It had been a long time since the Sacramento cops had been so very much in the limelight, and not all of them were comfortable with the situation.

Neither was the star suspect. The leather-and-steel wrist shackles Dorothea had been forced to wear by the L.A.P.D. no longer were buckled around her waist. Now she sported handcuffs, tightly securing her wrists at her back. Hidden amid the folds of her long red coat, the cuffs were not nearly as noticeable as the shackles had been. Her shoulders slumped in apparent fatigue and she kept her head lowered, ignoring the barrage of questions the reporters shouted at her: "Did you kill those people? Why did you do it?"

Dorothea was tucked into the back seat of a police car, with a very relieved Detective Cabrera still at her side. The caravan of cops, reporters, and photographers departed on the fifteen-minute drive to police headquarters downtown, where a second wave of newshounds were waiting. Upon her arrival there, Dorothea was booked on a single count of murder, that charge pertaining to the death of Bert Montoya.

The booking, fingerprinting, and other related procedures took more than an hour, and the sun was already peeking through the trees at the start of the new day before Dorothea could be lodged in a small, chilly cell at the adjacent county jail facility. Her jewelry, personal possessions, and the roughly three thousand dollars in cash she had been carrying at the time of her arrest had been confiscated.

Dorothea was arraigned later that same morning, Thursday, November 17, at 9:20 A.M. She stood, one hand on the railing in front of her, dressed in a very unfashionable orange jail jumpsuit buttoned to the neck, with "Sacramento County Jail" stamped on its back. She was drawn and haggard, her delicate facial features tightened by concern.

Sacramento Municipal Judge John V. Stroud asked her name.

"Dorothea Puente Montalvo," she answered, her voice quaking. Stroud then ruled there was sufficient evidence to warrant holding her with no bail, on the single count involving the unfortunate Bert Montoya.

Dep. Dist. Atty. Dan Kinter, scheduled prosecutor in court that morning, told the judge that special circumstances would be cited when additional counts of murder were filed. (Under California law, multiple homicides or homicide occurring as part of robbery are considered to be committed under special circumstances and can result in execution in the gas chamber.)

Dorothea nodded her head when the judge asked if he was correct in assuming that she could not afford to retain her own lawyer. Stroud ordered the public defender's office to represent her in the capital case.

AFTERMATH

In the middle bedroom, a rug has been removed and a large, dark stain is visible on the wooden floor. Candies wrapped in yellow paper fill a glass jar on a table, and an empty can of Wizard Light Lemon Air Conditioner lies on its side on the floor. No other signs remain of the F Street horror.

14

For the first week or so after Dorothea's arrest and arraignment, the fever of interest that had accompanied the gruesome discovery was sustained. The crowds visiting her house were respectable in size and demeanor. People claiming to have known the suspect spoke with anyone who would listen, telling their stories.

Cabdriver Patty Casey frequently drove the woman she knew as "Mrs. Montalvo" on her errands. Dorothea was "generous to a fault." Casey sobbed while recalling Dorothea and her many trips to the Lumberjack hardware store on Florin Road to buy bags of cement. She would tell the cabbie she was making "home improvements."

Dorothea also bought a roll of new carpeting one day, lugging it home in the back seat of the cab and telling Casey about one room in her house that had a curse. "People were constantly dying in it. They died of bleeding ulcers and had other things that they bled to death from."

When Casey heard that Dorothea had been apprehended because of her contact with the man in the bar, she smiled, tears rolling down her cheeks, and wistfully observed, "Bless her heart. She went back to the same hustle."

Another cabbie, Bill Mobley, told of picking up Dorothea after some of her nighttime drinking sessions: "She would sometimes leave the bars quite drunk. She could cuss up a storm."

One of the more fascinating stories was that of John Sharp, the tenant at Dorothea's who tipped off cops that the landlady had asked him to lie about Bert Montoya's disappearance.

According to Sharp, two days before that first leg bone was discovered Dorothea had gone to Sharp within hours of the deadline established by Moise and Valentine for filing their missing-person report on Bert. She made an urgent request.

Dorothea felt comfortable with Sharp. She had been good to him during his year at the house and thought he owed her something in return. The consideration that she had shown to him in the past caused Dorothea to hope Sharp would lie for her now, in a very important situation.

She pleaded, "John, the police are coming, looking for Bert. Tell them I was gone Thursday and Friday, and Bert moved out on Saturday."

She told him she would make it worth his while.

When Officer Richard Ewing arrived the next day, Dorothea took him to Sharp's room. Sharp told Ewing, "Yes, sir, I think I saw Bert on Saturday, and there was a pickup truck in front of the house being loaded with his furniture."

Shortly after he had provided Dorothea's alibi, Sharp nailed her by slipping the note to Ewing.

Homer Myers, seventy-four, was one former tenant at Dorothea's who didn't spare the hyperbole when relating his adventures under her roof.

Myers would often do favors for Dorothea, responding to her requests. Those favors included moving heavy bundles from one location to another and digging holes in the backyard. She told Myers that the holes were for tree planting or garbage. Myers never thought much about it.

Myers said that most residents of the boarding home exchanged very few words. Many would disappear without a word, but as Myers says, "Folks were always coming and going." Therefore, a tenant's sudden absence would not be a topic of much interest. If one *was* missed, a quick explanation from Dorothea was more than sufficient: He's up north, she moved in with her daughter. Almost any story would terminate further concern.

A two-year resident at Dorothea's, Myers had moved out after a terrible battle with the landlady. He had refused to sign over his checks to her, maintaining his right to independently manage his own financial affairs.

Thinking back, Myers commented: "I feel real lucky just to be here talking. I guess I could have ended up in one of those holes I dug."

Interest in Dorothea and her story was not limited to local media. Television movie producers, checkbook in hand, shuttled on Hollywood/Burbank-to-Sacramento commuter flights seeking to buy story rights to the Dorothea drama from anyone and everyone who had ever crossed paths with the suspect.

Dorothea herself (much to her chagrin) was ignored in the rush to ink, but others were signed. Neighbor Will MacIntyre, tenant John Sharp, cabdriver Patty Casey, and social workers Judy Harper Moise and Peggy Nickerson each put their signature to contracts with the hope of someday being portrayed in a made-for-television movie. The options brought each of these people a check for

$1,500, with the promise of at least $10,000 more if the teleplay made a network run.

Entrepreneurs pocketed unexpected but welcome profits from the brisk sale of Dorothea-related memorabilia. One young man purchased reproduction rights to a full-page color photograph of Dorothea that appeared in Sacramento's daily tabloid newspaper, the *Union,* and had the photo screened onto T-shirts with the bold imprint, SHE DIGS SACRAMENTO. He claims to have cleared a thousand dollars in quick profits.

Ricardo Ordorica, owner of the house of F Street, went before the city council to make a claim of nine thousand dollars, saying the police had made a terrible mess out of his house. He noted that the cops had "pulled up all the carpeting, removing some; ruined furniture; tore out grass and ripped apart a tool shed; tracked mud all over the house's interior, broke up a concrete driveway," and generally destroyed the property. The council expressed its sympathy and denied Ordorica's claim, telling the hapless homeowner to sue them if he wanted any remuneration.

Back in Los Angeles, tipster Charles Willgues had become a celebrity, with television camera crews, reporters, and photographers trooping through his small apartment that Dorothea had so wanted to visit. He answered, over and over, each question asked by the journalists. And when everyone had taken enough pictures of the happy hero at his own place, they all trooped over to the Monte Carlo I bar, where Dorothea had consumed her vodka and grapefruit juice just hours earlier. More pictures were taken, more jokes about Dorothea were exchanged, and a few newsmen's expense accounts were exercised.

Somebody asked Willgues how he felt about everything.

"I'm not really happy about putting someone in jail," he said sadly. "I am happy in a way, though. I believe in justice. I feel like I'm a good citizen."

* * *

Peggy Nickerson was not to share his happy perspective. For the first few days of the F Street drama, the various social workers who had spent the previous months and years working with Dorothea became the object of intensive and almost reverential treatment by the media.

Then, midweek, the attention turned accusatory toward the most unlikely person: Peggy Nickerson. The St. Paul's social worker who had "discovered" Dorothea and recommended her place as a possible home for Bert Montoya came under the public microscope, abruptly, unexpectedly.

Along with the understandable (but completely unwarranted) guilt she was feeling because of Bert's death, Nickerson suddenly found herself pinned in the harsh glare of critical examination by just about everybody.

The media had learned that, back in July, Nickerson had misled Kathleen Stadler, the state licensing program analyst who had investigated Dorothea. At the time, Nickerson still held Dorothea in high regard, and perceived Stadler's questions to be unwarranted prying by a nosey state employee. Since then, Nickerson's opinion of Dorothea had changed—but the media didn't know that.

Word had also leaked out that Nickerson had been "warned" about Dorothea some months earlier by Polly Spring, the county social worker, but that Nickerson had decided to ignore the warning. The critics began to examine her judgment with the wisdom of hindsight, and she began a journey through a unique kind of hell.

California's biggest newspapers headlined Nickerson. SOCIAL WORKER'S AGONY—SHE IGNORED A WARNING, heralded the *Los Angeles Times*. And the hometown *Sacramento Bee* proclaimed, SOCIAL

WORKER SAYS LANDLADY WAS KIND. The stories flatly told how Nickerson had tailored her responses to Kathleen Stadler, and graphically speculated on the results.

Nickerson quickly hired lawyer Peggy A. Christiansen of the Sacramento firm Turner and Sullivan to respond to questions regarding her client's actions. Christiansen issued a statement:

> In no way could [the conversation between Nickerson and Spring] be construed as a "warning." Ms. Spring said nothing to indicate she had any concern about placing people into [Dorothea's] home, but merely made the remark in passing. Had Ms. Spring expressed any real concern, my client would have taken it seriously. My client answered all of [state analyst] Stadler's questions truthfully and is comfortable that all of the information she provided was factual.

Nickerson was not the only one preparing for battle. After the arraignment, Dorothea's court-appointed lawyers were faint with fury over the events that had occurred since her arrest—the media-sponsored, photographed, and thoroughly videotaped flight back from Los Angeles, and the ongoing slurs from Kearns.

Deputy public defender Kevin D. Clymo, a tall, burly man with a thick, swooping moustache, horn-rimmed glasses, a balding pate, and a taste for wearing rumpled tweed, met with the media to lambast them and the police department. With his assistant, Peter Vlautin, standing next to him, Clymo ranted about the "impropriety" of cops to have held her, in contact with the press, for an extended period of time without her having had benefit of counsel. Such a situation, he said pointedly, could not be in the best interests of his client.

"It's unheard of to have a suspect transported with reporters before she's talked to an attorney," he said, noting that Dorothea's right to remain silent probably had been jeopardized. "I can give you all my feelings in one word—unfair. Whatever we are able to do legally, we will do. What are the limits, what are you willing to do to make a buck and a headline?"

Vlautin added that the Sacramento Police Department had "enlisted the aid of the news media to create a circus atmosphere. I don't know where the blame lies, but it is not right!"

Vlautin, however, was a realist. Faced with a future of working by necessity with the media, he thought this was a very unappetizing way to begin a case—in a hissing match with reporters. So before the press conference was terminated, he assured everyone present that "the only thing we can tell you now is that our client denies killing anybody and the true facts will come out in the courtroom, not in the hallways of the courthouse."

Police Chief Kearns, meanwhile, drew heavy criticism from executives of media outlets that had not been invited along on the airplane trip. They were outraged by the cops' cooperation with their competitors and demanded an explanation. The chief had to take a private meeting with them to try to soothe their anger. Kearns told them he knew nothing about the chartering of the jet, nor of the police department's decision to take advantage of the offer.

The news executives had no reason to doubt him. They could easily see that this was a once-in-a-lifetime opportunity that had slipped completely out of the chief's control, and many left the session pitying the sweating cop.

The two media outlets that engineered the controversial coup were quick to defend their own actions regarding the jet's use, with news editors claiming that the journalists had only been following their instincts in getting the whole story as fast as possible.

From television station KCRA, Bob Jordan, the man who had ordered the chartering of the Lear jet, said, "Our job is to aggressively cover the news and to run after things when they happen, and frankly, I'm quite proud of what we did." Jordan said that when Dorothea wanted the in-flight interview to stop, it did. He said his reporter, Boyd, asked the suspect "only general questions."

From the *Sacramento Bee,* managing editor George Baker opined, "Our role was that of an observer. I think we would have betrayed our readers if we hadn't done this." The cost of the plane was shared between the two news entities, and the police simply were offered the chance to ride back with them, "and they accepted," Baker said.

The *Bee's* ombudsman, Art Nauman, chimed in that it was the local police, and not the media, that had the black eye. "There's nothing unethical about chartering a plane and exploiting your resources. The police should have known they were setting themselves up," Nauman concluded.

Vlautin later subpoenaed all of the people on the jet, as well as recordings, videotape, film, and notes accumulated during the controversial ride home to Sacramento. Serious legal rights and obligations could have been violated by the unique circumstances of the early-morning flight, setting the stage for a protracted (and for taxpayers, expensive) courtroom battle with the prosecution regarding the technicalities and principles involved. A question exists, too, as to the resulting evidence that might be allowed to be introduced during trial proceedings.

15

The capture of Dorothea Puente in Los Angeles was viewed by the media as a fluke, one that occurred without the slightest bit of assistance from the Sacramento cops—rather, perhaps, in spite of them. To the great chagrin of Police Chief Kearns, the print reporters and electronic *Wunderkinder* of TV were proclaiming to the world that he and his boys had botched the case terribly. And they were particularly curious about the airplane ride back to Sacramento. Did everything point to Kearns' own bad judgment? The chief himself wondered if he could do anything right. Yet his anger was directed not inward but at his tormenters—the media—and at his own subordinates.

Immediately following Dorothea's capture, Kearns attempted to explain why he remained, almost stubbornly, at the Los Angeles police chiefs' conference. Even as he rationalized his own actions, he felt obligated to defend every procedure that his officers followed during their handling of the quickly evolving events on F Street.

Kearns waxed poetic: "You have to realize," he said to eager reporters (even though he knew in his gut they wouldn't realize anything, ever), "that at the time [of Dorothea's flight, she] was being extremely cooperative. We couldn't have even gone on her property without her permission."

That was quite true. Only through the smooth efforts of Detective Cabrera had investigators been granted access to the F Street grounds in the first place. Cabrera had skillfully convinced the landlady to allow the revealing holes to be dug. Yet Cabrera, his partner Brown, and the other two key, on-site officers, Jorgenson and Enloe, were about to begin a long and unanticipated stint of martyrdom. The chief of police had not the slightest intention of admitting to any of his own errors.

Kearns was quite put out, he didn't mind telling some of his underlings. He had figured on early retirement with a nice city pension. Then he wanted an appointment to a cushy political job, maybe chief of the state police or highway patrol commissioner. He figured he had a decent shot at it if the next governor happened to be his man, Pete Wilson, the senator from San Diego. The criticism from the media and the kidding from his peers was not what Kearns needed.

He leveled his verbal weapons in a backbiting attack on his underlings:

> Dorothea had been talked to by detectives and [they] established a dialogue, and I feel that what occurred was that the detectives became too familiar with the suspect, and too trusting. Sometimes in law enforcement we find ourselves bending over a little bit too far to protect the rights of the suspects or individuals in criminal cases, and that's what occurred here.

Local reporters then got wind of the fact that police had heard from parolee Brenda Trujillo ten months earlier regarding deaths and impromptu burials at Dorothea's house. When he was questioned at a press conference about the Trujillo incident, Kearns professed to be unfamiliar with the case, and felt compelled to confer at some length with a nearby aide before answering:

> That was information in another homicide case where [Trujillo] was charged and the information pointed to [Dorothea] as well as to several others. There was no continuity in the report [by Trujillo] and there wasn't any other evidence to indicate there was a problem at that address.

Plunging ahead onto dangerous legal turf, Kearns casually tossed off another inflammatory response when asked if police had formally ended their search for bodies in Dorothea's yard. Was it possible she might have buried other bodies elsewhere?

"I wouldn't put it past her," said the chief. "If someone is going to kill seven people, why stop there?"

It was one of several prejudicial statements Kearns made regarding the case. He then offered the prediction that she would be charged with "at least" seven murders in the deaths of those people found buried in her yard.

All hell broke out at the Sacramento Police Department following Kearn's determined flight from responsibility. A number of officers were called on the carpet as Kearns attempted to shift the blame from his own shoulders to those of others further down the line of command. Career cops began watching their butts.

By choosing this course of action, Kearns violated the basic code of the men in blue: Back your brethren. Kearns panicked in front of the cameras and microphones, and before the dust at F Street had even cleared, the chief had committed the most unpardonable of wrongs. Within hours of Dorothea's jailing, internal politics at the police department started getting very nasty indeed.

The *Sacramento Bee's* critical editorial questioning certain police decisions made during the heat of the F Street discoveries stung Kearns. He hadn't liked it one bit that the editorial appeared on the same day he arrived home from the conference, copies literally being hawked in his face at the airport.

He was also a bit concerned over the content of a subsequent newspaper article polling members of the city council. Some of those elected officials hinted that heads might roll if culpability for the embarrassment could be assigned. Kearns knew that swift work was needed on his part to insure that his neck was not among those being threatened.

In the immediate aftermath of the investigation into the sensational case, Cabrera and Brown became primary targets in their superiors' frantic scramble to remain untouched by the pall of public blame. Similar fates awaited Lt. Joe Enloe, the department-appointed spokesman on the scene during the excavation, and Sgt. Jim Jorgenson, who with Cabrera had brought Dorothea home aboard the chartered Lear jet.

Cabrera, Brown, Enloe, Jorgenson, and others were required to submit to interviews conducted by the department's internal affairs division and were grilled on numerous issues. So, in addition to the usual written incident reports, the men were obligated to repeat the story, over and over, detail for detail, to fellow officers who suddenly appeared to be serious adversaries. Jobs, careers, and futures were all on the line for those cops who had been selected for the sacrifice.

Cabrera was prodded about his reasons for initiating the original police investigation. His questioners honed in on the matter of the shovels: If he was the guy who had made the unilateral decision to take shovels to Dorothea's that morning, then he must have *known* something, right? He must have known that bodies were buried there. He must have known information he was not sharing with them.

The detective patiently repeated what he had been saying all along: How could he have known anything? He was playing a hunch. All he had was a tip or two, from a citizen and a murder suspect. At what conclusion was he supposed to arrive, based on the information he had been given? As for the shovels, his team was always well prepared.

Then the Internal Affairs fellows wanted to know why Dorothea had been allowed to walk away from the F Street house on that fateful Saturday morning, prior to discovery of the second body. That incident had made the police department look silly and had become a particular thorn in the chief's side. Kearns may have thought he might be able to lay the blame for it on Cabrera's shoulders, partly because it was convenient and partly because his top aides encouraged him to. According to the field investigative unit, here's how it happened.

Because of Kearns' absence, Asst. Chief Jerry V. Finney was the cop in charge in Sacramento the morning of Saturday, November 12, when Dorothea decided to flee. Dep. Chief Lee Dohm, head of investigations, had been to the site several times during the mass excavation and had been updated by field detectives on the scene ever since the first bones had been found. Capt. Michael O'Kane, reporting directly to Dohm, was at the site.

The embarrassing sequence of events (which remains a topic of heated dispute) was set into motion by Dorothea herself. From a window in her upstairs apartment, she saw Cabrera walk to a spot where it is assumed she knew another body was buried. As the detective sank the shovel into the soft ground, Dorothea walked outside to the porch and hailed Cabrera. Looking him straight in the eye, Dorothea had asked the only question that mattered under the circumstances: "Am I under arrest?"

The detective hesitated. Despite the discovery of a human bone in Dorothea's yard, he knew the cops' official mandate had been a search for a recently missing male. The bone unearthed the previous day had been that of a female. Cabrera and his fellow investigators had maintained constant contact, from the very beginning, with Tim Frawley and George Williamsom of the district attorney's office regarding proper procedures for this warrantless search of Dorothea's premises.

In fact, every single on-site action taken by Cabrera and his associates had been considered in advance, approved by the prosecutor and his deputies, and endorsed by police higher-ups. And up until then, the D.A.'s men had been able to perceive no reasonable cause to detain Dorothea.

As he walked with her down the stairs, Cabrera spotted his superior, Captain O'Kane, strolling around the crime site and nodding sagely, hands clasped behind his back.

"Wait here a minute," he told Dorothea, and he walked over to the captain.

At O'Kane's request, Cabrera provided him with an update of Frawley's and Williamson's most recent thinking on the matter of detainment: There was insufficient evidence, at the moment, to justify the detainment of anyone, Dorothea included. O'Kane told Cabrera that no arrest could be made—at least not one that would stand up in court.

Cabrera then returned to where Dorothea was standing to inform her of the findings. "No. You are not under arrest."

"In that event, I'd like to go have a cup of coffee at the Clarion," Dorothea said, "to talk to a nephew who works at the hotel."

"No reason why you can't," Cabrera said.

"And, oh, by the way," Dorothea continued, gesturing toward the crowd bunched at the yellow-ribboned police perimeter, "I'm afraid of all those people."

"No reason why you should be," Cabrera replied. Under the watchful eye of a battery of news cameras, Cabrera escorted her to the outer edge of the cluster of spectators, and she made herself history for the next few days.

With big, black headlines and raised eyebrows on the evening news, the local media howled. It looked to them like there was a scapegoat in the crowd, and they were going to hunt it down and identify it for the public.

During the heat generated by the events of the week, Kearns had caved in to the media's demands to know who screwed up. He had announced that some officers were responsible for making bad decisions, but that neither he nor his top brass were those officers.

Later the same day that Kearns made this statement to the media, he had summoned Brown and Cabrera to his office. Upon their arrival, he said he was "doing this as a courtesy" to the men, and proceeded to show them a videotape of his performance during that morning's press conference. It was Kearns' way of telling his detectives that the dung was about to hit the fan, and that when it did, he wanted both of them standing right in front of it.

Rank-and-file cops throughout the department were astounded by what happened during the next few weeks. In an apparent attempt to placate city council members and a growing list of critics (and perhaps to cleanse his own tarnished professional reputation), Kearns and his henchmen began hunting for pigeons among their subordinates, pointing the big finger straight at the field unit: Enloe, Jorgenson, Brown, and Cabrera.

Internal probes, sudden and unexpected ill will, threats to careers, transfers, and reassignments dominated the Sacramento Police Department's private activities for several months.

16

The first to be sighted in Kearns' cross hairs was Joe Enloe, the lieutenant in charge of the crime scene at F Street. Kearns' second target was Jim Jorgenson, the supervising sergeant.

Enloe and Jorgenson both joined the police department in 1965, making them twenty-three-year veterans. Enloe was a lieutenant in the larceny/fraud section in 1984, and in Internal Affairs for two years until his long-awaited transfer to the homicide/assault division. Jorgenson earned his spot in the section in 1987, a hand-picked selection of Deputy Chief Dohm.

As assignments in the Office of Investigations go, the homicide/assault team is considered the most desirable and prestigious, and Enloe and Jorgenson were happy to have finally made the grade. The pair seemed cut from the same physical pattern, both solidly built. Jorgenson was the larger of the two, with a round face and gentle eyes. Both were soft-spoken but tough, capable, and experienced.

Two weeks after the discovery of the bodies at Dorothea's, Enloe and Jorgenson knew their ordeal was about to begin. They were ordered to explain their actions at the crime scene by immediately responding in writing to Dohm's and O'Kane's order for a full explanation.

Enloe's report, contained in a memorandum dated November 29, 1988, began by summarizing his subordinate detective Cabrera's experiences leading up to the discovery of the first human bone on Friday, November 11. Enloe was summoned to the scene at about 11:10 A.M., about ten minutes after the grisly find.

He had checked with Detectives Brown and Cabrera to ascertain that the scene had been sealed, and agreed with the decision to call in a forensic anthropologist to help recover the body.

Enloe wrote in his memo that Jorgenson had arrived at the scene just before he did. He noted:

> Judging by the clothing and the relatively small size of the exposed bones, I suspected the skeleton to be that of a petite woman. I was confident it was not the remains of a robust Alvaro Montoya. Sergeant Jorgenson and I concerned ourselves with protecting the scene from the impending rain as we waited for information from the interviews being conducted by Brown and Cabrera.

Enloe cited the calm being displayed by Dorothea at that time as one reason he did not immediately suspect her:

> During [Dorothea's] interview, she remained very calm and composed. She again gave consent for the officers to continue the search of her property, maintaining that she had nothing to hide. She gave reasonable explanations for the digging she had caused to be done in her yard.

> She gave reasonable explanations for the cement that had been poured in the yard. She explained that [Ben Fink] had gone back to Marysville. She also insisted that [Bert] Montoya was not dead. She said she had last seen him on the previous Saturday.

When Cabrera and Brown had completed their first interview with Dorothea, and she had been returned to her house, Enloe got an update from the detectives. They told him that they had asked her about John Sharp's claim that she had requested Sharp to lie about Bert Montoya's whereabouts. They said they had also queried Dorothea about Brenda Trujillo's accusations concerning bodies and burials.

Enloe reported on his discussion with Cabrera and Brown:

> [Dorothea] stated that Sharp had made up the story . . . because he was mad at her for evicting him. She stated that Brenda Trujillo's remarks regarding [Dorothea] killing people were nothing new. She said she had refused to allow Trujillo to move back into the boarding house. Trujillo threatened to tell police about the "killings." [Dorothea] told her to go ahead. [Dorothea] then acknowledged that she had called Crime Alert [a telephone tip-the-cops service] regarding Trujillo as a murder suspect.

Dorothea proposed that her call to the police was the likely reason for Trujillo's continuing animosity toward her.

Enloe also pointed out that the version of events being so calmly outlined by Dorothea had been corroborated by information from Mervin John McCauley. McCauley had claimed to have seen Montoya the previous weekend, and he backed Dorothea's statement that Montoya had left with a relative.

While setting up the crime scene, Enloe had carefully thought out the situation. In his subsequent, formal response to his superiors' allegations, he reviewed the data he had been given up to that time and described the thought processes that had driven his decisions of the day:

1. [Dorothea] gave a voluntary consent for her parole officer and detectives to search the yard, telling them she had nothing to hide.

2. Two people corroborated her statement that Montoya had been at the boarding house the past weekend. Sharp's report that [Dorothea] had asked him to lie became suspect. I believed him, but she may have had another reason [for the request].

3. When a body was found in the yard, it appeared to be that of a female, not that of Montoya, about whom the [missing person] report had been generated.

4. The advanced decomposition of the body suggested that it had been in the ground for a much longer time than either Montoya or Ben Fink had reportedly last been seen.

5. There was absolutely no information, known to us at the time, that suggested any women were missing, or that any women were associated with the boarding house.

6. I did not give the comments made by Trujillo a great deal of weight. . . . She was in custody because of [Dorothea] and she knew it. She had also told the detectives that she heard [Dorothea] had killed people and no one had done anything about it because of her close contact with police.

7. The boarding house was occupied by at least four men in addition to [Dorothea]. Others were known to

have come and gone. John McCauley, as well as any other roomer, could have been responsible for burying the body.

8. There were no obvious signs of trauma observed on the exposed portion of the skeleton, thus no apparent cause of death.

9. Consent to search the property was given by [Dorothea] with the understanding that it was free and voluntary. To have arrested her almost immediately thereafter would have seriously jeopardized the validity of the search and perhaps the entire case against any suspect ("fruits of poison tree" doctrine).

10. [Deputy] District Attorney Tim Frawley was consulted and agreed that there was not probable cause to arrest [Dorothea].

Enloe responded to the accusation that he "endangered the safety of the public" by not making a timely arrest of Dorothea:

No surveillance [other than reserve officers at the scene] was placed on [Dorothea] during the night because it was not considered necessary. She had been cooperative and gave no visual signs of anxiety or fear. She told the detectives on at least two occasions that she had nothing to hide and her actions and demeanor portrayed that. She agreed to a polygraph examination to be conducted on Monday.

There was also the question regarding the possible culpability of one or more of the others living at the house. If John McCauley was lying about seeing Montoya on the [previous] weekend, perhaps he was the culprit. Donald Anthony is an ex-con who lived in the boarding

> house and had disappeared, leaving all of his belongings behind. Julius Kelley, another tenant, recently released from a mental hospital, could also be considered a suspect. He reported that he saw Montoya the previous weekend, also.

Jorgenson's written response echoed Enloe's recollection of events. But despite their explanations, and in spite of the facts, Enloe and Jorgenson were informed that Kearns had ordered an Internal Affairs investigation into their work on the crime scene. To make matters worse, specific allegations of "misconduct" and "errors in judgment" had been leveled against each officer.

Deputy Chief Dohm summoned Enloe and Jorgenson separately to his office in mid-December and told them they would be reassigned shortly. Both Enloe and Jorgenson say Dohm told them the reassignment was the result of their actions in the Dorothea Puente investigation.

Apart from allowing Dorothea to leave her house that fateful Saturday morning, Enloe and Jorgenson were criticized for the events of the chartered Lear jet flight back to Sacramento following Dorothea's Los Angeles capture.

According to the official department line, "Enloe and Jorgenson escorted or permitted [Dorothea] to be escorted onto an airplane chartered by a local television station and occupied by reporters. During the flight back, she was allowed to be questioned by at least one of these reporters about her alleged involvement in the crimes." As a result, "the public was left to wonder about the competency of the Sacramento Police Department."

Their reassignments were to two of the least popular of the investigative units; Enloe went to special tasks, Jorgenson to larceny/fraud. Each man considered this a severe insult to his professional standing.

Following the Internal Affairs investigation, Kearns and Assistant Chief Finney decided on the remainder of the department's official course of action: Jorgenson would receive a written reprimand from Kearns, while Enloe would get his reprimand from Finney. Enloe also got passed over for his captain's stripes. All in all, these were hardly reassurances of a job well done.

Enloe and Jorgenson, infuriated by the reassignment action against them and calling it punitive, filed grievances against Kearns and several of his top aides.

The field cops were not without support from within the ranks. Twelve fellow officers have indicated their willingness to testify on their brethren's behalf in formal proceedings.

Apparently, the people of Sacramento did not think the action of Enloe and Jorgenson had placed them in any particular danger. During the heat of the public scrap between Kearns and his troops, a readers' poll appeared in the morning tabloid Sacramento *Union*, the west's oldest newspaper, asking the question: "Should the Puente investigators have been reassigned?"

Nearly eight of ten readers responded with an emphatic "No."

17

Today, more than a year later, the house is devoid of all occupants, a door conveniently left unlocked to admit curious trespassers. The residence's interior displays mute evidence of the human beings who lived there and of those who just visited.

On the lower floor's dining-room table sits a claw hammer, used by police to pry at wallboards. A wooden kitchen chair is propped against the back door.

The upstairs apartment where Dorothea and McCauley lived is reached by either the front stairs or a narrow back stairway. The apartment has three bedrooms, two sharing a connected bathroom; a living room with a fireplace; and a kitchen.

A copy of a police search warrant rests on a coffee table. It lists various items seized from the house as possible evidence: numerous pills and prescription bottles, a letter addressed to "Mr. Bert Montoya," plastic gloves, a roll of duct tape, a cellophane-wrapped book.

The police left Dorothea's booze supply intact. Half-liter bottles of her favorite alcoholic beverage, vodka, along with gin, bourbon, and some Bloody Mary mix, rest on an oak buffet.

Dorothea's reading taste goes to romances, mysteries, and other paperback novels, stacked carelessly in a two-tier, dark-wood bookcase standing next to the oak buffet. The Book of Mormon perches atop the television set. A cheap print of the painting "The Last Supper" decorates a wall.

In the middle bedroom (the location, tenants had said, of foul and lingering odors), a rug has been removed and a large, dark stain is visible on the wooden floor. Candies wrapped in yellow paper fill a glass jar on a table, and an empty can of Wizard Light Lemon Air Conditioner lies on its side on the floor.

No other signs remain of the F Street horror.

But the events of the city's most extraordinary murder case cannot be forgotten.

Today, the scent of blooming flowers masks the once-heavy pall of death at 1426 F Street. Dorothea's rented house sits empty, its brick and wrought-iron gates chained and padlocked. The tiny, patchwork yards where police found Bert and the others lie barren, stripped of sod by searching police. Plainly visible from the street are several long indentations, holding only the occasional wet evidence of rainstorms, and several dandelions. A trash container adorned by an unfinished holiday wreath is behind the chained gate. Plastic bags are stuffed under the stairwell, assorted junk moved from the house. The Victorian house next door to Dorothea's and three other properties on the block are up for sale, but that's not particularly uncommon for the area. Mostly, things have returned to normal.

On the first anniversary of the macabre discoveries, nearly a hundred revelers gathered at the F Street house for a raucous midnight party that left the property strewn with garbage.

The statue of St. Francis of Assisi has disappeared.

Conversation around Henry's Lounge has turned to baseball and the lottery, but can easily be diverted to anecdotal recollections of the well-dressed woman who often bought drinks for the house. At Joe's Corner, a regular patron snorts disdainfully that, "People come in, want to know where she sat. Can you imagine that?" Also at Joe's, they proudly point out that the sixty bucks remaining on Dorothea's tab at the time of her arrest went to help defray some of the expenses of Bert's funeral.

Because there were so many government entities with blushing cheeks over the whole affair, there has emerged a veritable fountain of fact liberally tinted by imaginative alibi . . . an uncommon glimpse of government at work.

Michael F. Coonan, an ombudsman and patients' rights advocate for elderly and mentally disabled people, working under joint private and public grants, prepared an extensive and insightful report on the incident in which he observed:

> The fact is, it didn't take much to fool these professionals. About 25 different professional staff from at least ten separate public and private agencies were involved with and fooled by Dorothea Puente. Many of these professional staff simply did not do their jobs. Others made referrals of no value and others did not believe or take seriously complaints. . . .

It's probably going to be difficult to change things. Coonan adds that "one of the fundamental problems which feeds this system of abuse is the give-away of cash grants [SSI, General Assistance, etc.,] to dependent, isolated, and incompetent people." A system that is supposed to provide a measure of protection for these people—Coonan calls it the "safety net"—is not working. Government has created the illusion of monitoring and supervision, and that illusion has become the biggest of all impediments to meaningful change.

Numerous lawsuits aimed at forcing the Social Security Administration to alter its procedures relating to representative payees have been filed, most notably one by the Legal Services of Northern California against Otis R. Bowen, secretary of the U.S. Department of Health and Human Services, and Dorcas R. Hardy. It is essentially the same action the nonprofit organization has been pursuing for years, but Legal Services lawyer Curtis L. Child thinks the Puente case has highlighted the problem and that the series of lawsuits he has initiated might now be fruitful.

Interestingly, the only job casualties have occurred in the private sector.

Peggy Nickerson, who placed numerous tenants in Dorothea's room-and-board home, resigned during the media circus and the tumultuous investigation following discovery of the bodies.

Beth Valentine of Volunteers of America sang "Amazing Grace" at Bert's funeral and then quit her job. She later returned to take a different position with the organization.

Judy Moise delivered Bert's eulogy and then considered resigning. After some time off, she decided to resume her social work career.

"For a while there I felt like my life was on 'hold,' " Moise says of the aftermath. The media glare had been unexpected and brutal, and she briefly believed that she had "fattened Bert up to deliver him" to his death.

"It changed my life. I'm not sure what it is," she thinks. "I felt for a while that people would really be against me, and I felt a lot of shame. I do have guilt. . . ."

Moise once thought she and Dorothea had a great deal in common: They both were independent and somewhat rebellious, worked outside the system whenever necessary, appeared to be helping the same kind of people. "I saw a lot of kindness in Dorothea that was believable. What I didn't see was her complexity," says Moise.

Lawsuits against Nickerson and her former employer, St. Paul's Senior Center, have been filed by several relatives of victims. Also targeted for litigation are the owners of the F Street property, Ricardo and Veronica Ordorico. This suit, filed by Robert Fink, brother of victim Benjamin, contends the Ordoricos were "negligent" in renting the house to Dorothea. In addition to these woes, the Ordoricos continue making mortgage payments while the house sits unoccupied, virtually unsellable.

The man arrested as a possible accomplice at the time of Dorothea's journey to Los Angeles (subsequently released for lack of evidence) is being groomed by the prosecution as a key witness. Mervin John McCauley is said by police sources to be an important part of the prosecution's case against the landlady.

State narcotics officers in December arrested Sacramento physician Dr. José A. Herrera, 72, and charged him with dispensing prescriptions without proper licensing. Herrera, whose office is only three blocks from Dorothea's house, is suspected by the Sacramento County district attorney's office of unlawfully prescribing drugs, including Dalmane™, to Dorothea and others over a period of several years.

Bill Johnson, the Volunteers of America social worker, a devout Christian, lives with the constant memory of his friend Bert Montoya, and takes what solace he can in his firm belief that Bert "is with God now."

TRIAL:
The People v. Dorothea Puente

"I didn't kill anyone. Those people were all my friends, how could anybody believe I'd harm them?"

18

From the very moment the first bones had been found by parole agent Jim Wilson and his probing shovel, investigators had been faced with the chore of preserving, to the highest degree possible, the integrity of every single piece of evidence that might exist at the scene. Evidence relating to the identities of the bodies would have particularly far-reaching legal implications.

The human remains needed to be removed from Dorothea's yard with proper respect and extreme care. No tangible clue as to the identity and (if possible) cause of death of each individual could be overlooked.

Certain structural characteristics of that first body, which had almost completely decomposed to a skeletal state, would provide valuable information for the team of experts who had been assembled to assist police in the necessary but unappealing chore that lay ahead.

Because the skeleton of this body appeared to be complete, certain elements of identification could readily be made. Forensics people like to say that there are 206 bones and thirty-two teeth in a human being's body, and every piece has a story to tell about its owner's life and death. The resulting "book" on the body is called an osteobiography.

Forensic anthropologists Rodger Heglar of San Diego and Chuck Cecil of San Francisco began a cursory examination of the bones, which were wrapped in woolen cloth and tattered clothing. When it had been buried, the body was clad in a long-sleeved orange blouse, dark jacket, and low-heel shoes. The first task was to identify the corpse's sex.

The skull was the initial object of examination. Light brown hair still clung to it. Absent from the skull were the prominent brow ridges and the large mastoid bones behind the ears that are found in males. This was a female. The teeth were missing, indicating the woman had used dentures.

The ridge of the nose was high and prominent, indicating the woman was Caucasian. (In Negroids and Mongoloids, the nasal opening is broader; a smoothed-down nasal margin would be further indication of a Mongoloid.) The basilar joint, at the bottom of the skull, had fused, as had the cranial sutures, indicating that this person had been aged at death.

Enough dirt had been cleared away from the skeletal remains to allow a closer look at the neck area. There, the bone to which neck muscles once were attached appeared smaller, consistent with those belonging to females.

Next, Heglar and Cecil studied the femur, the large thigh bone, looking for indications of wear at points of juncture. No cartilage was visible, a factor helping to verify age and of vital importance if the remains were to be promptly and correctly identified.

Calipers were applied to the femur, and its precise measurements were entered into a computer that delivered to the scientists a reasonably close estimate of age. (A known correlation exists between the height and length of the femur bone, making possible an accurate computation of age.)

Further excavation allowed measurement of the foot joint, its size providing additional verification of the skeleton's probable sex. Clues to the size and stature of the person also were revealed by characteristics of the foot bones and by the length and girth of certain major bones.

Also factored into the forensic study were observations from the pelvic examination, which provided almost certain identification of the sex and age of the individual at death. (The surface of one of the pelvic bones, the pubis symphysis, changes in a very predictable way and has a distinctly different appearance when a person is 19, 25, 35, and so on until very old age.)

Through these visual methods of examination, the two forensic experts could ascertain with a reasonable degree of certainty that the first body found was that of an elderly female, about seventy-five to eighty years old, small of stature. She had been dead for a year or less.

The second body recovered was also that of a female.

But when the third was pulled from its muddy grave, amid pieces of cloth and foam rubber, investigators were fairly certain that it was the corpse of a male.

A white tag was placed on the right big toe of the body: SACRAMENTO COUNTY CORONER, CASE NO. 88-3381. These remains followed the previous two to the coroner's offices, but it would be the first to undergo autopsy. Speed was of the essence: If this body was that of the missing man, Montoya, it would tie into the missing-person report and would be a tangible link to Dorothea.

At 1:00 P.M. Tuesday, November 15, an autopsy was begun on Case No. 88-3381 by Dr. Gary A. Stuart, while Heglar conducted a simultaneous anthropological study of the remains. Witnessing the work was David W. Smith, resident in pathology at Veterans Administration Hospital, Martinez, California.

A green blanket, covered with soil and a white substance (later identified as lime), completely encased the body. Edges of the blanket were sewn together with red and yellow string. The blanket was tied in a knot at the head of the corpse.

Heglar and coroner's assistant Robert Wood carefully cut the blanket, immediately under which were two layers of medium-gauge clear plastic. A single piece of blue cloth, wrapped almost entirely with heavy, silvery duct tape, was under the plastic. Three more layers of plastic, then a light blue quilt, were cut.

On the surface of the quilt were four brown bugs, noted the examiners, who then placed the insects in formaldehyde.

A folded blue plastic tarp, with metal grommets laced with thin white rope, surrounded the body. The head and face were covered with black plastic material. These were cut away, exposing the remains.

The preliminary determination told the medical men that they were working on a Caucasian male, 50 to 60 years old, 64 to 65 inches in height and weighing 128 pounds. Hair remaining on the skull was light brown or blond. No obvious tattoos or scars were evident, but the doctors could detect evidence of "apparent healed nose bone trauma."

The body was clad in a white T-shirt imprinted with block letters spelling "Canon," dark gray trousers, jockey shorts, and blue-striped white socks.

External examination of the body was described by Dr. Stuart in his subsequent report, partially excerpted:

> When first examined after removal of the wrappings, but prior to removal of the clothing, the hips are extended

with slight flexion of the knees. The arms are raised at the sides of the head with the elbows flexed.

The body is that of an adult male. There are the advanced changes of decomposition. Those changes include malodor, slight, soft tissue swelling, patchy brown coloration of the skin and subcutaneous tissue, loss of hair in the pubic region, and minimal oral purge. The remains are cold. Over the head, face, anterior cervical area and chest bilaterally, there is a granular, dark brown material. Most of the skin has a light tan and brown-gray coloration.

The scalp hair is fine and relatively straight. A few scalp hairs are dark. [The hair] measures two-three inches in length. Frontal balding cannot be determined because of the skin slippage secondary to decomposition. There is possible occipital balding. The eyes are softened and decomposed. The cornea are turbid. The irises and pupils are not well visualized. Palpation of the calvarium, facial bones, zygomatic area, nasal bones, maxilla, and mandible reveals no obvious recent fractures. Five anterior lower teeth, right and left, are very loose in the mandible. These are removed and submitted to the forensic odontologist. Over the face, sideburns and moustache region [some] beard is evident, but most facial hair is missing due to decomposition.

. . . no scars, anomalies or other significant antemortem abnormalities. Palpation of the bones of the hand, forearms and arms reveal no obvious fractures. There is extensive skin slippage over the palmar surfaces of the hands and fingers. The fingernails are soiled. The toenails are unremarkable except for slight thickening. The back is normal.

* * *

In order to make a positive identification of the remains, the pathologists had all the corpse's fingers removed, and Dep. Laura Synhorst drove the appendages to the state Department of Justice's Latent Fingerprint Section. That concluded the day's examination.

The state attorney general's fingerprint specialists receive several difficult identification cases each month. But because of the degree of decomposition of Coroner's Case No. 88-3381, getting prints from the fingers was particularly tricky: These fingertips were badly decayed, and persistent oozing of body fluids made the prints smear easily.

In this instance, the print experts tried several techniques. First, the appendage was dusted with black powder in an attempt to lift a print, as might be done with a living person. Having no success with this method, technicians removed the skin from two fingers. One was pressed between glass slides and microscopically photographed. The remaining skin segment was dusted "flat" and then pressed onto a clear sheet of plastic. The plastic was then turned over, and the print impression photographed in reverse, like a transparency.

This latter effort proved successful.

When the autopsy on Case No. 88-3381 was resumed, the internal condition of the body came under examination.

Examined first were the neck area and the organs of the upper chest cavity. From Stuart's report:

> The neck muscles show no hemorrhages or significant focal dislocation. The hyoid bone, larynx and cricoid cartilage reveal no fractures although the larynx is very flexible. Thyroid gland is small, symmetrical and red-brown.
>
> The pericardial sac is free of fluid. It contains a small

> amount of soft fatty yellow material. . . . The heart weighs 200 grams.

No abnormalities of the heart or cardiovascular system were noted by Dr. Stuart. No foreign objects were found in the larynx, trachea or windpipe; no tumors were evident. The stomach, liver with attached gallbladder, both testes, brain, heart, lung, kidney, fat, spleen, aorta, skin, and muscle tissue were removed for closer study by pathologists and toxicologists. Also gathered for a microscopic look were some rib fragments, body and head hair, and mucus from the nasal passages. A long-healed broken nose was detected by further scrutiny, the damage indicated by a roughening of the nasal bones.

No signs of trauma were seen on the head. The brain was shrunken, softened, and discolored to gray-green, and weighed six hundred grams.

Coroner's deputies received Bert Montoya's medical records from a 1984 surgery at the University of California, Davis, Medical Center. Those records indicated Montoya had a mastoidectomy in 1984, and a subsequent reexamination of the skull showed matching evidence of such an operation.

Several days after completion of the autopsy, the California Justice Department's Joe Sypnicki, of the Latent Fingerprint Section, notified Coroner Charles Simmons that their efforts had borne fruit, and a positive identification of the body had been made through a print match: It was, without any doubt, Alvaro (Bert) Montoya.

Edward Smith, the coroner's deputy who had first answered the call to Dorothea's house, telephoned the sad news to Bert's eighty-two-year-old mother, Theresa. Her long-missing son had been found.

The disturbing investigation took its toll on a wide variety of people who found themselves haunted by its memory.

Joyce Underwood, thirty-four, had been a clerk in the Sacramento police's property room for four years at the time the bodies were discovered. It became part of her job to handle the macabre materials from the mass gravesite that were gathered for future analysis and possible courtroom display.

One night she was given a pair of rubber gloves and an "odor-eater" mask and was dispatched to the morgue. For more than four hours she watched as different items—clothing, body bags, pieces of sodden blankets—were systematically labeled by a coroner's assistant.

"It was a shocking experience and the smell was horrible." She retched when she had to load the sacks into the rear of her black police van.

"My hand became hot, like it was on fire," recalls Underwood. "I felt angry, evil spirits floating and surrounding me, suffocating and strangling me."

Two months later, she was sent back to what she by this time was calling "the room of hell"—the morgue—to get more sacks of evidence. "I cried and threw up," she says, and then her job was threatened by an angry supervisor.

Since that occurrence, Underwood says she has "been unable to feel clean no matter how many times I shower. I'm preoccupied with death."

She got no sympathy from her boss, Police Lt. Rich Kupper, who commented, "If she's queasy I can understand that, but we still have to go and get stuff. All property room clerks become involved with a lot of unpleasant things, homicide evidence being one of them, but it's part of the job."

All in all, it was not an enjoyable time for Underwood. She eventually sought reassignment to another department as a result of her experience, and quit the police department when she was not accommodated.

Eight months after the bodies were found, toxicological results were received by the coroner. The body contained various levels of the prescription drugs diphenhydramine, loxapine, flurazepam, amitriptyline, and carbamazepine. None of the substances were found in lethal quantity. All are drugs commonly taken by elderly people.

Diphenhydramine is a common antihistamine, marketed under the brand names Sominex™ and Nytol™. Carbamazepine is an anti-seizure compound. Loxapine, an antipsychotic agent, can be very dangerous when taken in concert with any other drug. Amitriptyline is a mood-elevating antidepressant, and consumers are warned explicitly not to take double dosages.

(Only one of the substances, flurazepam,* commonly called Dalmane™, was eventually detected in each of the seven bodies found at Dorothea's. Dalmane™ is a sedative with hypnotic, depressant actions. An accidental overdose, even as small as double the prescribed dosage, can be life-threatening, and immediate emergency aid is suggested by its manufacturer. Symptoms include delirium, unusually fast heartbeat, shortness of breath, difficulty in breathing, and coma.)

After Montoya, identification was completed on the other six people found at F Street. One was Benjamin Fink, whose brother, Robert, had worried about him during the excavation. The first body found was Leona Carpenter, 80. The others were Betty

*According to The American Society of Hospital Pharmacists, in their publication *The New Consumer Drug Digest* (1985), flurazepam may cause a host of undesired effects, including intestinal problems; hallucinations; depression; allergic skin reactions; and nervousness. The drug may worsen such conditions as asthma; emphysema; chronic lung, kidney, or liver disease; and depression. Consumption of alcohol while taking flurazepam may increase the chance and severity of side effects. The drug may be habit-forming and potentially dangerous if taken in large amounts or over a long period of time. In addition to these precautions, tampering with the dosage of this drug may have serious results.

Palmer, 80; Dorothy Miller, 65; Vera Faye Martin, 65; and James Gallop, 64.

The interpretation of the results of the autopsies and the numerous, detailed forensic studies of the bodies will become the centerpiece of both the prosecution and the defense in Dorothea's upcoming trial.

19

With Dorothea sitting in jail and the autopsies finally completed on all seven disinterred bodies, the juggernaut of justice has started rolling in earnest.

The police have done their best to shrug off the distracting public and internal turmoil the department was experiencing in order to concentrate on the important business at hand—that of finding and organizing a vast amount of evidence. The district attorney's office on the one hand, defense lawyers on the other, have begun their lengthy, painstaking preparations on the case involving the woman suspected of being a rare female serial killer. Each side knows it walks uncommon legal ground, and that the eyes of the world will watch with keen interest when the curtain finally goes up on Dorothea's trial.

For six months following the excavation, there was relative quiet. Then, in April 1989, prosecutors filed additional charges—eight more counts of murder. Up to this time, Dorothea had been held without bail on charges alleging just one murder, that of Bert Montoya. Now she would stand accused in the deaths of all those found in her yard—and two others.

The body of Everson Gillmouth, seventy-seven, a former resident at Dorothea's boarding house, was found in 1986 on the banks of the Sacramento River in Sutter County. The decomposing body was enclosed in a rough-hewn, wooden, coffinlike box, half in, half out of the water. Prosecutors claim to have a witness to the dumping of Gillmouth's body, a onetime friend of Dorothea's named Ismael Florez. Florez is said to have helped build the box, place Gillmouth's body inside, and transport it to its eventual dumping spot.

The ninth murder charge tagged to Dorothea involved the 1982 death of her then-roommate, Ruth Monroe. Monroe was sixty-one when she collapsed at the 2100 F Street residence. The coroner found in her system a high concentration of codeine and acetaminophen, both prescription painkillers. The death was almost listed as a suicide, but friends of Mrs. Monroe's raised allegations causing investigators to pause: The deceased was allergic to codeine, never would have knowingly taken it for any reason. The official cause of death remained undetermined until the prosecutor decided to add the late Mrs. Monroe to the list of victims already attributed to Dorothea.

Shortly after Mrs. Monroe's death, Dorothea was arrested and subsequently sentenced to her state prison term for drugging victims, forgery, and theft. At the trial, prosecutors knew about the circumstances of Mrs. Monroe's death, but were unconvinced that sufficient evidence existed to justify a related charge against Dorothea. According to police, confirmation of Mrs. Monroe's supposed allergy to codeine still has not been established. But when the bodies were found at the F Street house, the Monroe file was reopened and sent to the district attorney for review. Subsequent filing of the additional charges followed. Prosecutors also took another look at the death of Eugene Gamel, overdose victim at Dorothea's in 1987, but stayed with the original finding of suicide.

Eight months after the bodies in the yard were found, Coroner Charles Simmons issued his final determination: There was no way to establish cause of death in any of the seven corpses unearthed at F Street, and there never would be. Therefore, Simmons could not say if any of the seven had been murdered. He officially declared the cause of death in each to be undetermined.

Lacking a specific cause of death assignable to any of the alleged murder victims may be a problem for the prosecution, but not an insurmountable one.

The prosecution faced other major obstacles. There were reportedly no eyewitnesses to directly support the prosecution's allegations of murder, and thus the case would have to be constructed completely on circumstantial evidence.

The findings of indeterminate cause of death were not the least bit surprising to defense attorney Kevin Clymo and his associate Peter Vlautin, who had already predicted that result. Clymo also noted, wryly, that many defendants have "burned" on circumstantial evidence. But, he said, he woke up with a smile on his face the morning after the coroner's announcement.

Supervising prosecutor George Williamson appeared unruffled by the lack of a specific cause of death determination, reflecting at all times the righteous indignation of the accuser in making his public comments.

From the beginning, Coroner Simmons had been placed in a very awkward position. Even before the vans arrived bearing the seven bodies, he knew that the people found in Dorothea's gardens had been taking lawfully dispensed prescription drugs. Ranging in age from fifty-two to eighty, all had health problems of one kind or another. Traces of Dalmane™ were found in each of the seven, as anticipated. Extensive toxicological testing was conclusive: There were no indications of excessive presence of other drugs in any body.

Simmons said his coroner's office had hoped to find such a high level of some drug in the systems of the supposed victims that any finding of accidental death could be ruled out. But that did not happen.

The coroner's report did spark some legal maneuvers, however, despite the seeming nonchalance by both the defense and the prosecution. Clymo immediately withdrew a motion he had made earlier in the month in which he had demanded the prosecution's "penalty phase evidence," evidence that would be introduced to prove the existence of special circumstances. The request for penalty phase evidence would be premature at this point, said Clymo and Vlautin, because the available evidence was "insufficient."

Clymo's next statement to the media defined the very core of defense efforts to prevent the state's attempt to execute Dorothea Montalvo Puente: "There is no death penalty for unlawful burial."

There is, as the lawyer noted, "a big difference between people who have died of natural causes and are buried, and people who have been murdered and are buried. The seven people found in Dorothea's yard died of natural causes." This will be the claim of the defense.

Clymo was candid about his client's motive: She buried the people in order to continue receiving their monthly benefit checks.

The confrontation between the defense and prosecution will center on a legal concept known as *criminal agency*—a criminal act by one person that results in the death of another. Criminal agency does not have to be proved beyond a shadow of a doubt. If the preponderance of evidence points to guilt, there's guilt. Even the existence of a noncriminal alternative explanation does not require a jury to reject the criminal agency theory. But getting a jury to agree to convicting a little old white-haired woman on the basis of circumstantial evidence, no matter how strong, might be a bit difficult.

The prosecution has announced it will introduce into evidence as much of Dorothea's criminal history as the presiding judge will allow.

Clymo will need to counter as much of that history as possible. Lacking that historical information, moreover, a judge might be more receptive to Clymo's contention: If the coroner cannot determine cause of death, where is the crime of homicide? Upon what will the prosecution rely to prove its case? Where are the "strong circumstances?" Clymo has conceded that the number of bodies that were buried in Dorothea's yard works against her. One or two might be explainable, but seven?

Prosecutor Williamson and his team have not been shy about voicing their claims that significant circumstantial evidence, coupled with the facts in the Monroe and Gillmouth cases, is "compelling." All Williamson has to do is prove that any one of the deaths was by criminal means. If he proves more than one murder, Dorothea may face the gas chamber.

From the beginning, Williamson's and Clymo's comments were part of a truly remarkable aspect of the case against Dorothea Puente: a high degree of cooperation with the media exhibited by both the prosecution and the defense. Both sides provided for public consumption a rich supply of quotable quotes relating to the supposed guilt, and presumed innocence, of the suspect.

As far as defense attorney Clymo was concerned, there were

important gains to be made by addressing several questionable issues. Regarding Dorothea's sudden and rather furtive trip to Los Angeles:

> It's safe to say that when Dorothea left Sacramento, it was at a time when spotlights were shining twenty-four hours a day on her house. She pretty much knew that there would be no way in the world she could have any peace of mind, or peace and quiet. So she just took the cash she had and left.

Clymo was not speaking from knowledge garnered from newspaper clippings; he had driven past the house at 1426 F Street during the very time Dorothea was in Los Angeles, and he had witnessed the scene. His comments were born of direct observation.

A month after Dorothea was jailed, Clymo won a motion to allow her to skip personal appearances in court if it was not necessary for her to make some kind of formal response. This was a small but important victory for the defense team; Clymo and Vlautin do not want Dorothea any more visible to the public than is absolutely necessary. Yet there is much to be done in the preparation of her defense that will at least require Clymo's appearance in court if he is to offset what he knows are widely held, preconceived public notions relating to the case.

Because jewelry had figured so prominently in Dorothea's checkered criminal past, Clymo thought it worthwhile to regain from the prosecution her wristwatch, rings, a Susan B. Anthony dollar collection, and the $3,042.55 in cash she had in her possession at the time of her arrest. If these were held until the trial, Clymo guessed, a jury might learn of it and misinterpret it.

He won his plea, and Municipal Court Judge John Lewis ordered prosecutors to return her belongings. Williamson said he would, after he had photographed everything and assured himself that nothing had belonged to any of the deceased whose deaths were attributed to Dorothea. The belongings were not given to Dorothea in jail, but Dorothea now had the right to determine who would safeguard them for her.

Clymo also attempted to "clarify" Dorothea's reasons for carrying the uncommonly high amount of money. He told the judge that she "had cash because she and a couple of friends had gone on a gambling trip to Las Vegas a few days before this thing blew up."

Clearly Clymo was trying to gain a long-term advantage for his client by inserting into the public consciousness any notion that might help dispel suspicions regarding Dorothea's actions. At the same time, he was attempting to inject a little doubt into the prosecution's theories.

20

In a sensational case punctuated by the bizarre, one facet emerges as perhaps the strangest of all: When Dorothea departed the chaotic scene in front of her house, she was fleeing what must have been a very upsetting situation. Yet before she could travel beyond the long arm of the law, she had slipped right back into the same routine that had already caused her so much trouble in life.

Despite the fact that she was headline news all over the state, Dorothea was drawn to that blue-collar bar in that lower-income part of Los Angeles like a moth to a flame. Her determined effort to befriend and date Charles Willgues was the clue that tipped off the pensioner to her identity and quickly resulted in her late-night arrest.

Why would Dorothea, in what might well have been a frightened flight for her life, repeat her modus operandi almost in plain sight of the world? Was the accused serial killer begging for capture?

Dr. Donald T. Lunde, a California psychiatrist who specializes in criminal behavior and was one of three court-appointed psychiatrists who examined Patricia Hearst during her trial, differentiates between "mass murderers" and "serial murderers" in his book *Murder and Madness:*

> In common usage of the term, *mass murderer* is applied to someone who kills a number of people, usually for no apparent reason or for an apparent but perverse (often sexual) reason. Psychiatric and legal literature sometimes make a distinction between *mass murder* and *serial murder,* with mass murder referring to a crime in which a number of victims are killed, usually by one person in a single episode . . . and serial murder referring to a number of murders by a single person over a period of months or years. Each killing is usually a discrete episode, but there is usually a common method, motive, or type of victim.

The answer might be rooted in that part of her past that is now on the public record. Her frequent brushes with the law and her felony convictions brought her into contact with her share of psychiatrists and psychologists, causing her behavior to be placed under intense scrutiny at various times in her life. Accounts of these sessions shed some light on her thinking, and may help explain some of her actions in a variety of particularly stressful circumstances.

Her personal psychiatrist, Dr. Thomas Doody, once described Dorothea as a "seriously disturbed woman." Several specialists, including a psychologist familiar with criminal behavior, suggested in official reports that Dorothea exhibited schizophrenia dominated by histrionic, narcissistic, and antisocial personality disorders. Her actions during the past thirty years, particularly those of her last few days of freedom, indicate the doctors may be right.

According to many criminal psychologists, personality disorders differ significantly from most psychological disorders, the latter generally being traceable to one (or a few) specific incidents in one's life. Personality disorders, on the other hand, involve an identifiable pattern of lifelong development that permeates both behavior and thought. This in turn colors an individual's whole sense of being, self-image, and internal rules for dealing with fellow human beings. A person thus afflicted has a completely distorted view, both of self and society.

Dr. Lunde notes that "some psychotic conditions have a known organic cause." One such condition is hyperthyroidism, and Dorothea is known to suffer from, and has been treated for, thyroid problems.

Some of Dorothea's more visible affectations were her preference for bright, boldly colored clothing; her abundance of flashy (but real) jewelry; and her tendency toward grandiose descriptions of herself and her activities. A person displaying elements of histrionic personality disorders tends to be overly dramatic and excitable, exaggerating almost everything and insisting upon being center stage. Many more women than men are diagnosed as having this disorder. Easily provoked to sudden fits of temper, histrionic people form friendships quickly but soon begin to make unrealistic demands on others.

Dorothea's narcissistic tendencies were manifested in her flamboyant behavior (buying drinks for everyone in the bar with a fat wad of cash), her constant exaggerations (claiming to be a surgeon or nurse), and her overwhelming concern about how she was perceived by others.

The narcissist's concern for him- or herself all but eliminates the capacity to feel any emotion for people. For this reason, it is possible that the apparent empathy Dorothea showed for certain tenants, such as John Sharp and Bert Montoya, was feigned.

Dorothea's antisocial behavior was evident from the time she was nineteen years old. That was when she was first arrested and convicted of forgery, an activity she not only continued throughout her lifetime, but accelerated.

In most aspects of life, criminal psychologists contend, antisocial people are amoral, often flagrantly violating the rights of others and usually breaking the law. These people will admit to no culpability when caught in their transgressions, as they inevitably are. They are completely incapable of feeling guilty. They find it easy to concoct complex schemes but always lose control of those schemes. They minimize their errors, are incapable of learning from past mistakes, and have great trouble forming personal attachments.

Over years of psychoanalysis, Dorothea has made a habit of minimizing her transgressions, and once told a police officer who was arresting her that she often forgot committing the criminal acts of which she was accused.

Individuals afflicted with personality disorders may lead outwardly normal lives, and become the last to admit that they might need professional treatment.

Because antisocial behavior so often involves criminal activity, it is the most studied personality disorder. An outdated term for an antisocial criminal, *psychopath,* has been supplanted by the term preferred in modern analysis, *sociopath.* If the actions of a sociopath are reinforced during his or her life (resulting, for example, in financial success), the behavior dominates.

Dorothea does seem to deviate from the classic antisocial pattern in one important way: Most of the crimes for which she has been convicted were committed for the purpose of financial gain. (If present charges against her stand up in court, the pattern will have continued to an almost predictable conclusion.)

Her repeated forays into the board-and-care business reflect a taste for risk that was satisfied by undertaking bold actions she knew were forbidden to her. She flaunted her behavior in front of her own parole agents, perhaps daring them to catch her.

This same tendency was, perhaps, the motivating factor that propelled her toward the Monte Carlo I bar in Los Angeles and into her revealing conversation with Charles Willgues. Both were continuations of her standard method of operation.

The early deaths of her parents are thought to have figured heavily in Dorothea's psychological development. Sigmund Freud theorized that underdevelopment of the superego (in effect, one's conscience) likely would result in some form of antisocial behavior. Because the personality of an individual is more or less completely formed by the age of six, it can be assumed that the death of Dorothea's parents prior to her fifth birthday had a negative impact on her psychological development. She lacked the influence of the same-sex parent and enjoyed very little security in her early home life; instead she struggled for survival, working in the fields to pick cotton and fruit from the age of three.

In one published study, 60 percent of the antisocial individuals examined had endured loss of parents as children. For one who grows up in underprivileged circumstances, the rules governing a life of crime may be just as workable as those pertaining to middle-class America.

In other words, by clinical definition, Dorothea may have had a few recognizable reasons for ending up as she did, a psychological disaster.

Against this backdrop of mental instability is an imprisoned Dorothea, who has written two novels since she was arrested, for the specific purpose of proving to her lawyers and anyone else who will listen that she is, in her own words, "not insane." She was ordered by her team of defense lawyers to undergo extensive psychological analysis, and she subsequently was examined on several occasions by a Los Angeles psychiatrist.

"Everyone was surprised that I tested so high," she says proudly. "They didn't think I would."

Dorothea fears the unpleasantly ironic possibility that future legal proceedings might categorize her as mentally ill, and that she might end up institutionalized. For that reason she has resisted efforts of lawyers Clymo and Vlautin to base any part of her defense on her mental condition.

21

As she sits in jail awaiting trial, Dorothea worries about life's little things. For one period that lasted several weeks, she had no money for shampoo and was forced to do without it. She frets about what people think of her and wonders why she hasn't heard from many old friends. And she thinks about her future.

Since her arrest, Dorothea has maintained a stoic public silence. But on July 11, 1989, she began making a series of telephone calls to me. These took place over several months. During one of these conversations, the third, Dorothea made some startling admissions that went to the very heart of the charges against her.

She has not remained quiet willingly. She had completely different plans. From the outset, though, her public defense attorney, Kevin Clymo, made it perfectly clear to her that if she followed her inclination to discuss her case with anyone but him, Associate Attorney Peter Vlautin, or Chief Investigator Dave Howard, she'd be on her own.

Dorothea, of course, wants nothing more right now than to shout "not guilty" to the multiple murder charges as loudly and as broadly as she can. Faced as she has been with very public pronouncements by Police Chief Kearns presuming and prejudging her guilt, Dorothea's desire to articulate her innocence is understandable. But Clymo believes her pretrial utterings could unnecessarily endanger his preparation of her defense.

She adhered to this demand as best she could, but eventually Dorothea grew edgy. She had some things to say, and she planned to say them. And she just had to talk to someone other than her legal team.

The first collect call from Dorothea came at 5:01 P.M., from her new quarters at the Consumnes River Women's Facility, an element of the Sacramento County jail system.

The contact took me by surprise; until this moment, Dorothea and I had been corresponding only through the mail. I had been requesting an exclusive interview from Dorothea for an article about the F Street events, soon to appear in *California* magazine. Even then, Clymo was our intermediary. As a result, I was completely unprepared to tape record the conversation and so began scribbling hasty notes.

Among Dorothea's first words were, "Promise me you won't tell Kevin that I'm calling." The request posed inherent problems. Clymo and I had agreed to play by a certain set of rules, with my clearly stated eventual goal an exclusive interview with Dorothea. This situation was one that the public defender obviously would not condone. And that was unfortunate for me, because I would have liked nothing better at the time than to hear the details of her own story.

But why was Dorothea calling? What did she have to say? Why would she want to skirt Clymo and establish contact with a reporter? Her wishes seemed to take priority, and with this rationalization firmly in mind I agreed to abide by her request, at least for the moment.

Her main concern that day was her perceived conflict with deputy public defender Peter Vlautin, who at the time was working almost exclusively on Dorothea's case while Clymo was temporarily occupied by another.

Vlautin had just departed from a conference with Dorothea, and the visit had agitated her. She expressed a newly found disdain for him. "I asked him if they had any recent letters from you and he looked me right in the eye and told me no, they hadn't, and he acted like he didn't know what I was talking about. Well, Kevin's been real up-front with me so far, and I know right away Vlautin's lying to me, but I don't know why. That's why I'm calling. I don't like that man."

"Maybe he's just trying to do the right thing for you," I suggested.

She wouldn't tolerate any support for Vlautin, however slight.

"He stutters."

"What?"

"He stutters. I don't know if he's smart or not, but he doesn't sound very smart."

(The comment is typical of Dorothea's vituperative attitude, a patent impatience with other people's failings that she exhibits willingly and quite frequently.)

She then politely offered her thanks for my accepting her collect call, noting she could call every other day after 6:00 P.M. or later, "when we're allowed in the walkway." She was being held in virtual isolation under constant supervision, and was making the telephone call while she could see the jailhouse guard upstairs was not sitting at his console.

I told her that regardless of what she might think, everything we said was being taped—if not directly monitored—by her captors, and we should converse accordingly.

Abruptly, she asked, "Can you send me some money?" She had

not been able to wash her hair with real shampoo for weeks, her commissary account having run dry. "All my friends . . . I don't hear from anyone anymore except you, and . . . what bad things they're all saying about me." She related some stories she had heard, and lamented that "everyone's making money off me but me, some people I don't even know."

I told her the case was very sensational.

"Yes." Her voice turned pensive. "I know it is."

At this point she reiterated her innocence: "Dan, I didn't kill anyone. Those people were all my friends, how could anybody believe I'd harm them? I couldn't kill anybody."

Remembering my agreement with Clymo and feeling a burst of conscience, I broke into the monologue. "Dorothea, I don't think we should be talking about your case just yet."

She agreed, and changed the subject. She started describing her various cellmates ("mostly 51/50s* and other hard cases"), her jailers ("they're okay, I like the night shift best"), and the accommodations ("the cell is so small you can only lay down, there's no chair, and there's nothing to do but read, I read a lot.").

Dorothea terminated this first of several telephone conversations after nine minutes, saying that she "had to go, right now." I promised to send some commissary money, and mailed cash and a letter that same day.

Both came back ten days later, marked "undeliverable." Complying with jailers' instructions on the outside of the envelope, I removed the metal paper clip from within and mailed via overnight delivery a new letter and a U.S. postal money order for one hundred dollars. It would not be made available to her for eleven more days.

*51/50s are inmates thought to be criminally psychotic, who pose a danger both to themselves and to others and thus are isolated and kept under constant scrutiny by guards. The term derives from state statute designations.

In the interim, another phone call came from Dorothea, at 6:08 P.M. on July 18. We made small talk while I quickly hooked up the tape recorder.

During the subsequent thirteen-minute conversation, transcribed verbatim below, Dorothea again denied the charges facing her and talked about granting me a formal, in-person interview:

BLACKBURN: Well, let's talk abut that for a second. Ah, how do you propose to move forward on that?

DOROTHEA: Okay, it'll be after my two-one, my prelim trial.

BLACKBURN: Okay, that comes up September twelfth.*

DOROTHEA: Right.

BLACKBURN: Right.

DOROTHEA: After that's over with I'm going to see if you can't get on my visitor's list, because, really, they've kept me too isolated. There for a while I was really tripping out that I couldn't get decent letters in. I got terrible letters in the beginning.

BLACKBURN: Well, I imagine you were hearing from people who had no reason to be contacting you, really.

DOROTHEA: I didn't even know them. There was nothing from friends, notes from people back east who said they had lived with me, rented a room from me, shacked up with me, and that's something. I've never lived with a man. I've always had to marry them to go to bed with them. I think when you knew me, you never saw me come into the bar with anyone, you didn't see me leave with anyone. And, ah, that's one thing that Kevin and them couldn't get through their head at first, but the more they talked to me and the more they talked to other people, although people went on national TV, and said I did this and did that, they found out they were liars.

*The preliminary hearing referred to subsequently was rescheduled to be held in Sacramento Superior Court in February 1990.

BLACKBURN: Well, you run into a lot of different people who do a lot of weird things—

DOROTHEA: Uh-huh.

BLACKBURN: —in relation to something like you were charged with. It was a very sensational circumstance, as you know.

DOROTHEA: Right.

BLACKBURN: And the thing got out of hand and it got out of hand real fast.

DOROTHEA: And if Channel 3 hadn't gotten involved it wouldn't have been so bad.

BLACKBURN: Well, and yeah, of course that was something that you had no reason to expect, uh, the police surprised everybody by allowing that thing to occur.

DOROTHEA: I know it. Now they really don't know what to do with my case, you know.

BLACKBURN: There are very . . . there were a lot of mistakes.

DOROTHEA: Um-hum.

BLACKBURN: —And I think they jumped real fast in arresting you.

DOROTHEA: Yeah, yeah, they did, and they took stuff out. And I never asked to go for a walk, they offered to walk me past the lines.

BLACKBURN: Yeah.

DOROTHEA: —And another thing, they took my rugs out of my house, they took—emptied [unintelligible]—what happened to all my furniture? I had beautiful furniture.

BLACKBURN: Uh-huh.

DOROTHEA: I had before I went to prison, and before I got arrested, and my clothes and stuff, they . . . my jewelry, that one ring I've had since I was fifteen years old, and it was my grandmother's before that.

BLACKBURN: Oh, lordy.

DOROTHEA: Well, I think if, you know, it wouldn't hurt to talk to

Kevin. Do you remember seeing my jewelry on my left hand? I think that—

BLACKBURN: Oh, yeah, I remember your jewelry on your hands.

DOROTHEA: And my Seiko watch.

BLACKBURN: And all those things are now gone?

DOROTHEA: That's what we went to court today for, to get them back, but they want another two weeks. And it took, it's taken eight months, I've been down eight months and two days. It's taken eight months for the damn coroner's report, and eight months . . . Well, it took them six months to admit they had my jewelry and money.

BLACKBURN: Well, you—

DOROTHEA: They've got my bank books, you know, under lock and key.

BLACKBURN: Yeah.

DOROTHEA: We're not even asking for that now because they're going to use that for evidence, but they can't because it was my money.

BLACKBURN: Well, they didn't really know how to react to any of this thing, it, uh—

DOROTHEA: And if I ask Peter anything . . . I don't get along too good with him, but they say he's supposed to be an excellent attorney. Kevin hired him, but he makes me nervous. He stutters, and I'm a very calm, cool, collected person, and he jiggles the whole time we're talking. And if I ask him a question . . . I asked him about you and two weeks ago, he says, oh, no, they never met with him. Well, I knew that you did because Kevin had told me.

BLACKBURN: Oh. But was Kevin with him at the time?

DOROTHEA: No.

BLACKBURN: Oh, okay.

DOROTHEA: And then—

BLACKBURN: What's this lawyer's name?

DOROTHEA: Peter Vlautin, he's the other attorney.

BLACKBURN: Okay, He's a, a public, public defender?

DOROTHEA: Yeah, yeah.

BLACKBURN: Okay, yeah.

DOROTHEA: Because even Melvin Belli, I knew his wife Bella real good, he wanted my case.*

BLACKBURN: Yeah, you don't want to get involved with that.

DOROTHEA: I don't.

BLACKBURN: No.

DOROTHEA: That's the reason I took the two public defenders, is because they've made a model of my home.

BLACKBURN: Kevin's very good.

DOROTHEA: Yeah.

BLACKBURN: Kevin I mean, I mean this is just my opinion, but, ah—

DOROTHEA: Yeah, I've written two books, not about my trial, but two novels.

BLACKBURN: He's only interested in one thing, and that's your welfare.

DOROTHEA: I know it.

BLACKBURN: And that's a very rare thing to find, even in a private lawyer.

DOROTHEA: Well, he believes in me, because everything I've told him has been the truth.

BLACKBURN: And that's the way to stay with it, too.

DOROTHEA: I told him, I told him right from the start: I'm going to be very honest with you about everything.

BLACKBURN: Yeah.

DOROTHEA: You know.

*Belli, the bellicose legal institution from San Francisco, went on television to claim that Dorothea had contacted his office with a plea that he represent her. Dorothea heatedly denied this, saying instead that it was Belli who initiated the contact.

BLACKBURN: Well, that's your best bet, because that's the way he can help you then, and deal with the thing and that way he's not surprised.

DOROTHEA: Everything that I tell him is the way it has been, you know.

BLACKBURN: It's the surprises that, you know, cause the problems, and you know that, too.

DOROTHEA: I know.

BLACKBURN: How are you bearing up?

DOROTHEA: Oh, okay. I miss hearing from my friends, I mean, you'd be surprised how many deserted me, like C., who used to work at Henry's, who I had to kick out.

BLACKBURN: Well, uh—

DOROTHEA: Oh, she talked so terrible about me, and I was so good to her. I used to wake her up, fix her breakfast, draw her bubble bath, and her boyfriend too, you know, I let him move in, and they drank so damned much I just couldn't put up with it.

BLACKBURN: Well, you were dealing with a lot of people who needed a lot of help.

DOROTHEA: I know it.

BLACKBURN: Yeah. And, ah, maybe next time you're just going to kinda—

DOROTHEA: There won't ever be a next time (slight sob). I'll end up marrying somebody—

BLACKBURN: Stay by yourself . . . yeah.

DOROTHEA: —just to get out into the country or something. I don't even know what I'm going to do when I . . . if . . . if and when I get out, because there's no place I can go without being known.

BLACKBURN: Well, if you didn't do this, you're going to get out.

DOROTHEA: I didn't. I didn't.

BLACKBURN: You're out. You know, that's gotta be that way.

DOROTHEA: Well, this is running your bill up.

BLACKBURN: Don't worry about that. Let me say something to you, okay? In relation to the future as you think about talking to people. . . . Kevin knows when in the future you should tell your story. Let Kevin be the guide to that, okay?

DOROTHEA: Well, I think he knows that.

BLACKBURN: I think he's got a good sense of timing, and he has your best interests at heart, again, which is very uncommon for a lawyer right now.

DOROTHEA: I know.

BLACKBURN: You've got someone who really cares about doing his job, which is to take care of you legally. In the end you have . . . really have two choices as far as what people think about you. You can either just—

DOROTHEA: That's why I contacted you.

BLACKBURN: And, ah.

DOROTHEA: And when I see Kevin in a couple of weeks . . . he won't be over for a while, Peter will be over again this week, and the social worker comes on Friday. Sometimes I see her, sometimes I don't. Usually by Friday I'm so burned out by the ding-a-lings I'm . . . that I'm in with . . . my cell block . . . it's two murder cases and then some real bad armed robberies, and then the 51/50s.

BLACKBURN: Uh-huh.

DOROTHEA: And we're in almost total lockdown except for our dayroom time right now, and most of them are interested in funnies. You know, they're not interested in the news or anything.

BLACKBURN: Yeah. Do you have certain hours that you can call? Do they limit—

DOROTHEA: Every other day I'm out at this time.

BLACKBURN: About this time, which is . . . what, now, six o'clock.

DOROTHEA: Yeah.

BLACKBURN: So.

DOROTHEA: I try to call after six anyway, on account of rates.

BLACKBURN: Okay. So if you were to call me—

DOROTHEA: Well, if I call even after eight but I don't know what your schedule is.

BLACKBURN: Well, it's always fine, there's no problem. I'm around here in the evening, usually, because I'm working. Ah, okay, let's see—

DOROTHEA: I'll be out again Thursday but I won't call you this week again.

BLACKBURN: Well, you can whenever you feel like it. That's one of the things I said in my letter. Call me whenever you feel like it and call me collect.

DOROTHEA: Okay, I just, well, I have to.

BLACKBURN: I know that. There's no way I can call back, is there?

DOROTHEA: No.

BLACKBURN: So that's just the way we'll do it. My letter, sent, you know—

DOROTHEA: I'll probably get it tonight.

BLACKBURN: Okay. They sent the other back, then?

DOROTHEA: Well, they won't send this. No, the money came, they told me that.

BLACKBURN: Did they send back the first letter and everything?

DOROTHEA: Everything, yeah.

BLACKBURN: Okay. I'll just—

DOROTHEA: Put it in another envelope and remail it.

BLACKBURN: I'll just turn around and remail it for you and I'll put it in the right form.

DOROTHEA: And on the money order or certified check make sure my number's on it.

BLACKBURN: Yes, I put that all down. Okay, all that'll be on the certified check.

DOROTHEA: Yeah.

BLACKBURN: Okay, do you, ah, do you think they listen to these phone calls?

DOROTHEA: No. No.

BLACKBURN: Okay.

DOROTHEA: 'Cause I'm watching control.

BLACKBURN: Good. Okay. They could—

DOROTHEA: They could, but I only call when they've all left control.

BLACKBURN: Oh. Okay.

DOROTHEA: Yeah.

BLACKBURN: This'll be interesting. I want you to call me whenever you feel like it.

DOROTHEA: All right.

BLACKBURN: And I will set up some writing and we'll stay in touch both ways. I know that they are watching what's written, so, ah this may be the way to communicate.

DOROTHEA: Right.

BLACKBURN: Okay?

DOROTHEA: Okay.

BLACKBURN: All right.

DOROTHEA: Bye-bye.

BLACKBURN: Keep your chin up.

DOROTHEA: Thank you.

BLACKBURN: See you. Bye-bye.

DOROTHEA: Bye-bye.

Two days later, a letter from Dorothea arrived, the first of three. In it she apologized for using pencil: "I'd never write with one on the outside, but we have to here, it's a 4″ long pencil, they even cut our toothbrushes down to about 4″." Then she complained about the continuing media coverage of her case: "I hate when I hit the newspapers and TV, but guess that's the way things will be for a while."

When Dorothea next telephoned my home, July 30 at 6:00 P.M., I was en route back from Sacramento, so my wife accepted the call and began taking notes.

She would have called sooner, Dorothea reported, but she had been ill and believed she may have suffered a slight heart attack. This was the first time she had felt well enough to get up and make a telephone call.

She had a reason to call, she said. "I want Dan to find an entertainment lawyer and handle all the rights" to her own version of the story, and to scrutinize possible avenues of sales. She talked about retaining 70 to 75 percent of revenues from any such sales and mentioned that she had offers from numerous media outlets, including *People* magazine and the *National Enquirer.*

She repeated her wish for personal visits: "I don't want anything going through the mail. They read it all and I don't want anything going out until after (her upcoming preliminary hearing)." Then, saying "someone's coming for me," she hung up.

I received a chatty letter postmarked August 6, in which Dorothea noted that "tomorrow is commissary day, I can't wait." She hadn't had shampoo for two weeks, "and you really have to wash your hair every other day in here, at least".

In her next call, which came Sunday, August 10 at 8:16 P.M., Dorothea was in an upbeat, talkative mood, and we conversed for thirty-four minutes. She was pleased with at least one member of her defense team, investigator Dave Howard, whom she learned was very thorough in his work. "[He] even talked to the [foster daughters] I raised. He didn't tell me that; I heard it through the prison grapevine."

She recently had been psychologically examined by a psychiatrist from Southern California, she said, and her lawyers "were shocked, I tested so high. I've written two novels since I've been in, that [attorneys Clymo and Vlautin] have in their possession. I wrote them to prove I could do something constructive under stress. I wanted to prove that I wasn't crazy, you know."

After a brief discussion of the best times to meet with her in prison ("after 10:00 P.M., so we can visit for an hour"), Dorothea turned to business.

She was bothered, she said, by something public defender Vlautin had said to her during his last visit. "He says he has a friend who should handle all my business when the time comes, to serve as the lawyer" in any future contract negotiations that might occur. She viewed this as a conflict of interest, expressing the belief that Vlautin should be concerned with only one thing, defending her.

Further, she said, she had a very specific financial need; she wanted to earn sixty thousand dollars before she went to trial.

"That's the amount of money, it's what I need to pay back, it's what I stole, in the checks, you know. If I can make—what is it, restitution?—before the trial, then maybe they'll believe I didn't kill those people, and I didn't. They were all my friends, I couldn't do something like that."

We discussed possible ways of generating this kind of money through the marketing of her story.

Then she requested some particular novels be sent to her (which by prison regulation must be ordered directly from, and sent by, each book's publisher). That reminded her of her own collection of books at home. "I had books; I read a lot, you know. I had this one from Susan Atkins, she was in the adjoining cell when I was in [Frontera] state prison, and she gave it to me, an autographed copy. It was called *Child of Satan, Child of God* and I haven't even read it, it still has the cellophane wrapper on it, but they took it anyway, for evidence, I guess."

It was at this point that she made this eye-opening comment in relation to the people whom she is accused of murdering: "You know, all of those people were legally dead before . . . before they were . . . you know . . . buried. I wouldn't kill anyone."

Before concluding, Dorothea said that she planned to tell attorney Clymo of our phone conversations. That, I said, was a very good idea.

"He'll be angry with both of us," I warned her.

"That's all right," she replied.

This would be my final contact with Dorothea outside the courtroom. When I next met with Clymo in his office, he closed the door and walked slowly back to his desk before speaking. My prediction to Dorothea proved correct. The lawyer was furious, believing he had been circumvented. It made no difference to him whatsoever that Dorothea had initiated the telephone calls. He thought I had violated the spirit of our verbal agreement by even accepting the telephone calls.

I tried to assure him that no confidence had been breached, that Dorothea and I (usually) kept away from discussion about her case, and that we had done so at my behest.

Then I suggested that Dorothea would not have telephoned me in the first place if she hadn't been so angered by his associate Vlautin's untimely proposal regarding her future business dealings. (Many media and entertainment entities have tried to reach Dorothea, all dangling cash offers, but Clymo's orders preclude her from discussing any agreement for the rights to her story. Clymo believes that such action on Dorothea's part would help prejudice her case even more than it is already.)

I told Clymo that Vlautin's comments had been construed by Dorothea as a potential source of conflict of interest, and that she seemed to have a valid complaint.

Clymo blanched at this. Then he said that any comments his

associate might have made to Dorothea during their jailhouse discussions obviously had been misinterpreted.

He added that he had informed Dorothea of the many reasons why she should discontinue the calls and not talk to me any further, and said that she had agreed this time to assent to his wishes.

Clymo is a rare bird these days: a lawyer in charge of defending a major capital murder suspect, surrounded himself by frenzied media interest, yet showing no interest in cashing in on his client's woes, and refusing to participate in self-promotion. The reasons he has conducted himself in such an outwardly upright way probably are quite similar to the ones that first propelled him toward a life as public defense counselor.

He is narrow in his professional purpose—he wants to prevent the state of California from following through on its expressed threat to execute his client, Dorothea Montalvo Puente, by strapping her into a chair and enveloping her in a deadly cloud of poisonous gas. Any efforts at self-aggrandizement, or any histrionic pleas of Dorothea's innocence, would jeopardize this objective. Clymo knows the case will be won or lost on the presentation of facts, within the confines of a courtroom, to a jury of his client's peers. There is nothing to gain, for him or Dorothea, in trying this case in the media. It will be a trial of tactics that he must control. He intends to do just that.

Shortly after our exchange, Clymo told local newspaper reporters that his client's version of events leading up to the gruesome discovery in her yard would cast doubt on her accusers' allegations of capital murder.

Whatever the decision of a future jury, Dorothea's story already has altered—in some cases, significantly—the way in which the daily activities of government are conducted.

And there aren't many people who can boast that achievement.

EPILOGUE

This has been a dark and depressing tale, ripe with the dank scent of death, repellent yet gripping. But if even a small measure of reform in the national policy of care for the aged can be accomplished by its telling, then there will have been purpose where none was evident.

Through the recounting of her story, Dorothea Puente—admitted thief and forger, possible murderer—teaches a valuable lesson. The incongruity of her outward appearance as a kindly landlady and her inner landscape of delusion and amorality invites a close examination of society's role in her actions. For if we fail to look beyond the macabre and sordid events of her alleged crime, the real issue—the wrong-headed, narrow, and often silly bureaucratic procedures of the Social Security Administration (SSA)—will remain unexplored, buried deep in the topsoil of America's collective conscience.

By her actions, Dorothea helped open official eyes to certain

SSA management deficiencies, skeletons in the nation's closet. The bureaucratic loopholes through which she maneuvered to accomplish her deeds still exist, threatening to endanger the lives of older citizens all over this country.

The blame for this ongoing error can, in fairness, be placed upon many shoulders. But there is no time for finger-pointing. People are dying because certain public policies have proven to be flawed. The relatively simple corrective procedures that still elude politicians and policy makers must be initiated, accelerated, and quickly accomplished.

Demographic studies suggest that any problem of the elderly soon will become the problem of the masses. Because of a decrease in fertility and an increase in longevity, America's population is aging. Today, there are nearly 30 million people over the age of 65 in the United States, comprising 12 percent of the total population. These numbers will continue to grow through the year 2050, when more than 67 million elderly will represent 21.8 percent of the nation's whole.

Modern societies grapple constantly with the problem of caring for and feeding fellow human beings who cannot fend for themselves, by various means and with varying results. The vexing quandary, "Are we our brother's keeper?"—a question that has confronted civilizations throughout history—assumes a much larger measure of significance in the America of the future.

As a people, Americans generally have concurred with the Founding Fathers' noble concept of government's true function: that of providing protection for, and assistance to, the weak, the old, the incapable.

This objective has been traditionally accomplished by the payment of taxes by all producing members of society; the citizen writes a check for annual taxes and then expects the government to identify, locate, address, and solve all of the nation's social problems.

Yet, actual practice produces markedly different results. It should come as no surprise that the money always gets spent, but the desired objective is not always reached.

In 1974, one of the many proposals adopted by the Ninety-third Congress of the United States seemed to make pretty good sense and appeared to be expedient and humane. But this revolutionary and supposedly money-saving shortcut by the federal government has turned out to be anything but economical. In fact, it has become a cause of despair and even violent death for Americans fifty-five and older.

Anxious to exploit the new miracle technology of the computer, Congress authorized direct mailing of Social Security and Supplemental Security Income (SSI) payments and other monthly benefit checks to recipients at their homes all across the country. By replacing the old methods of distribution, much time and many federal tax dollars were to be saved—or so went the conventional wisdom.

Under the old, cumbersome, hands-on system of benefit-check distribution, federal assistance was remitted to counties nationwide in the form of annual subsidy grants. County governments established welfare departments, which in turn hired social workers to handle individual cases. In this way, recipients of these benefits were regularly seen in their living environments by the caseworkers, and assistance could be provided on a very personal basis. A caseworker could easily observe how benefits were being spent for any recipient.

With the new federal direct-mail plan, the work load of these county caseworkers was lightened considerably, resulting in a slow but steady decline in the numbers of such county employees.

There is an inherent and major flaw in the direct-mail system of fund distribution, however: Some of the nation's benefit recipients are mentally or physically incapable of handling their own financial affairs. Statistically, there are many more of these people wandering the streets of America today than ever before.

During the early days of John F. Kennedy's administration, the young president accomplished something he had dreamed of for years. He signed legislation that placed thousands upon thousands of former mental patients back into American communities. This was given the lofty identifying term *deinstitutionalization,* and the revolutionary practice was hailed as a major reform in the mental-health industry.

For many of these mentally disturbed people, the return into society's mainstream was possible only because of the rapid advances in tranquilizing drugs. Instead of high walls and guards, which cost money, people with mental problems were just drugged heavily, a much more fiscally convenient arrangement. All of a sudden, there was a pill for every ill.

Through a program utilizing the regular administering of pharmaceuticals, most onetime asylum inmates could be doped into a state of semiconsciousness and, thus controlled, could live among the general population without significantly disrupting it.

The result of this policy, as well-meaning and humane as it seemed at the outset, is a sad statistic: Nearly half of the people sleeping on the streets in America today suffer some kind of mental illness. The big problem with the policy is the assumption that communities would be receptive to these people. The opposite has proved to be true. The burden of long-term care has fallen on the families of former patients, and families often prove incapable of doing the job.

To offer all possible assistance to these people in their efforts to function outside the asylum, Congress decided to require that a "representative [or substitute] payee" be named on benefit checks addressed to people who had been branded by the government as incompetent.

This representative payee, ostensibly, would be a family member or close friend who could be trusted to cover the usually meager financial obligations of the recipient.

Lawmakers also hoped that the payee system would keep recipients from using their monthly checks to perpetuate their chronic alcohol or drug addictions.

Today, Social Security estimates that 43 million Americans receive direct benefits or supplemental benefits (for the poor, aged, blind, or disabled). One of every ten recipients, 4.7 million in all, is determined to be legally incapable of handling his own financial matters, and thus requiring a representative payee.

Consequently, representative payees across every state of the union receive two *billion* dollars monthly from the U.S. government to bank, account for, and distribute.

The law creating representative payees was forged with apparent compassion, and was a specific attempt to assure that benefits truly did help recipients. But the new statute came equipped from the beginning with structural cracks that remained, until recently, out of sight and thus out of mind.

For starters, no law, rule, regulation, or requirement governs the selection of these representative payees. There are no efforts to verify any response from a prospective representative payee, even the most obvious: Have you ever been convicted of a felony such as fraud, theft, robbery, or murder?

In this fetid atmosphere, criminality has flourished. The potential for the harvest of aged and dependent victims has been created; helpless individuals who receive $400 to $575 monthly are easy pickings for the unscrupulous.

Several Social Security employees, speaking out despite expressed threats of official retribution, tell of abductions, beatings, check forgery, and slavery among aged, infirm, and poor men and women. The victims in these horror stories are recipients of Social Security and SSI benefits who live at board-and-care homes and have been assigned substitute payees.

In widespread cases, there is a systematic selling of these defenseless people in a black market involving boarding-home operators and unwitting social workers. The victims are shuttled around in cargo vans, traded like so many stocks and bonds to the highest bidder.

The federal government tends to minimize the problem. Its apologists insist that most recipients requiring representative payees use the services of family members. This would wrongly suggest that a close, personal bond usually eliminates larceny.

One of the most common (yet difficult to detect) abuses of recipients is actually perpetrated by relatives. Documented cases abound: Children, grandchildren, nieces, nephews who have been designated as representative payees spend the money on their own drug or alcohol addictions.

Others, upon becoming a representative payee, move into the home of the beneficiary, often without the beneficiary's permission. Thus taxpayers and the helpless elder support the freeloading payee. (While she was still licensed as an in-home caretaker for elderly patients, Dorothea lived for many years in this manner.)

To the Social Security Administration workers, family situations such as these can easily be made to appear quite appropriate and aboveboard. The representative payee's occasional report will show that the money is being used for the recipient's food, lodging, utilities, and other living expenses.

Because of tangled bureaucratic procedures, it has proven very difficult for government entities at any level to monitor use of SSA and SSI money through the direct-mail process. And because of this difficulty, it is almost impossible for local jurisdictions to locate (much less arrest and punish) the swindlers who prey on these unfortunates.

Some local SSA jurisdictions make a regular practice of appointing representative payees before notifying the actual recipient that he or she has been ruled incompetent. Often, the first time the benefit recipient hears of the payee appointment is upon checking with the Social Security Administration regarding missing benefit checks.

Even more incredibly, bunglers at the SSA have managed to pervert the system by deciding that incompetent benefit recipients will simply *be deprived of their benefits* if they should lose their representative payee and, for reasons beyond their control, are unable to immediately find another.

Members of Congress are beginning to hear stories like the following, which help illustrate how deeply the cancer goes:

• For nearly a year, a homeless SSI recipient had her benefits suspended because she lacked a payee. During that time she visited her Social Security office five or six times a month, only to be told that it was her responsibility to find a payee in order to receive the money due her. While her benefits were suspended and she was living on the streets, she was kidnapped, beaten, and raped.

• A Social Security office approved a man as substitute payee without investigation even though his only identification consisted of release papers from the county jail, and despite a warning from a social-service agency that the prospective payee was an alcoholic.

• SSA approved a liquor store manager as a payee, and he keeps an open tab for his beneficiaries and then reimburses himself—at premium prices—from their monthly benefit checks.

- SSA approved a substitute payee who gave them the wrong Social Security number. Then when the payee disappeared with six thousand dollars in benefits intended for someone else, SSA stated for the record: "There isn't anything that can be done."

Clearly, the people for whom these assistance checks were intended would have been better off if the government had not intruded into their lives and made decisions that were not, in the final analysis, in their best interests. The bighearted solution often becomes a big problem.

The emerging horror stories prompted one congressman to observe that "we spend more money on our dogs than we do to feed and house our fellow human beings." This is probably true, but there is a powerful stack of tax money that *is* being spent on failing efforts.

Supplied with SSA's own estimate that fully 20 percent of the Social Security and SSI benefit dollars entrusted to substitute payees are somehow misused—four hundred million dollars monthly!—a logical person might conclude that some changes need to be made in the way the law is administered and the money distributed. But no changes are forthcoming.

To make matters worse, for the last twenty years there has been a steady decline in the percentage of federal, state, county, city, and local agency budget amounts allocated to the needs of the elderly. And since 1974, when Congress took its computerized shortcut, the ranks of U.S. citizens over age sixty-five have ballooned a whopping 28 percent.

Along with the increase in numbers of people in this age bracket comes a parallel increase in the mentally or physically disabled population. Fewer institutions exist to care for the needy. In 1955, more than 560,000 people were in mental institutions nationwide; in 1975, there were fewer than 150,000. That translates into a frighteningly high number of mentally ill people who now find themselves on the streets of America's communities.

Into this volatile fiscal environment, then, walked a man with a plan. He was the fortieth president of the United States, Ronald Reagan, and during his two terms he successfully promoted a parsimonious federal spending plan that would be dubbed *Reaganomics*.

The idea was to grant greater tax breaks to the nation's economically comfortable population, at the same time spending fewer federal tax dollars on the nation's helpless.

By simultaneously reducing the overall level of government spending (went the theory), private enterprise would be stimulated and good old Yankee ingenuity would solve any problem that might evolve. Advocates of Reaganomics found ready allies among the wealthiest political contributors in America, and encountered little opposition from the poor.

Year after year when budget time rolled around, the first categories to endure cuts were social-welfare subsidies to local governments. With less money to go around, more and more tax-supported mental institutions, hospitals, community halfway houses, and other facilities for aged, infirm, mentally ill, and dependent people were closed down. And with no place to go, the former occupants of these facilities ended up living on the streets, where hundreds of thousands of them can be found today.

Reagan, an immensely popular political figure with older citizens during his two-term tenure, may in the future be perceived as a politician whose efforts substantially diminished the quality of life for whole generations of Americans. Certainly his policies, and similar ones of the succeeding Bush administration, have done little to improve the plight of the aging. Reform has been difficult:

Federally mandated programs and their modes of administration seem set in concrete, and the voice of the poor is weak.

To fill the gap created by the continuing closure of so many public institutions, private entrepreneurs have opened thousands upon thousands of boarding homes where the financially able can receive room, meals, and other basic sustenance.

Because of the existence of government assistance such as SSI benefits, almost anyone, no matter how poor, can qualify for the amount of money needed to live in one of these privately operated homes. If an individual can manage his or her own money, he or she simply pays boarding costs monthly like any other bill.

If a boarder is incompetent, however, the operator of a boarding house may become representative payee for the recipient. This was the case with Bert Montoya and his payee, Dorothea Puente.

Many homes have multiple boarders, and as a result the monthly income to a single residential establishment may be in the tens of thousands of dollars.

By reducing the level of services to boarders, an operator can substantially increase his or her level of profit. Few, if any, standards for these private homes are established under existing law. Consequently, many occupants of nonregulated homes survive under needlessly inferior and unhealthy living conditions, while their monthly support checks continually disappear, misappropriated by callous and greedy providers of very minimal board and care.

A Washington, D.C., ombudsman for the elderly, Beverly A. Bryant, summarized the problem to a congressional subcommittee:

> Residents in board-and-care homes are among the most vulnerable of the elderly and mentally impaired in the United States. While some [residents] may go about the neighborhood and community portraying some de-

> gree of independence, many are mentally and physically impaired, often frail and elderly. [During numerous investigations] we often uncover some irregularity with [substitute payees' handling] of residents' finances.

For its part, the Social Security Administration prefers alibi to change. Called by that same congressional subcommittee to testify in the aftermath of the Sacramento tragedy, Louis D. Enoff, Social Security's deputy commissioner, said his agency "is aware of some problems in the representative payee program," but he downplayed the importance of those problems.

"We believe we generally accomplish our objective of appointing responsible and caring payees," he told members of the subcommittee without so much as a smile. Enoff said SSA is "reevaluating policies and procedures" but then added that old bureaucrats' battle cry: "Further study will be necessary to identify all the problems."

For decades, Social Security administrators have been fending off lawsuits aimed at changing representative payee procedures. The problems have been evident and solutions suggested, but SSA's response has been little more than a cold shoulder.

Senior citizens' law group advocate Neal S. Dudovich believes the benevolent intent of the representative payee system has been completely lost.

"SSA's determination that a beneficiary needs a payee is more often tantamount to [his either being] sentenced to months as a homeless beggar in the streets, . . . [or to becoming the victim of a payee holding] a government-approved license for financial and physical abuse," he told congressmen at the hearing.

Testimony pointed to at least four major failings of the current system: Benefits are not properly paid to those who are eligible; potential payees are not investigated or screened; payees are not monitored; and no effort is made to recover funds that have been improperly spent by a payee.

Congress is considering adoption of standards that could help halt the widespread abuses. Many of these reforms will be adapted from a successful prototype in use in the state of Michigan.

Recommendations that might be considered:

- Specific rules and criteria need to be developed by SSA for its own use in addressing possible solutions.
- Recipients of SSA benefits must be notified in advance that a representative payee will be appointed, so they can present evidence on their own behalf or object to the person being appointed. Requests for reconsideration must be processed in a timely manner.
- Criminal-record checks should be run on prospective payees, and interviews should be conducted by Social Security employees to determine their suitability.
- Statements of physicians are relied upon heavily in evaluating the functional ability of a beneficiary. Specific criteria should be developed to prevent inequitable use of this practice. In documented cases, some physicians have been found to have financial interests in board-and-care homes where they have sent "incompetent" recipients.
- A neutral party should visit the beneficiary upon the filing of an application by a prospective representative payee. The meeting should be conducted with the predetermined view that a beneficiary is capable of handling his or her own financial affairs unless evidence to the contrary exists.
- Annual accountings must be provided to SSA, reviews must be conducted, and irregularities investigated.

• An efficient method for removing unacceptable payees must be designed. Ideally, a system for recovering misused funds from a payee would be established to help dull the criminal appeal of this practice.

One outspoken Social Security employee in California, Jose L. Sanchez, says that

> for what happened in Sacramento, SSA and Congress must share the blame. The incident is not an isolated occurrence. For too long, we at Social Security have known of existing and potential exploitation of beneficiaries.
>
> The representative payee program is a sham. It is not responsive to the needs of the recipient and the system is ripe for abuse. The SSA totally ignores the problem, has even intentionally kept its dirty little secret from public scrutiny. I am not alone among my fellow employees in taking this position.

Some strides have been made by the American Association of Retired Persons (AARP) to solve the problem of outlaw payees. The national organization has established, with congressional blessing and financial assistance, a pilot program in Washington, D.C., to train its members for volunteer work as representative payees. If it is successful on its initial, limited basis, the program will be expanded to all chapters nationwide, providing a safer alternative to many of those who need assistance in managing their financial affairs.

But any efforts of government at the federal level must be matched by those of individual states. Stung by their proximity to the F Street debacle, California legislators have greatly intensified their efforts to improve the system. Dorothea's deeds were simplified because state law, too, was slack.

Legislation is now being considered that would assign responsibility for representative payees to the state's Department of Social Services. Counties would assume responsibility in the event that payees mishandle or steal funds. A bill of rights is included in the California plan, to insure the right of benefit recipients to be treated fairly, equitably, and with courtesy. If that does not occur, a legitimate claim may be made against counties, or even the state.

The gap in Social Security laws has been overlooked for decades by those in positions to provide solutions; they usually prefer more politically popular crusades. It is a problem of long standing, one that most likely still would be ignored today if not for the horror that surfaced on November 11, 1988, on a peaceful, tree-lined street in downtown Sacramento, California.

More than any other single event, the discovery of human remains under the meticulously manicured lawn of the matronly, sweet-faced boarding-home operator has set the stage for sweeping changes in national policy regarding the operations of the Social Security Administration.

Perhaps, in the end, that will be the true legacy of Bert Montoya and the half-dozen souls who shared his uneasy resting place in Dorothea's yard.

APPENDIX A

SEQUENCE OF EVENTS: THE F STREET DISCOVERY

1985

Dorothea Puente is released from state prison; moves to 1426 F Street.

1988

Early February
Judy Moise and Beth Valentine learn from Peggy Nickerson about a marvelous rooming house in downtown Sacramento.

Mid-February
Alvaro "Bert" Montoya is moved into the rooming house, "owned" and operated by Dorothea Montalvo Puente. Dorothea becomes Bert's "substitute payee" on regular checks and vouchers he receives from the county.

Early March
Brenda Trujillo complains to her state-appointed psychiatrist, Dr. Angela Curiale, that Dorothea is stealing Trujillo's SSI checks.

Late March
Dr. Curiale learns that parolees are digging holes at Dorothea's rooming house. Dr. Curiale advocates an investigation of Dorothea.

April 8

Brenda Trujillo claims that Dorothea is "trying to poison" her.

Late April

Polly Spring tells Peggy Nickerson: "That woman is crazy." Nickerson disregards information about Dorothea.

Early June

Mary Ellen Howard is alarmed by a string of obscenities from Puente.

Mid-June

Judy Moise and Beth Valentine are informed about Dorothea's past, but discount the information.

July 6

Kathy Stadler, State Deptartment of Social Services, investigates the level of care provided by Dorothea; pronounces her okay.

Early August

Nickerson decides "on a gut feeling" not to place any more clients with Dorothea.

August 11

Bert returns to Volunteers of America's Detox Center and is returned to 1426 F Street by VOA's Bill Johnson.

Mid-September

Judy Moise attempts to contact Bert at Dorothea's.

October

Dorothea reports Bert "has been calling her from Mexico."

November 1

Judy Moise and Beth Valentine threaten to report Bert as a missing person to the police.

November 7

Moise receives several phone calls from "Michel Obergone, Bert Montoya's brother-in-law."

Moise and Valentine immediately file the missing persons report.

November 8

Sacramento police officer Richard Ewing is told by a tenant that Dorothea had asked him to lie.

November 9/10

Det. John Cabrera is telephoned by Judy Moise.

November 11

Dets. Cabrera and Terry Brown and federal parole agent Jim Wilson discover the first of seven bodies buried in Dorothea's well-kept yard.

November 12

Dorothea is escorted through police lines; boards a Greyhound bus for Los Angeles.

The second and third bodies are discovered in Dorothea's backyard.

November 13

The fourth and fifth bodies are discovered in Dorothea's backyard.

November 14

The sixth and seventh bodies are discovered in the back and front yards.

November 15

Dorothea is arrested at the Royal Viking Motel in Los Angeles.

November 17

Dorothea Montalvo Puente is charged with the murder of Alvaro "Bert" Montoya.

March 31, 1989

Dorothea is charged with an additional eight counts of murder, for the deaths of the bodies discovered at 1426 F Street and two additional deaths.

Appendix B

California Department of Corrections, Parole Outpatient Clinic Montalvo (Puente), Dorothea W-17456

Discharge Summary
March 25, 1986

Present Impression: Montalvo offers no evidence of psychotic or suicidal ideation. Her affect appears to be appropriate for time and place, although somewhat depressed. Her IQ appears to be in the normal range. She appears to disassociate herself from any of the crimes for which she has been arrested and convicted. She continues to minimize the importance of what she did or her responsibility in any of them. Her lifestyle to date consists of refurbishing and remodeling her home in the Sacramento area. She indicates that this remodeling is being paid for by her nephew, who owns the house.

Although Montalvo doesn't evidence any symptoms of psychosis, that being hearing voices or having delusions of grandeur, it appears that she is still a disturbed woman. Her contacts with P.O.C.* have been extremely conscientious and dependable. She is also still under the care of Dr. Doody in town and is receiving several medications for several physical conditions as well as an antidepressant. She is taking digoxin, Lasix, throxine, Premarin, and potassium.

*Parole Outpatient Clinic

There does not appear to be any reason to continue this woman on parole. Her prognosis for success in the community is good if she does not work with people who are dependent on her for their welfare. It would also be contraindicated for her to have a roommate who would be receiving any kinds of funds or to leave children in her care, who might also be receiving some sort of financial support. If these are plans that Montalvo has, it would be practically impossible to prevent her from doing so once she is off parole. She is still being followed by Federal Probation and so would be supervised somewhat in the absence of parole. . . .

RECOMMENDATIONS: Discharge from P.O.C. and discharge from parole.

APPENDIX C

EXCERPTS FROM THE CALIFORNIA DEPARTMENT OF CORRECTIONS (PAROLE) PROBATION REPORT, DOROTHEA PUENTE, JUNE, 1982

I. Present Offense

. . . Defendent exhibited . . . a high degree of callousness. This is demonstrated in the record by the age of the victim, MALCOLM McKENZIE, 74 years old, who had his ring taken while he was incapacitated.

RULE 421(a)(3): The victims were particularly vulnerable. . . .

RULE 421(a)(7): The defendant was convicted of other crimes for which consecutive sentences could be imposed, though concurrent sentences are likely to be imposed. This is demonstrated by the fact that the record shows the defendant to be convicted of Grand Theft, Grand Theft From the Person, Forgery, and Administering a Stupefying Agent.

RULE 421(a)(8): The planning and sophistication with which the crimes were carried out, and other facts, indicate premeditation. This is demonstrated in the record by taking MALCOLM McKENZIE by cab to his home. . . . and pretending to be from the "Sacramento Medical Association."

Rule 421(a)(12): The defendant took advantage of a position of trust and confidence to commit the offense. This is demonstrated in the record by acting as night nurse . . . and pretending to be from the "Sacramento Medical Association" in order to gain the confidence . . .

II. Defendant's Statement

The defendant was interviewed at the Sacramento County Jail for purposes of this presentence report. At that time, the defendant expressed remorse for all the victims that lost some of their possessions as she reported that she could see that they were either needy people or had a right to continue to possess their property. She indicated that she, too, had suffered as a child and disliked seeing other individuals suffer likewise. The defendant reported that she had relatives in Mexico that depended upon her financially and that she feels extremely saddened that she is letting them down as she is now unable to help them financially. Throughout the interview, the defendant mentioned her relatives dependent on her and her disappointment, in herself, in letting them down.

Regarding the victim . . . in Counts One and Two, the defendant indicated that she did not take any of the items from her apartment, although she admitted taking the two checks and forging them. She was quick to point out that she had made restitution, but she could not reasonably explain her actions as she reportedly did not need the money that bad.

Regarding the victim . . . in Count Three, the defendant indicated that she was confused as to her actions in this offense, but she nevertheless denied that she had ever been in the victim's apartment and denied taking any items from her. She indicated that she had only seen this victim at the beauty shop which they both patronized.

Regarding the victim . . . in Counts Four, Five and Six of Information #63695, the defendant first admitted to this writer that she had administered a drug but could not recall what it was composed of. After first indicating that she had no explanation for her behavior, she then changed her story and denied administering any drug at all. She indicated that she had been invited to the victim's apartment to drink socially and that the victim had given her the wrapped pennies with the victim's name and phone number on the wrapper to buy beer.

Regarding the victim McKenzie, in Information #63029, the defendant reported that she took two checks from his checkbook and forged them. However, she could not explain her actions. She denied administering a drug to McKenzie and also denied taking any items from his apartment.

The defendant explained that she pled to certain counts made against her as it was simply part of the plea bargain arrangements.

Officer's Comment: During the probation interview, the defendant expressed remorse for her actions by expressing concern for the victims and their suffering. However, in this officer's opinion her expression of remorse was diluted by her attempts to manipulate the interview. While this officer was explaining the reasons for the interview, the defendant, after noting this writer's Hispanic surname, interrupted to explain that she, too, was of Hispanic descent. Further, although the defendant appeared distraught and tearful throughout the interview, it was apparent to this writer that she was extremely observant of the notes that were being made during the interview and, at one point, asked for explanation of a particular word that this writer had written in his notes. The defendant appeared to attempt to read, upside down, the officer's notes, as she sat on the opposite side of the interview booth.

III. Criminal Record

The following information is taken from a United States District Court presentence report, dated December 14, 1978.

Prior Convictions: *April 27, 1948, Forgery/Fictitious Checks, Riverside Police Department:* According to United States Probation Department sources in Riverside, California, no arrest summary was available due to the age of the report, but arrest and conviction information was verified by the Federal Probation officer in Riverside. *Disposition:* One year county jail, six months suspended, three years probation.

April 25, 1960, Residing in a House of Ill Fame/Vagrancy, Sacramento Police Department: Arrest reports are unavailable. *Disposition:* The defendant was ordered to serve 90 days in the county jail for residing in a house of ill fame and received 90 days suspended for vagrancy. She was placed on five years summary probation. Regarding this offense, the defendant indicated to a Federal Probation officer, according to the Federal Probation report, that she was staying with a friend at the time of the offense and did not realize that the house was a brothel.

September 19, 1978, Forging United States Treasury Checks (18 USC 495), FBI #5111377: Federal investigation was initiated in response to a claim by a payee that she had not received, negotiated, endorsed nor participated in the proceeds of a United States Treasury check, dated August 4, 1975. . . .

V. Social History

. . . **FAMILY SITUATION:** The defendant reports that she is the youngest sibling of 18. Fourteen surviving siblings reportedly live in Mexico and depend on the defendant for financial help. They reportedly are not aware that she is in jail. Montalvo claims no relatives in the United States.

Montalvo reports that she was four years old when her father died and five years old when her mother died. She reportedly was raised by her grandmother and aunt until she was 13, in Fresno. She then went to Mexico to stay with an older brother but returned to California at age 15½ and soon thereafter married a Fred McFall. Her husband reportedly passed away two years later as a result of a heart attack and she then married Axel Johansson in 1952 and divorced him in 1966.

In 1976, she married Pedro Montalvo in Reno, Nevada. She reported that they experienced extremely serious problems and he was physically abusive. She reportedly obtained an annulment in 1977, but later returned to him for one year. The defendant indicated that, although she became pregnant during the first two marriages, she was unable to bear children and experienced several stillborn births.

The defendant's Federal Probation file also indicates that she married a Robert Puente in 1966. This marriage reportedly ended in divorce in 1970 as, according to the Federal Probation file, she reported that her husband was much younger than she and that the age difference caused their separation.

AGENCY AND/OR COLLATERAL CONTACTS: PSYCHOLOGICAL/PSYCHIATRIC/ MEDICAL. The defendant reported that she is currently experiencing several ailments for which she is required to take a number of drugs. She takes Dioxgin and Nitrostat for an adverse heart condition. She takes Laxix, 40 milligrams daily, for high blood pressure and Tagamet for an ulcerous condition. Additionally, she takes KCL three times daily for potassium retention. Additionally, she is prescribed Ativan, by her psychiatrist, for "nerves."

The defendant's Federal Probation file indicates that she had surgery on numerous occasions for such things as definitive thyroid, abdominal hysterotomy, jejunal ileo bypass for morbid obesity and surgery on the tip of her nose with skin grafts in 1974 for basal cell carcinoma.

The defendant has, in the immediate past, been under the care of Thomas E. Doody, M.D., a psychiatrist. According to the defendant's Federal Probation file, he had diagnosed her condition as "schizophrenic, chronic undifferentiated type", and had described her as a very disturbed woman. In a recent letter to the Federal Probation officer, Dr. Doody indicates that he has seen the defendant make progress in her mental condition, although there has been episodes of anxiety and some depression. The defendant was reportedly found unconscious in her home on September 30, 1981 and rushed to Sutter General Hospital. She reportedly had taken an overdose of Metrobarmate (Miltown), which she reportedly did not use routinely. The defendant asserted at that time that there was no suicidal intent and accused a woman she befriended of poisoning her. There was no alcohol reported in the toxicology report. The defendant was transferred to Sutter Memorial Psychiatric Unit and evaluated. The evaluation, however, indicated no signs of serious depression or risks and she was sent home. Dr. Doody indicated that the defendant had multiple physical problems, and of special concern was her body's inability to regulate its potassium level. The doctor further indicated that one explanation for her behavior is the presence of "disassociative disorder."

FEDERAL PROBATION: As indicated previously, the defendant was granted probation in Federal Court on December 12, 1978 for a period of five years. On May 5, 1982, a probation violation petition was requested by the Federal Probation officer, alleging that the defendant had violated her conditions of Federal Probation as a result of charges filed in Sacramento County alleging theft, petty theft and forgery, in the current case.

Federal Probation Case file entries indicate that in 1981, the defendant made voluntarily restitution on a check fraudulently passed in Sacramento by the defendant in 1977. Secret Service agents also investigated the defendant on a Federal check passed in Stockton in 1979. In that incident, the U.S. District Attorney decided not to prosecute as the defendant voluntarily made restitution.

A quarterly evaluation entry in the defendant's Federal Probation file, dated December 1, 1979 to March 31, 1980, indicates that during that period the defendant was suspected by doctors at the Medical Center of poisoning a patient, Esther Bussby. Bussby had been hospitalized several times in a short period of time and, apparently, tests revealed several medications within her system beyond prescribed dosages. At that time, the defendant resided with her. At the Federal Probation officer's suggestion, the defendant moved away from the Bussby apartment.

POLICE: Sacramento City Police Department report #81-18495, dated January 27, 1982, indicates that police officers were in possession of two personalized checks to Clair E. Maleville and Lauretta E. Chalmers. The checks were payable to Dorothea Montalvo and one was in the amount of $261 and the other one in the amount of $35. Both checks were reportedly signed by Ms. Maleville but she reported to investigators that she did not issue nor sign either of the two checks. Montalvo was questioned by police officers on January 27, 1981, and she stated that she had observed Ms. Maleville sign both checks. The checks were reportedly in payment for work she had completed. When asked by investigators if she had endorsed the checks, she replied in the positive and then changed her story to say that she completed all of the face information on the checks, excluding the maker's signature. The defendant was placed under arrest at that time, but this writer is unable to find any information regarding disposition of the arrest.

VI. Controlled Substances

The defendant reports that her use of alcohol is restricted to social occasions and that she does not abuse its use. She denies the use of any controlled substances except for legally prescribed drugs. . . .

VIII. Probation Officer's Conclusions

. . . The defendant is seen as undeserving of probation as she has concentrated her criminal efforts on a segment of the community that is the most vulnerable, the ill and elderly. Her criminal acts, therefore, are callous and unconscionable.

Her criminal activity occurred over a ten month period and included four victims. For this reason, consecutive sentencing to state prison is recommended. As the defendant was on Federal Probation at the time she committed the current offenses, it is recommended that she be committed to the high term of three (3) years in Count Two of Information #63695 and to consecutive terms of one-third of the middle term, eight

(8) months, in each of Counts Three and Four of Information #63695 and Count Three of Information #63029, for a total commitment of five (5) years.

Probation Costs: If the Court grants the defendant probation, it is recommended that probation costs not be levied at this time, as the defendant is unemployed.

Appendix D

Sacramento Police Department, Dorothea Montalvo Puente Detective John A. Cabrera

Summary of Initial Interview, November 11, 1988.

PUENTE, Dorothea Montalvo
Female White, 59
DOB: 1/9/29
Phone: 444-6059

1225 11/11/88 I contacted the above subject, Dorothea Puente, who had voluntarily been transported to the Hall of Justice, 813 6th Street for a follow-up statement regarding the finding of human remains in her backyard. Ms. Puente was taken up to the Second Floor Homicide Assaults Unit and placed into Room #5 for an interview.

(The following is a brief summary of a taped statement):

I asked Ms. Puente how long she had been living at the residence at 1426 F Street. She stated she had been living there from 1978 until May of 1982 when she was arrested. She then stated that she went to prison in that year in 1982 and was released in September 1985 and continued to live at the residence until the present. I asked Ms. Puente if she knew who lived in the residence before her originally and she stated she didn't know. Ms. Puente stated she lived there and collected the rent for her nephew Ricardo. I asked her who was the owner of the property and she stated her nephew Ricardo was the owner of the property and that she paid rent, but the utilities on the property were in her name. She stated also that there was kind of a verbal lease or agreement that she would live there.

I asked Ms. Puente at that time if she could explain the disappearance of Mr. Montoya who had lived there. I stated the information we were getting was inconsistent. She stated she didn't think she would have to remember things regarding Mr. Montoya. I advised Ms. Puente that Mr. Sharp who lives at the residence also as a tenant stated he hasn't seen him, (Montoya), for three months. Ms. Puente then stated "I'm not lying." I also advised Ms. Puente that Mr. Sharp told us that she, (Puente), had told him at one point to lie for her. She stated "I did not." Ms. Puente went on to state that Sharp couldn't pay the rent and she asked him to move. Then Ms. Puente went on to state that Sharp paid her on the 3rd and then she asked him to move. I asked Ms. Puente about Ben and she stated Ben lived there two months. I asked Ms. Puente if John, (also known as Mervin McCauley), knew John. Ms. Puente stated she didn't know. Ms. Puente also stated that Ben went back to Marysville, but couldn't remember the month that he left, but she remembers it was summertime and he went back to Marysville.

Dorothea also stated that Mr. Montoya didn't want to see his social worker anymore. I asked Ms. Puente if she knew where Mr. Montoya was now and she stated she did not know where the man was going to take him. She also went on to state that she would like the police to put a tap on her phone and when the person called the police could get the number to where he possibly was. I also stated to Ms. Puente that she had been cooperative and had allowed us to search her premises and to also dig in the yard. She stated at one point she would have said no if she had anything to hide.

At this time I asked Ms. Puente about the concrete area just north of the shed located on the side of the residence. She stated that the concrete was put down in February. I asked Ms. Puente about an open trench in that particular area and she stated yes, there was a trench and it was for a sewer line. I drew a diagram on a piece of paper, so that Ms. Puente knew what area of the yard I was referring to. Ms. Puente went on to state after I told her that the trench was in an L-shape, she countered that and stated no, that it was a straight trench, approximately the size of the table that she was sitting at at this time, which was the interview table which is approximately 48 inches long. Ms. Puente stated that the trench was approximately 18 inches deep. Ms. Puente stated that this trench was dug while she was looking for a sewer and it was sometime in March that the hole was dug. I then asked Ms. Puente about the concrete patch just south of the shed showing her on the diagram that I had drawn. She stated the concrete in back of the shed had been put down over a year ago and the shed had been there over a year. I asked her why she put the concrete down and she stated that there was too much work for her to do and so she did. Ms. Puente stated that the shed was put up sometime after 1985.

I also asked Ms. Puente about the area in back of the residence where three trees had been planted. I told her that it looked like the trees were recently planted and that there had possibly been some digging back there. She stated yes, there used to be a chicken coop back there, approximately 1½ years ago, but they dug another trench for the sewer sometime this summer. I asked her what particular area they dug the trench and she stated the whole area, but they found nothing.

I also asked Ms. Puente about the lime that I thought I observed in the ground and she responded with yes, she was told by the people, she thought at Lumberjack, that if she put lime in the ground it would soften the dirt. She stated she did so. I asked her about the lime material that was possibly in the same hole where the remains were located this date and she stated she didn't know how it got there. I asked her who did the digging of the trenches and she stated John, (McCauley), did some digging and casual labor she hired did some digging.

I asked Ms. Puente if she had any knowledge of what was in the hole and she responded no. I asked Ms. Puente if John might have had information about what was in the hole and she stated no as she also stated no to if Mr. Kelly had any knowledge of what was in the hole.

I advised Ms. Puente at the time that nothing seemed to fit about the disappearances. I told her that I believed Mr. Montoya was dead and she responded "he's not dead." I then confronted her about the body in the yard and Mr. Montoya and she stated "sir, I have never killed anybody." She went on to state that she cared for Mr. Montoya. She also stated that Ben Fink had gone to Marysville again. Ms. Puente went on to state that she had not seen the body and she did not know anything about it. I then asked Ms. Puente were there any other bodies in her back yard and she responded with no. Ms. Puente stated again she would have told us not to search the yard if she had anything to hide. I advised Ms. Puente that I felt if we continued to dig in the yard we would find more. Again during the interview, Ms. Puente stated "sir, I have not killed anybody." I then asked where Mr. Montoya was and when did he actually disappear. Ms.

Puente then stated "SEPTEMBER." I then asked her was that the last time she saw him and she stated no, Sunday was the last time she had seen Mr. Montoya.

At this time I asked Ms. Puente if she would take a polygraph test and she stated she would take one Monday because she was too nervous now to take one.

. . . At one point Ms. Puente asked me did I really think she was guilty. I advised her that somehow she was involved and she stated that she hadn't killed anybody.

Report of Departure, November 12, 1988.

PUENTE, Dorothea
Female White, 59
ADD: 1426 F Street

0820 11/12/88 While at the residence of 1426 F Street following up on the previous day's find of possible human remains, I was summoned by Ms. Puente who was at her residence. She asked me if I would come up for a moment and I did so. Ms. Puente then stated "Mr. Cabrera, I've lived here since 1980. You can ask Ricardo. I thought 1978, but it's 1980." I then told Dorothea that I would add that to my information.

0840 hours, Ms. Puente again summoned me up to the porch area of her residence and stated that she had lived at this residence 1980 or 1981, but in 1978 she was at either 2100 F Street or she was living in Stockton, CA. with her ex-husband. At that time I again advised her I would add the information to my fact sheet.

Dorothea again stated before I left the porch area that she didn't know why she told me 1978, but that somebody else lived there when she had gone to prison, but the guy who lived there was dead in Mexico and had died recently. She stated his name was Jesus Mendoza and her nephew Ricardo would know about it.

0845 hours, again I was summoned up to the porch area of Ms. Puente who at that time asked me if she could go for a walk, that she would like to walk over to the Clarion Hotel with John McCauley to visit her nephew. At that time I asked her if she needed an escort out of the immediate area and she stated yes, she would appreciate that. I escorted her down the stairs and down to the corner of 14th and F where we then walked southbound on 15th Street down to the corner of 15th and G. There, I told her I would leave her and John McCauley who was also accompanying us and when she decided to come back she could have John come in and summon me if she felt that the news media was going to corner her and ask her questions. She stated she would do so when she was ready to come back.

Appendix E

Sacramento County Superior Court Excerpts of Testimony by Malcolm McKenzie

Trial Proceedings: *People of California v. Dorothea Montalvo (Puente)*, June, 1982

Q. . . . Is that here in the County of Sacramento?

A. Yes, it is.

Q. What did you do when you got to your home?

A. I laid down on the bed. I was out.

Q. When you say, "Out," what do you mean specifically?

A. I didn't know what I was doing, or things to the effect.

Q. Could you move?

A. I couldn't move my body or talk, but I could see and hear.

Q. What did you see this woman defendant do inside of your home?

A. Well, she took a red suitcase I had and was filling it up with bushel pennies, memorial pennies, and different things around my apartment.

Q. All right. When you say, "Bushel pennies," approximately what was the value of those pennies?

A. Well, it's pretty hard to say. They were worth quite a bit at one time, but now you never see them any more.

So, they might be increased in value. I just don't know.

Q. Can you put an approximate value on them?

A. Well, I would say maybe a hundred, a hundred and fifty dollars.

Q. The other coins that you mentioned, what would the approximate value of those coins be?

A. Well, that was about forty dollars in nickels and maybe five dollars in dimes and half dollars. . . .

Q. Had you given this woman the defendant permission to remove anything from your home?

A. None whatsoever.

Q. Or to sign those checks?

A. What?

Q. Or to sign those checks?

A. No way.

Q. Did she take anything from your person that night?

A. She took a ring off of my little finger.

Q. And what kind of ring was that?

A. It was a diamond ring.

Q. And what was the approximate value of that ring?

A. Well, it was given to my older brother fifty years ago, and he gave it to me, so the ring could be about seventy, eighty years old.

Q. And do you have an approximate value for that ring?

A. Well, the value was sentimental, so—

Q. What kind of ring was it?

A. It was a small diamond ring.

Q. Did you give her permission to take that ring off your hand?

A. No, I did not.

Q. Did she stay in your home?

A. Did she stay? No.

Q. That night? Did you see her leave?

A. I saw her go out the door. . . .

APPENDIX F

EXCERPTS, CORONER'S REPORT ON ALVARO MONTOYA

FIRST NAME	MIDDLE NAME	LAST NAME	CASE NO.
Alvaro	Gonzales	Montoya	88-3381

On November 11, 1988 at 1128 hours, Coroner Investigator Edward Smith was notified by Sacramento Police Detective Faust that SPD Detectives were present at 1426 F Street, the site of a possible buried body. At 1147 hours, Smith, along with Gary A. Stuart, M.D. and Robert M. Anthony, M.D., Forensic Pathologists, arrived at 1426 F Street. Upon their arrival, SPD Detective Terry Brown and Federal Probation Officer Jim Wilson were digging in an area in which a human body appeared to be buried. Officers Brown and Wilson were advised that digging should be suspended and a Forensic Anthropologist consulted before digging was resumed. Preliminary SPD information indicated that there was a possibility that multiple bodies might be buried at this site.

Rodger Heglar, Ph.D., Forensic Anthropologist was contacted and requested to assist with the excavation. On November 12, 1988 at 0730 hours, a briefing was held, which included Dr. Heglar, Sacramento Police Department personnel and Deputy Coroner Smith as to how the excavation would proceed.

During the day of November 12, 1988, Coroner Case #88-3372 (later identified as Leona Carpenter) and Coroner Case #88-3374 (later identified as Dorothy Miller) were removed from the ground and transported to the Coroner's Office.

Because of the possibility that there were additional bodies buried in the yard and because Deputy Coroner Smith was on the last day of his weekly shift, I was contacted at home on 11-12-88 by Chief Deputy Coroner Bowers and I was advised to report to work at 0730 hours on 11-13-88 in preparation to arrive at 1426 F Street at 0800 hours for a briefing by Deputy Coroner Smith.

On November 13, 1988 at 0806 hours, I arrived at 1426 F Street and met with Dr. Heglar, Charles Cecil, Anthropologist (who had been called in to assist Dr. Heglar), SPD Detectives and Deputy Coroner Smith. I was shown the two sites from which bodies had been removed the previous day and directed to another area in the rear southwest corner of the yard. Pieces of cloth and foam rubber protruded from the ground in this area. Dr. Heglar and I dug at this spot from approximately 0830 until 0930 hours.

At approximately 0920 hours, Charles Cecil informed me that he had uncovered a small section of what appeared to be a greenish colored blanket material in the rear part of the yard, approximately 6 feet from the rear fence. I moved to this area and began assisting Cecil in removal of dirt from the area until we unearthed a large bundle wrapped in a greenish colored blanket. There were pieces of a light pinkish colored material attached to the middle portion of the bundle. The body was lying in an east/west alignment with the appearance that the head end was to the west. After most of the bundle was exposed, Gary Stuart, M.D. was requested at the scene.

Following Dr. Stuart's arrival, Cecil and I continued excavation around the body until removal could be effected. J. Morris and Sons Mortuary Transportation Service was requested and arrived at 1330 hours. An identifying 3 × 5 inch card with Coroner Case #88-3381 written on it was placed inside the body bag used for removal. A toe tag, also labelled 88-3381 was attached to the blanket material before removal was made at 1340 hours. A large piece of plywood was used to aid in the removal and transport of the body. Dr. Stuart remained at the scene during removal of the body.

The body was transported to the Coroner's Office by J. Morris Transport.

On Tuesday, November 15, 1988 at 1300 hours, an autopsy examination was begun on the deceased. Gary Stuart, M.D. performed the autopsy and Rodger Heglar, Ph.D. conducted an anthropological study of the remains.

At that time a preliminary determination was made that the deceased was a caucasian male, 50 to 60 years old, 64 to 65 inches in height and 128 pounds. Hair color was possibly light brown or blond. There were no obvious tattoos or scars, however, there was apparent healed nasal bone trauma. The deceased was clothed in a white or beige T shirt with ¾ inch block letters—"Canon," dark grey or black trousers, jockey shorts and white socks.

The body had been wrapped in numerous layers of different types of fabric and plastic, some layers sealed with duct tape.

On November 16, 1988, the deceased's fingers were removed by R. Wood, R.N., F.N.P. and I transported them to the State of California, Department of Justice Latent Fingerprint Section in an attempt to obtain a positive identification of the deceased.

On November 23, 1988 at 1625 hours, this office was contacted by Joe Sypnicki, DOJ Latent Prints and advised that a positive fingerprint comparison had been made of our case 88-3381 and Alvaro Gonzales Montoya.

On November 24, 1988 at 1000 hours, Deputy Coroner E. Smith notified the deceased's mother, Theresa Montoya, by telephone of the positive identification.

Subsequent pathology and toxicology studies revealed that although the deceased's tissues tested positive for several different drugs, the cause of death was "Undetermined." The classification of this case will also be "Undetermined."

—Laura E. Synhorst

C.R. Simmons, Coror

CORONER OF SACRAMENTO COUNTY
CORONER'S INVESTIGATION

Case No. 88-3381

DATE	TIME	REPORTED BY:
November 11, 1988	1128	Sacramento Police Department
RECEIVED BY	**DEPUTY ASSIGNED**	
Smith	Synhorst	

CLASSIFICATION Undetermined

DECEDENT PERSONAL DATA
- 1a Name-First: Alvaro
- 1b Middle: Gonzales
- 1c Last: MONTOYA
- 2a Date of Death: FND 11-13-88
- 2b Time: FND appr 092
- M [x] F [ ]
- 4 Race: White
- 5 SSN: 436-66-8076
- 6 Date of Birth: 9-8-36
- 7 Age: 52
- 8 Marital Status:

RESIDENCE
- 9a Usual Address: 1426 F Street
- 9b City: Sacramento
- 9c County: Sacramento

PLACE OF DEATH
- 10a Place of Death: Found - yard of residence
- 10b County: Sacramento
- 10c Street Address: 1426 F Street
- 10d City: Sacramento

CAUSE OF DEATH
- 11: UNDETERMINED

INJURY INFORMATION
- 12 Accident, Suicide, etc.:
- 13 Place of Injury:
- 14 At Work?:
- 15a Date of Injury:
- 15b Hour:
- 16 Location:
- 17 Describe how injury occurred:

RELATIVES
- 18a Names (Relationship): INFORMATION WITHHELD
- 18b Address: INFORMATION WITHHELD
- 18c Phone: INFORMATION WITHHELD

NOTIFICATION
- 19a Who Notified: Mother
- 19b How Notified: By telephone
- 19c By: E. Smith
- 19d Date: 11-24-88
- 19e Time: 1000

DESCRIPTION
- 20 Height: 64½
- 21 Weight: 128
- 22 Hair: Brown
- 23 Eyes: Unknown
- 24 Teeth: Own
- 25 Tattoos/Scars: None

IDENTIFICATION
- 26 Remains identified by or how identified: Department of Justice fingerprint comparison
- 27 Other Investigators: SPD Homicide Detectives
- 28 Remains Removed By: J. Morris Transport

PROPERTY
- 29 Property: Y [ ] N [X]
- 30 Receipt #: 10586
- 31 Released/Sealed by: DNA
- 32 Keys: Y [ ] N [X]
- 33 Other:

CASE SUMMARY

34

From November 12 through November 14, 1988, seven bodies were recovered from the yard of a Victorian style house located at 1426 F Street, Sacrament The house faces north on F Street.

Six of the bodies were recovered from the ground in the east and rear yards of the lot with the seventh body recovered from the small yard area directly in front of the house.

The seven bodies were eventually identified as:

1. Leona Carpenter 88-3372
2. Dorothy Miller 88-3374
3. Alvaro Montoya 88-3381
4. Benjamin Fink 88-3382
5. James Gallop 88-3384
6. Vera Faye Martin 88-3394
7. Betty Palmer 88-3395

The following is a summary of the events Deputy ~~surrounding reporting of the cases,~~ recovery of the bodies and their subsequent identification.

APPENDIX G

EXHIBIT MM, DECLARATION OF JUDY MOISE AND BETH VALENTINE

Briggs, et al v. Bowen, et al, March 17, 1989.

We, JUDY MOISE and BETH VALENTINE, do hereby declare:

1. We are outreach counselors for Volunteers of America in Sacramento. Our job entails advocacy, referral, counseling and assessment for the metropolitan Sacramento homeless community. We work directly as a team on Sacramento streets and in the low-rent hotels. We serve homeless mentally disabled individuals and actually approach them and offer our services.

2. A portion of our job is assisting homeless individuals in applying for and receiving Social Security and SSI benefits. As such we have both seen at least 30–35 homeless people in the last year who are eligible to receive Social Security and SSI benefits but are not receiving them because they do not have a representative payee and Social Security will not pay them until they find a payee.

3. We are constantly told by individuals we talk to on the streets and at the hotels that they are told by Social Security that they will not be paid their benefits unless they find a representative payee on their own. These persons frequently ask us to serve as their payees so that they can get their benefits. We try and find payees for these people by contacting community agencies. There are only two County agencies in Sacramento that provide payee services. They are Sacramento County Case Management Service (CMS) and Adult Protective Services (APS). However, they

cannot meet the current demand for representative payees that exists in this community.

4. More significantly, we frequently see people who have to resort to strangers and often untrustworthy individuals to be their payees. We know that these payees charge exorbitant amounts to be payees, spend the benefits on themselves or they simply disappear with the money. The beneficiaries are often fearful to report the misuse because they know Social Security will suspend their benefits and they will be left with nothing at all. That is an incredibly cruel alternative for these people to face.

5. Finding a payee for many of the people we deal with is a totally unrealistic task that they are often not equipped to handle.

We declare under penalty of perjury under the laws of the State of California that the foregoing is true and correct.

Executed on March 17, 1989, at Sacramento, California.

Appendix H

Excerpts, Senate Bill 1130 Social Security Act*

101st Congress, 1st Session, S. 1130

To amend titles II and XVI of the Social Security Act to improve supervision of representative payees on behalf of beneficiaries under those programs.

IN THE SENATE OF THE UNITED STATES
JUNE 6 (legislative day, JANUARY 3), 1989

Mr. Pryor (for himself, Mr. Riegle, Mr. Heinz, Mr. Moynihan, Mr. Levin, Mr. Bradley, Mr. Glenn, Mr. Simpson, Mr. Shelby, Mr. Burdick, Mrs. Kassebaum, Mr. Reid, and Mr. Cohen) introduced the following bill; which was read twice and referred to the Committee on Finance

A BILL

To amend titles II and XVI of the Social Security Act to improve supervision of representative payees on behalf of beneficiaries under those programs.

**Publisher's note*: Amendments relating to OASDI (Old Age Survivor Disability Insurance) are virtually identical to the amendments relating to SSI (Supplemental Security Income) outlined in Appendix H, and have therefore not been reprinted.

Be it enacted by the Senate and House of Representatives of the United States of America in Congress assembled,

SECTION I. SHORT TITLE.

This Act may be cited as the "Representative Payee Abuse Prevention Act of 1989."

SEC. II. SCREENING AND INVESTIGATION OF REPRESENTATIVE PAYEES.

(a) AUTHORITY FOR CERTIFICATION OF PAYMENTS TO REPRESENTATIVE PAYEE.—

(1) AMENDMENT RELATING TO OASDI.—Section 205(j)(1) of the Social Security Act (42 U.S.C. 405(j)(1), is amended to read as follows:

"Representative Payees

"(j)(1) Upon a written determination by the Secretary that the interest of any beneficiary under this title would be served thereby, certification of payment may be made, regardless of the legal competency or incompetency of the beneficiary entitled thereto, either for direct payment to the beneficiary, or for his or her use and benefit to another person (hereafter referred to as the beneficiary's 'representative payee') with respect to whom the requirements of paragraph (2) have been met."

(2) AMENDMENT RELATING TO SSI.—Section 1631(a)(2)(A) of such Act (42 U.S.C. 1383(a)(2)(A)) is amended to read as follows:

"(2)(A) Payments of the benefit of any individual may be made to any such individual or to his eligible spouse (if any) or partly to each. Upon written determination by the Secretary that the interest of such individual would be served thereby, or in the case of any individual (including an eligible spouse) referred to in section 1611(e)(3)(A), such payments shall be made to another person (hereafter referred to as such individual's 'representative payee'), including an appropriate public or private agency, who is interested in or concerned with the welfare of such individual, and with respect to whom the requirements of subparagraph (A) have been met."

(b) PROCEDURE FOR INVESTIGATION OF REPRESENTATIVE PAYEE.—

. . . AMENDMENT RELATING TO SSI.—Section 1631(a)(2)(B) of such Act (42 U.S.C. 1383(a)(2)(B)), is amended to read as follows:

"(B)(i)(I) Any certification made under paragraph (1) for payment to a representative payee must be made on the basis of an investigation, carried out either prior to such certification or within forty-five days after such certification, and on the basis of substantial evidence that such certification is in the interest of the individual entitled to such payment, giving priority to the immediate needs of the beneficiary.

"(II) The Secretary shall promulgate regulations which will encourage, where appropriate, face-to-face contact with the representative payee and the beneficiary.

"(ii) The Secretary shall develop and promulgate, through regulations, procedures to implement the investigation required in paragraph (a)(2)(A)(i), including, but not limited to—

"(I) verification of the Social Security account number; name; address; telephone number; and place of employment, if applicable accepted as part of any person's application for designation as a representative payee, unless such person's identification has already been established;

"(II) a determination insofar as feasible of whether any such applicant, has been convicted of a felony or misdemeanor under section 208, 1107(a), 1632, 1877, or 1909 of this Act, or convicted of a felony under any other Federal or State law, to the extent that such determination is consistent with, and not prohibited by, Federal and State laws; provided that the Secretary shall retain discretion as to excluding an applicant who is a spouse of the beneficiary or a parent with custody of a minor child or children;

"(III) a determination, based on all existing records maintained by the Secretary pursuant to the provisions of this Act, of whether the services of such person as representative payee have previously been terminated or suspended by the Secretary for—

"(aa) misuse of the benefits of the beneficiary for whom they were intended;

"(bb) conviction of a violation of section 208, 1107(a), 1632, 1877, or 1909; or

"(cc) failure to meet the requirements of this section.

"(iii) Large lump-sum payments of retroactive benefits shall not be paid to new representative payees, pending the completion of the investigation described in subparagraph (b). The Secretary shall develop and promulgate through regulation procedures under which the lump sum payments will be held pending completion of the investigation, and allowing for reasonable exceptions where the funds are urgently needed to meet the medical, shelter, and other basic needs of the beneficiary.

"(iv)(I) The Secretary shall maintain a centralized, current file, which shall be updated periodically on the basis of information derived pursuant to this paragraph and which shall be in a form which will be readily retrievable by all local offices of the Social Security Administration, of—

"(aa) the address and social security account number of each representative payee in receipt of benefit payments pursuant to this subsection,

"(bb) the address and social security account number of each beneficiary for whom each representative payee is reported to be providing services pursuant to this subsection, and

"(cc) the name, address, and social security account number of each person who has been convicted of a violation of section 208, 1107(a), 1632, 1877, or 1909, or whose services have previously been terminated by the Secretary for failure to meet the requirements of this subsection.

"(II) The Secretary shall, not less frequently than twice yearly, correlate the information described in substance (I)(aa) with the information described in subclause (I)(bb) to determine whether two or more individuals described in subclause (I)(bb) reside at the same address and whether benefit payments with respect to two or more individuals are being sent to the same address. If the Secretary determines in such correlation that two or more such individuals have or have had the same address or that such benefits with respect to two or more individuals are being or have been sent to the same address, the Secretary shall prominently display such correlation in the file referred to in subclause (I) and shall, upon request, transmit such determination to the agency of each State which the Secretary determines is primarily responsible for regulating care facilities operated in such State or providing for child and adult protective services in such State."

SEC. 3. SAFEGUARDS TO PROTECT BENEFICIARIES.

(a) NOTICE OF INITIAL DETERMINATION OF NEED FOR REPRESENTATIVE PAYEE.—

. . . AMENDMENT RELATING TO SSI.—Section 1632(a)(2) of such Act (42

U.S.C. 1383(a)(2)) is amended by inserting after subparagraph (B) the following new subparagraph:

"(2)(C)(i) The Secretary shall provide to each beneficiary, and to each person or persons authorized or otherwise entitled to act on his behalf if he is judged legally competent or is an unemancipated minor, a formal notice of the initial determination of the need for a representative payee. The notice shall—

"(I) be written in simple language, and shall be made orally upon request;

"(II) explain to the beneficiary his right to object to a determination that a representative payee is necessary, his right to object to the designation of a particular person as representative payee including his right to review the evidence upon which the proposed action will be based and to submit any additional evidence regarding the proposed action; and his formal appeal rights under the Act; and

"(III) be provided in advance of any benefits being paid to the representative payee."

(b) LIMITATIONS ON WHO MAY BE APPOINTED REPRESENTATIVE PAYEE.—

. . . AMENDMENT RELATING TO SSI.—Section 1632(a) is further amended by inserting after subparagraph (2)(C)(i) the following new subparagraph:

"(ii) No individual or agency who is a creditor of a beneficiary under this title by virtue of the provision of goods or services to the beneficiary in exchange for money may serve as such beneficiary's representative payee. The preceding sentence shall not apply to any person who—

"(I) is a relative of the beneficiary and resides in the household of the beneficiary;

"(II) is a legal guardian or court appointed agent for the beneficiary;

"(III) is a facility licensed or certified pursuant to State or local law; or is an administrator, owner or employee of a facility licensed or certified pursuant to State or local law in which the beneficiary is a resident, if the appointment of such facility or such individual is certified as a last resort only after good faith efforts have been and by the local social security office to locate an alternative representative payee; or

"(IV) establishes to the satisfaction of the Secretary, based on written findings and pursuant to procedures established by regulation, that he or she poses no risk to the beneficiary, that his or her relationship poses no substantial conflict of interest, that no other suitable representative payee may be established, and that he or she is not the representative payee for any other beneficiary.

"(iii) The Secretary shall make good faith efforts to locate a suitable representative payee for each beneficiary for whom a suitable representative payee cannot be readily established. To facilitate such good faith efforts the Secretary shall make available to all local offices of the Social Security Administration a current list, updated periodically, of all local nonprofit community-based social service agencies that provide services as a representative payee. Failure to maintain such list and/or make good faith efforts to locate a suitable representative payee shall constitute a failure of the Secretary to comply with the provisions of this subsection for purposes of clause (E)(ii)."

(c) PAYMENTS MADE DIRECTLY TO BENEFICIARIES UNDER CERTAIN CIRCUMSTANCES.—

. . . AMENDMENT RELATING TO SSI.—Section 1632 of such Act (42 U.S.C. 1383(a)) is further amended by adding the following new clause after clause (C)(iii):

"(iv)(I) If payment is being made directly to a beneficiary who is over the age of 18 or who is an emancipated minor and who has not been adjudged legally incompetent, and an application to receive representative payment is made on his behalf, the Secretary shall continue to make payments directly to the beneficiary until such time as the Secretary completes his determination about the ability of the beneficiary to manage or direct the management of benefit payments and the selection of the representative payee.

"(II) All benefits shall be paid directly to all persons over the age of 18 or to emancipated minors who are newly eligible for benefits and for whom the Secretary has determined that a representative payee is necessary, until such time as the Secretary has completed his investigation of and has selected the representative payee or until such time as the person has exhausted his appeals rights under this section. The preceding sentence shall not apply with respect to—

"(aa) lump sum payments described in paragraph (2)(B)(iii) of this section;

"(bb) such beneficiaries who the Secretary determines, based on a written finding issued pursuant to regulations promulgated by the Secretary, are likely to suffer substantial harm as a direct result of his functional inabilities if payments are made to them directly. In making a determination pursuant to this clause, the Secretary shall only consider functional deficiencies; medical diagnosis, age, or eccentricity shall not form the basis for the determination; and

"(cc) a beneficiary who is eligible for benefits solely on the basis of a disability and who is medically determined to be a drug addict or alcoholic, unless the Secretary determines that the best interests are otherwise served.

"(III) The Secretary shall promulgate regulations to provide for the immediate needs of all beneficiaries for whom he determines direct payment of benefits cannot be made pursuant to the provisions of clauses (C)(iv)(I), (II)(1), (II)(2), and (II)(3) of this subparagraph. Such regulations shall provide for direct payment to a landlord, health care provider, treatment facility or other long-term care provider upon written request of such landlord, health care provider, treatment facility, or other long-term care provider."

(d) ENFORCEMENT OF BENEFICIARY RIGHTS.—

. . . AMENDMENT RELATING TO SSI.—Section 1631(a)(2) of such Act is further amended by adding at the end the following new subparagraph:

"(E)(i) The Secreatary shall terminate or suspend the services of any person as representative payee under this subsection if the Secretary or a court of law determines that such person has acted in violation of this subsection or has otherwise not acted as representative payee in the best interest of the beneficiary for whom such person was authorized to perform such services, or who has misused the proceeds of any benefit payment under this title as determined by State or Federal law. Upon termination of such services by the Secretary, or for such time as such services are suspended, the Secretary shall—

"(I) secure for such individual the services of another person as representative payee under this subsection, or

"(II) make direct payment to the individual subject to the restriction in clause (C)(iv).

"(ii) Failure of the Secretary to investigate or monitor such representative payee pursuant to and in accordance with subparagraphs (B), (C) and (D) of this section resulting in misused benefits, shall constitute an underpayment of benefits under Section 1631(b) of this Act. The Secretary shall repay to the beneficiary the amount by which such beneficiary has been paid less than the correct amount.

"(iii) In the case of any termination of services pursuant to subparagraph (A) based on misuse of the proceeds of any benefit payment under this title by an individual serving as representative payee with respect to such payment, the Secretary shall make every good faith effort as described in regulations promulgated by the Secretary to obtain restitution of the misused funds, and to make available upon request to the beneficiary documentation of those efforts—

"(I) the Secretary shall assess a fine on the individual serving as representative payee not to exceed the amount of funds misused;

"(II) the Secretary shall decrease any payment under this subchapter to which such representative payee is entitled, or shall require such representative payee to refund the amount of funds misused; and

"(III) to the extent that funds are recovered under this clause, and the beneficiary has not been paid pursuant to clause (ii), the funds shall be used to reimburse the beneficiary.

"(iv) Any finding by the Secretary that results in a decision of no misuse of funds by the representative payee or no underpayment, of if the Secretary has not made a formal decision on a complaint of misuse within 60 days, shall be treated as an unfavorable decision referred to in subsection (c)(1), and the beneficiary shall be treated as an individual referred to in subsection (c)(1)."

SEC. IV. IMPROVED MONITORING, ACCOUNTING AND RECORD-KEEPING.

. . . AMENDMENTS RELATING TO SSI.—Section 1631(a)(2) of such Act is further amended by renumbering subparagraph (C) (as in effect immediately before the date of the enactment of the Act) and amending it as follows:

"(D)(i) In any case where payment under this subchapter is made to a person other than the individual entitled to such payment, the Secretary shall establish a system of accountability monitoring whereby such person shall report not less often than annually with respect to the use of such payment. The Secretary shall establish and implement statistically valid procedures for reviewing such reports in order to identify instances in which such persons are not properly using such payments.

"(ii) Clause (i) shall not apply in any case where the other person to whom payment is made is a State institution. In such cases, the Secretary shall establish a system of accountability monitoring for institutions in each State.

"(iii) Clause (i) shall not apply in any case where the individual entitled to such payment is a resident of a Federal institution and the other person to whom such payment is made is the institution.

"(iv)(I) Notwithstanding clauses (i), (ii), and (iii), the Secretary shall establish and implement a more frequent and a more detailed system of accountability monitoring for certain categories of high-risk representative payees to be determined by the Secretary. Such categories of high-risk representative payees shall include, but not be limited to, licensed or certified care facilities that serve as representative payees for residents; administrators, owners, and employees of licensed or certified care facilities that serve as representative payees for residents, and all persons not related by blood or marriage to the beneficiary to whom they are providing services.

"(II) The Secretary shall report to Congress within one year of the date of enactment of this provision its findings of which categories constitute high-risk representative payees, and its system for the additional accountability monitoring that will be required of such categories.

"(v) Notwithstanding clauses (i), (ii), (iii), and (iv), the Secretary may require a report at any time from any person receiving payments on behalf of another, if the Secretary has reason to believe that the person receiving such payments is misusing such payments."

SEC. V. FEASIBILITY STUDY.

. . . AMENDMENT RELATING TO SSI.—Section 1631(a)(2) of such Act is further amended by adding at the end the following new subparagraph:

"(F)(i) The Secretary shall conduct a feasibility study regarding the designation of the Department of Veterans Affairs as the lead agency for purposes of selecting, appointing, and monitoring representative payees for those individuals who receive benefits under this title and from the Department of Veterans Affairs.

"(ii) The Secretary shall report its findings to Congress within six months of the date of enactment of this subparagraph."

SEC. VI. REPORTS TO CONGRESS.

. . . AMENDMENT RELATING TO SSI.—Section 1631(a)(2) of such Act is further amended by adding at the end of the following new subparagraph:

"(G)(i) The Secretary shall make an initial report to each House of Congress on the implementation of the provisions of this section no later than May 1, 1990.

"(ii) The Secretary shall include as a part of the annual report required under section 904 of this title, information with respect to the implementation of this Act, including the number of cases in which the payee was changed, the number of cases discovered where there has been a misuse of funds, how any such cases were dealt with by the Secretary, the final disposition of such cases, including the penalties imposed, the number of instances in which it was determined that a payee was handling the funds of two or more beneficiaries who were under the services of the same or different representative payees were residing at the same address, and such other information as the Secretary determines to be appropriate."